VitalChecklist™

How to Improve Patient Experience Score?

First Edition

Chief Medical Author and Editor:

Dr. Harpreet Singh MD, FACP

- Chief Experience Officer—Michigan Primary Care Partners
- CEO and Founder—Vital Checklist and iCrush.org
- Board Certified Physician—Michigan Primary Care Partners
- USMLE Instructor—Vital Checklist Workshop for Step 2 Clinical Skills
- Clinical Adjunct Instructor—Central Michigan University
- Patient Experience Coach— iCrush Health and Wellness Seminars
- Speaker, Inventor, and Medical Author
- School—Sacred Heart Convent School, Ludhiana, India
- College—Arya College, Ludhiana, India
- Medical School—KMC Manipal, India
- Residency— MSU-Grand Rapids Medical Education Partners
- Residency— Spectrum Health, Grand Rapids MI and Mercy Health, Grand Rapids MI

Publisher:

Vital Checklist

Where is the research?

I have pitched my idea to healthcare clinics, hospitals, and outpatient offices nationwide. Everybody has asked me one question, "Where is the research on Vital Checklist?"

As expected, the healthcare industry wants proof of my work before they can implement it in their hospitals and clinics. However, I am a busy practicing clinician who firmly believes in the Toyota Production System Principle of *Genba*. This system entails the application must take place in real scenarios, in which healthcare professionals spend time at the patient's bedside, educating patients. This is the key for perfecting this Vital Checklist. To do a research project of this scale, I would need a team of patients, medical students and researchers to help me with the Vital Checklist. This is the reason I published my work in one book; so that I can get my work in the hands of patients and healthcare providers. I have provided this instrument for freeand you can visit it via iCrush.org. You can read numerous testimonials I have received on Healthgrades.com which support the effectiveness of this tool. This is a focus group study that was initiated with the sole purposed of educating my patients and implementing tools to improve their health.

Another question health caregivers have asked me, "Are you interested in doing research?"

Of course, I would love to partner with a hospital or a clinic and do a double-bind study with them. I am looking to hire research savvy people and prove my concepts on patient experience. If you know somebody who is interested to work with me, please email me at drsingh@vitalchecklist.com

Contributors

Associate Medical Author—Translated Vital Checklist in different languages

Dr. Jasmine Hundal (English)

Dr. Igor Vaz (Portuguese and Spanish)

Dr. Shree Shanmugam (Tamil)

Dr. Chintan Rupareliya (Russian and Gujarati)

Assistant Medical Author—Translated Vital Checklist in different languages

Dr. Lissette Himinej (Spanish)

Dr. Meghna Reddy (Telugu)

Dr. Krishna Sai (Telugu)

Dr. Dinesh Kumar (Punjabi)

Dr. Charu Dutt Arora (Hindi)

Dr. Udyavir Singh Grewal (Punjabi)

Dr. Rehan Malik (Urdu)

Dr. Shahena Nazeer (Malayalam)

Dr. Shobita Singh (Marathi)

Dr. Noni Rana (Punjabi)

Dr. Shafi Rana (Punjabi)

Dr. Omar Al-Janabi (Arabic)

Contributing Authors

Samrath Singh

Dr. John Lobo (Urology)

Dr. Gurneel Kaur Dhanesar

Dr. Krutika Srivastava (Marathi)

Reviewers

Emily Franckowiak (English)

Dr. Eduardo Cortes (Spanish)

Suresh Rupareliya, MSc. Ph.D.(Gujurati)

Dr.V.T.Alexandrovich,MD, MS (Russian)

Mrs. Ashu Arora MA MPHIL. (Hindi)

Maria Benit, PA-C (Russian)

Dr. Manimegalai V, MBBS (Tamil)

Mrs. Saleena Nazeer (Malayalam)

ThasniAbin, (Malayalam)

Mrs. Ajit Kaur (Punjabi)

Mrs. Parminderjeet Kaur (Punjabi)

Mrs. Kuldeep Kaur (Punjabi)

Proof read and Edited by

Christopher Burton

Penny McQueen

Book Design

Munish Ahuja

Sweekar Info Media

www.sinfome.com

How to contribute?

We are looking for awesome team players—students, nurses, physician assistants, nurse practitioners, and doctors to become part of Vital Checklist and iCrush.org Family. If you want to be part of this global project—Vital Checklist, please send us your contribution, and for every entry, you will receive an acknowledgment in the next edition. If your contribution is significant, then your name will appear as a part of contributors. If you want to share your acronym, checklist or art, please email us at hi@vitalchecklist.com

Content usage guidelines

Thanks for your interest in sharing our content. We are thrilled. Before you do so, here are some general rules. Please note, all of our content is copyrighted, and we operate under © All Rights Reserved clause. It means that if you do not abide by our usage policies, we have the right to pursue you legally.

What Vital Checklist and iCrush content can you use? And how?

Feel free to share links to any of our content on any website or social media channels. We appreciate the help of getting Vital Checklist concepts in front of more people.

Feel free to reference or quote up to 50 words of any of our text content in your own blog articles and presentations as long as you abide by the content attribution policy.

Vital Checklist cannot be shared, downloaded, distributed, reused and published in any form without written consent of our legal team. For commercial license, please contact our ipoffice@vitalchecklist.com

You cannot copy in full or in part any of our full-text content and our original copyrighted images and Vital Checklist without our prior consent. We love to know how Vital Checklist is applied around the world by patients and caregivers and we monitor for our Checklist mentions so we will know if you do not abide by our rules. You cannot monetize on the content we provide you free of charge. You cannot claim our content as your original ideas and publish as your own on your platform. Health caregivers can use the checklist to explain the concepts with these checklist but cannot make macros in the electronic health records. Please ask your electronic health record to contact us for licensing Vital Checklist.

Cite Vital Checklist and iCrush.org as a source

Cite Dr. Harpreet Singh MD as the author/creator of VITAL CHECKLIST

Link back to our original source you are referencing.

Dedication

To the United States of America where 54 dollars and 50 cents can take you so far.

To KMC, Manipal and Spectrum Health Hospital where I learned how to take care of patients

To my patients who gave me the opportunity to serve them.

To my parents—Anar Singh and Ajit Kaur, who taught me hard work will always pay, and if you are the best, people will find you

To my brother—Dr. Harvinder Paul Singh, who was and continues to be there for anything and everything. Without his emotional and financial support, it would have been an arduous journey.

To my wife—Aroma, my rock, who never questioned my long working hours and has been very patient while I write books.

To my daughters—Suhani and Sanjhvi, who still have a Disney trip on their bucket list.

To my family and friends who taught me to see the world with better eyes.

Foremost, God almighty, this formless one, for blessing me with all the opportunities to speak and overcome stuttering.

Preface

The Agency for Healthcare Research and Quality (AHRQ) is encouraging patients to ask questions of their health caregivers. On their site www.ahrq.gov, AHRQ elaborates on the idea of asking questions before, during and after their appointments. In my practice, I see that a majority of patients are still unprepared regarding managing their care and asking their questions, many of which don't ask the correct questions to their health caregivers. More and more patients are searching their symptoms on the Internet, which in many cases only confuses the patient further. Patients often accept Google's suggestions regarding their diagnosis and end up worrying about a disease that they more than likely don't have.

Why the confusion?

- This confusion is due to numerous websites providing symptoms of the disease and how the disease would present. However, most patients don't know which symptomis more relevant pertaining to their disease.

- Next, they don't know symptoms can overlap with various other diseases confusing the diagnosis.

- Not only that, after reading symptoms, patients think like a third-year medical student and believe they actually have an illness: stressing about the disease, resulting in depression.

- Just knowing the symptoms doesn't mean you have a specific diagnosis. Remembering the entire symptom checklist is important when recognizing a disease pattern.

During an office visit or in the hospital, patients will often forget to ask questions at the time of the meeting due to stress and will remember only after being discharged. These "door-knob" questions or "By the way, doctor!" questions, will delay the care of other patients sitting in the waiting area or waiting to be discharged. Although we recommend asking questions, sometimes random questions at the wrong times can become a bottleneck for the health caregivers, hospitals and clinics resulting in the delay.

Whether it'sthe health and wellness of the employees, population health of the communities or chronic care management for Medicare beneficiaries, everybody needs to be on the same page of how the disease presents. Every major healthcare or patient education website has symptom checkers. Symptom checkers are an excellent idea but what we propose is a symptom checklist to provide a focused approach to disease ailments, which has the enormous economic burden. We hope it will raise awareness to chronic diseases.

Our symptom checklist was developed for easy memory and recall. As this symptom checklist is vital for the patients' health, we therefore conceived the name Vital Checklist. We have used business concepts like Kanban Methodology, Agile Mindset, and Theory of Constraints to design our Vital Checklist and acts like the 24x7 information radiator. Our checklist is like a metaphorical 'rope' which pulls patients and caregivers out of the bottleneck by empowering patients. Whether it is a Lean Management, Agile Mindset or Theory of Constraints, our goal is to make this Vital Checklist easy to remember and difficult to forget. The left-hand margin of the page depicts the acronym, followed by the open-ended question and a blank area for patients to write their answers. Last but not least, we have a space for caregiver initials and a column for patient initial in order to show that the communication between them happened and was completed appropriately. These Vital Checklists, which will be translated in multiple languages will come in separate books in the near future.

To make patients and people more aware of the wide array of diseases in today's society, we have different modalities to activate different sensory functions--eyes, ears, touch, and taste. Given that everybody has different learning styles—visual, auditory, reading, writing, kinesthetic, or pictures; we will be providing Vital Checklist in the form of a book, YouTube video, 24/7 awareness touchpoint and 5k events. Primary chronic illnesses with enormous economic burden will have their own individualized websites. Why different sites for chronic diseases? Websites are the waterfront property and easy access to those sites will help patients to get educated, activated and engaged.

We have taken a leaf out from the Khan Academy and provided this checklist for free on our YouTube Video Channel for self-motivated and driven patients who want to improve health literacy. However, insurance companies want accountability from their beneficiaries, for which we have developed online certification courses for. We believe in shared value for the businesses, hospitals, outpatient clinics and patients. We want to deliver value-driven health!

Let's collaborate and listen to our patients first so that we can then educate, activate and engage with them, helping to improve their experience through the utilization of the Vital Checklist Patient Education Guide.

Harpreet Singh MD

Acknowledgment

Vital Checklist would not have been possible without the help of medical students. Dr. Jasmin Hundal helped me in coordinating with other team members, formatting the tables, rechecking all the acronyms, and was instrumental in handling the bibliography for this book. I want to give a special thank you to the following team members:

- Shreenivasan (translated in Tamil and formatted the tables)
- Chintan (translated in Russian and Gujarati),
- Igor (translated in Portuguese),
- Lissette (translated in Spanish),
- Sai (translated in Telugu),
- Meghna (translated in Telugu),
- Udhayvir (translated in Punjabi),
- Noni (translated in Punjabi),
- Shaffi (translated in Punjabi),
- Dinesh (translated in Punjabi),
- Charu (translated in Telugu),
- Shahena (translated in Malayalam),
- Omar (translated in Arabic),
- Rehan (translated in Urdu)
- Shobita (translated in Marathi)

Gurmeet Singh, Gagan Ahluwalia, and Munish Ahuja (sinfome.com) were instrumental in providing IT support. I am indebted to Dharminder Kumar, Munish Ahuja and Vakil Singh for designing this book in multiple languages, making it feasible to reach a much broader audience. I am very thankful to First Edition Design Publishers for printing this book. This book would not have been possible without Samrath Singh, Chris Burton and Penny McQueen, who reviewed my work. Jim Collins in his book has rightfully mentioned, "Having the right people in the right seats is important." I am genuinely grateful for everyone that played a part in making this book come to life.

I am truly grateful to Dr. Darryl Elmouchi and Dr. Paul Singh for reviewing this book and giving me the direction for this book. A big thanks to Smita Singh for providing valuable critique to the book. The pictures in this book are part of my previous book—Road to USMLE Step 2CS and were drawn by Dr. Himanshu Deshwal. Dedicated and intelligent medical students like Himanshu are a real treat to work as I can rely on them 110% all the time. I would like to thank Dr. John Lobo for contributing urology pictures.

Last but not the least, I am grateful to my wife—Aroma, who always pushed me to do better. This humungous task would not have come to fruition without her support.

Table of Contents

Section A

Introduction

1. How to use this book? What is the RBC Method?

Dr. Atul Gawande, Dr. Peter Pronovost, and Sully Sullenberger have already proved that checklists save lives. Dr. Gawande published his landmark research in the New England Journal of Medicine and demonstrated that by using this WHO Safe Surgery Checklist death fell by 47% and surgical complications fell by 36%. On the other hand, Dr. Peter Pronovost's Keystone Initiative saved 1500 lives and 100 million dollars by using the centerline checklist. Checklists are not only beneficial in the healthcare setting as proven by Sully Sullenberger, a distinguished pilot, who saved 155 lives by landing his aircraft on the Hudson River with the help of a checklist. This Hudson Miracle was only possible because of the astuteness of the pilot and the co-pilot who utilized a checklist after their aircraft was struck by a flock of birds, causing engine failure. Repeatedly, it has been shown that implementing and utilizing a checklist helps. We now have a checklist for healthcare providers that support standard protocols, guidelines, and reminders for the health caregivers to help ensure things do not get forgotten during emergencies and stressful conditions. These reminders for health caregivers come in the form of tangible touch points, emails, and messages. However, when it comes to the patients, we do not have checklists or reminders. We have the expectation that they will remember complicated medical jargon in 15 minutes of their clinical appointments or the last 30 minutes of the discharge process. Health caregivers are mandated to do CME's, retake board examinations and attend conferences in order to refresh their knowledge. However, when it comes to patients, we expect that they will remember everything taught to them within their 15-30 minutes appointment, which can often be rushed by medical professionals. I have read thousands of business books, watched numerous TED talks and read many journal articles to develop a method for teaching patients; I call this RBC Method.

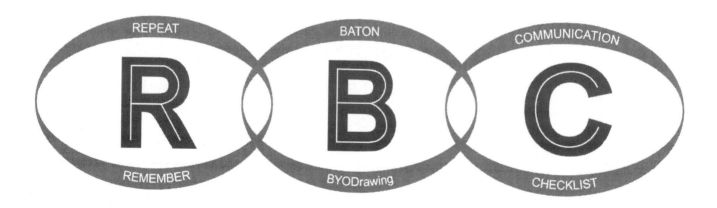

Figure: RBC Method ™

Medical knowledge is vast and for this experience to engrain into our brains, we need constant repetition, which is only possible with 24x7 tangible touchpoints. The letter "R" in RBC method stands for Repetition and is derived from John Medina's book Brain Rules. In his book, he explains the concepts of repeat to remember and remember to repeat, thus transferring things from short-term memory to long-term memory. 33.7% of information is forgotten in the first 24 hours; so how can we expect a patient to remember voluminous information given at the time of discharge? We need to implement a call to action checklist for which 24x7 tangible touchpoints are present at the bedside. The letter "B" in RBC method is derived from tangible touchpoints or a baton. In the world of marketing, we give souvenirs out for the sole reason that we want people to remember. Similarly, giving a tangible touchpoint in the form of a simple checklist, communication cards, communication boxes or t-shirts serves as a bridge between hospitals and home. As I am a big proponent of drawing your own two-dimensional pictures to explain the disease concepts to the patients and therefore I believe health caregivers should draw the pictures and these simple line diagrams help patients to visualize their disease and take better care of themselves. Thus, the letter "B" also stands for BYOD: Bring Your Own Drawings. Do not be a pamphlet doctor! The strategy behind this RBC methodology is adapted from the book—Blue Ocean Strategy which I have explained in detail in my upcoming book—Doctor in no hurry! Last but not the least, the letter "B" stands for the Blue Ocean Strategy. behind this RBC methodology is adapted from the book—Blue Ocean Strategy which I have explained in detail in my upcoming book—Doctor in no hurry! Last but not the least, the letter "B" stands for the Blue Ocean Strategy.

This baton or a drawing is not only a memory tool but also a communication tool for easy conversation with patients. It is through this process that the letter "C" of RBC comes into play. Not only the letter "C" stands for communication, but also it stands for checklist which is the core of our company. In medicine, RBC means red blood cell and naming a theory by the same name will help healthcare providers to remember this theory easily. For this reason, I have specifically chosen red colors, and because of the Blue Ocean Strategy, the words are written in blue. This RBC methodology will help patients to ask more questions and is inevitably summed up in the title of the book—Vital Checklist:

However, these problems should not be asked at the tail end of the discharge or when the doctor is about to leave the room. Asking "doorknob questions" or "by the way doctor questions" delays the care of other patients. When these questions occur, the doctor now has to log into the electronic health records and document chief concerns, history of present illnesses, change assessments and treatment plans. Patients might think it was only 5 or 10 minutes that the doctor overspent with them, but the time adds up when this occurs with every patient. We want patients to be proactive with their health and asks questions in an upfront manner. The patient should be prepared to ask questions right from the beginning. Rather than reading magazines or watching TV in the waiting area, if they are ready with their questions and problems, it will make the doctor's life much more manageable, and the meeting will be more efficient. We can only make management lean if both parties are involved—health caregivers and patients. To make RBC methodology more useful, I have taken a leaf out from Khan Academy.org and flipped it for healthcare by making a Youtube video on iCrush diabetes. As diabetes is going to be a pandemic, we have dedicated a separate domain name iCrushdiabetes.com to educate patients for free.

We have used Kanban Methodology to design our Vital Checklist. All checklists require validation from the health caregiver and the patients, keeping both parties accountable. The first column of the checklist represents a letter which forms the acronym, mnemonic or a super-word which usually represents the disease. The second column represents the symptom of that illness and below it is a question followed by a space to answer the question. Validating the checklist should only be done if the patient has responded to all the questions. Let's make patients' lives safe, healthier and happier by holding each other's hands and saving healthcare dollars for America, as well as the rest of world. Let's shun the assembly line approach to medicine and stop draining our GDP for healthcare. We did not become doctors to practice "conveyer-belt" style medicine. Start educating patients about their health so that they are prepared to ask questions and give a thorough history, helping us to reach a better diagnosis and create more effective treatment plans.

2. How will this book save healthcare dollars?

How will this book be beneficial for doctors, hospitals, and clinics?

How will this book keep patients safe?

I have repeatedly been told that by training patients to ask more questions, our workload will increase. "Dr. Singh, we are already inundated with electronic health records and now you are going to train patients to ask more questions."

However, I have a different view point. I always ask this question: "Do you know why hospitals are going towards lean methodology?" My friend had no answer. Lean is designed and constructed to prevent waste. I am in no way a lean expert, but after reading books, I have used bits and pieces of lean in various aspects of practice. I use a checklist, Kanban, and value mapping from lean. For me, lean also stands for:

L: Listen
E: Educate
A: Activate
N: eNgage with patients.

This is one of the primary reasons I am starting a Lean Patient Experience Course.

We already know why patient experience is important. We also know what has to be done to improve patient experience scores. However, we don't know how we are going to improve this aspect. I explained to my friend that patient experience could not be improved without patient education. They are closely connected to each other. Let me explain this philosphy to you by means of an example.

Have you ever noticed CT scan of the abdomen and pelvis with per oral and IV contrast ordered without a proper history? Do you ever wish you had proper history from the patient? Do you think it is fair for a radiologist? Do you think it is safe for the patient to get an IV contrast study? Do you think it is fair for the patient to be exposed to the radiation? What about the prior authorization for the CT Scan? Why are so many insurance companies denying the tests? Is it because of the over ordering and erroneous ordering in this process? This is where the waste and lean comes to play, as I explained to my friend.

Now on the other hand, if you ask the patient the history of the abdominal pain, you may be able to pinpoint the type of the test that the patient will need. Let me explain this to you with a multiple-choice question:

A 66-year-old patient comes to the clinic and complains about 5/10 dull pain in his left flank. This pain is a constant pain which doesn't come and go (non-cramp pain) and has been going on for the past three days. The pain is present 24-7, stays on the left flank and is getting gradually worse. There is no specific time of the day in which the pain worsens as well. He was pushing a lawn mower when this pain exacerbated and the pain does not radiate anywhere. The pain does not get worse or better with food or passing stools. The pain does not increase or decrease in passing urine as well. According to the past medical history, the patient is a smoker and has a 40-pack-per-year history of smoking. The patient also has a history of drink hard liquor as well. His colonoscopy done at 60 years of age was negative. He has a significant family history of colon cancer, and one of the relatives was recently diagnosed with colon cancer. What is your next step?

A. CT- Scan of the abdomen and Pelvis with IV and PO Contrast

B. Blood work and Urinalysis

C. Colonoscopy

D. Ultrasound of the left kidney

Answer B is the correct answer; from less invasive to more invasive. Results of the urinalysis reveal that patient has hematuria, proteinuria and red blood cells in the urine, for which creatinine is normal.

Now the patient returns to the clinic for the results but also has increasing pain. You do a bedside ultrasound and found that patient has mild hydronephrosis in the left kidney. What is the next step?

A. CT Scan of the abdomen and pelvis with PO and IV contrast

B. CT Scan of Kidneys with IV contrast a.k.a. CT UROGRAM

C. CT Scan of Pancreas with IV contrast

D. Colonoscopy

Answer B is the correct answer. Why would you do CT UROGRAM? You would do so because the patient has hematuria, proteinuria and large amount of RBC.

You may be able to detect a kidney mass on a CT scan of the abdomen and pelvis, but this is not the correct test. Why is the ordering of the exact test essential?

If your suspicion is kidney mass, then you will order a CT Scan of the kidneys with a n IV contrast. Why is this important? A dedicated kidney CT scan requires a 100-second scan delay after the IV contrast while the CT Scan of the abdomen requires a 70-second scan delay. Therefore, getting the correct history and ordering the correct test is of utmost importance.

Now, what about if the patient presents with mesenteric ischemia history. The test to diagnose this is a CT Angiography. A CT Angiography requires a 25-second delay after the IV contrast is injected. If we just ordered a CT Scan of the abdomen and pelvis, this may be a wrong test and you may be unable to diagnose the problem for the patient. You would also be exposing the patient to the radiation, wasting health care dollars and provide a poor patient experience. Getting a proper history from the patient is an art and we must train medical students, physician assistant students, nurse practitioners from the start. We are already testing medical students with USMLE Step 2 Clinical Skills. What about the physician assistant students and nurse practitioners? Disruption is happening everywhere, especially in the healthcare field and we need to be ready as a nation for the shortage of physicians. We need to train smart, not hard.

Let's make smart patient smarter.

"My grandma smoked for 50 years and she lived to be 92.So why should I stop?" It's a story I hear practically every week in my practice and on this particular morning, as L.C.* sat on my examination table, it was no different.

She was 27-years-old, a mother of four and relatively healthy. Every time she came in for an appointment, I begged her to listen to what I had to say about smoking, yet she usually told me how her grandmother, who had smoked for 55 years had defied all the odds and ignored anything I had to say.

When patients walk into my clinic, my one of the open-ended question in their social history is "do you use tobacco in any form?" The answers vary from person to person but if they say "yes,"I'll ask if they know the side-effects of smoking. Most will cite heart disease, lung disease, cancer and death, but what I tell them is that there are so many other things to be worried about.

As doctors, we presume our patients know everything. We tend to forget that we achieved this knowledge only after years of dedicated study. The truth is that if we don't take the time to educate them, it can cost them their lives.

When I ask my patients who smoke if they want to quit, some are motivated to stop immediately, some aren't sure,and most have no intention to stop.

Since my female patient had absolutely no motivation to kick the habit, I thought long and hard about how to persuade her. I knew that if I gave her a pamphlet with information about quitting smoking, she would probably leave it in her car or throw it out. She needed and deserved more especially since she had her whole life ahead of her.

I also could never in good faith claim that I had actually educated her if all I gave her was a piece of paper. I could have checked the appropriate box in the electronic health record to boost my patient satisfaction scores, but what then would I have done to save her life?

I asked her if she'd be willing to learn about my LET'S CRUSH SMOKINGplan and to my surprise, she wasn't. She was running late and had to do some chore for one of her kids. Somehow that day I convinced her and that visit not only transformed my patient's life but my life also as I changed from being a doctor to a transformational coach. I took a pen, stack of papers and started drawing pictures and explained my "Let's Crush Smoking, Okay! Checklist"

The L-E-T-'S C-R-U-S-H SMOKING Plan

L-Lungs: I drew the picture of lungs and I explained that the lungs have several balloons (alveoli) filled with air and in close contact with blood vessels that continually exchange oxygen and carbon dioxide. If she didn't quit smoking, the damaged alveoli would become weaker resulting in one big balloon thus losing the surface area and this is where the gas exchange happens between carbon dioxide and oxygen. This reduction in the available area results in less oxygen and more carbon dioxide in the blood. This phenomenon is called emphysema. The tubes may also get inflamed and swollen, produce sputum, and obstruct the airway,which can lead to bronchitis.

L-Lungs

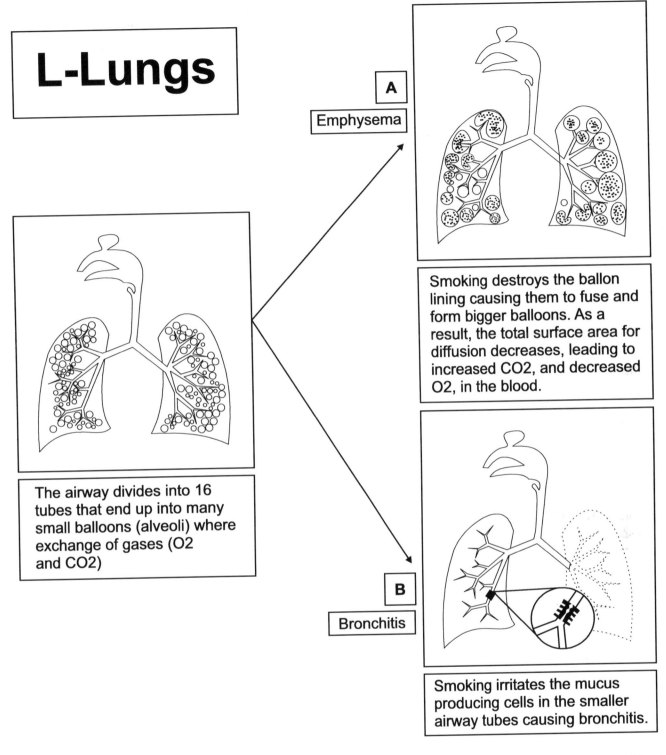

A | Emphysema

Smoking destroys the ballon lining causing them to fuse and form bigger balloons. As a result, the total surface area for diffusion decreases, leading to increased CO_2, and decreased O_2, in the blood.

The airway divides into 16 tubes that end up into many small balloons (alveoli) where exchange of gases (O_2 and CO_2)

B | Bronchitis

Smoking irritates the mucus producing cells in the smaller airway tubes causing bronchitis.

E-Endocrine: I explained to her that diseases such as type-2 diabetes and Grave's Ophthalmopathyare common amongst smokers.

E-Endocrine

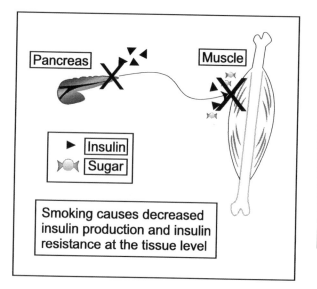

Pancreas ▲ Muscle

▶ Insulin
🍬 Sugar

Smoking causes decreased insulin production and insulin resistance at the tissue level

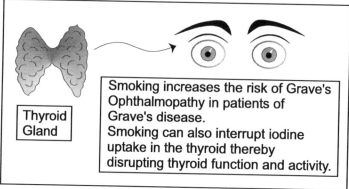

Thyroid Gland

Smoking increases the risk of Grave's Ophthalmopathy in patients of Grave's disease.
Smoking can also interrupt iodine uptake in the thyroid thereby disrupting thyroid function and activity.

T-Teeth

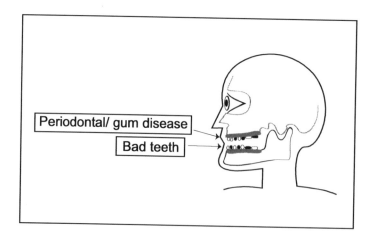

Periodontal/ gum disease
Bad teeth

T-Teeth: It is well known people who smokehave discolored teethfrom the nicotine. The enamel may get disturbed and this may also lead togum disease and bad breath.

S-Skin: I showed her how the skin contains specialized tissues called collagen and elastin that contribute to the strength and elasticity of the skin. Smoking disrupts these collagen fibersand elastincausing wrinkles. Thisdisruption can also happenin the ligamentum flavum andthis strong ligament connects the lamina of the vertebral bodies thus giving support to the back. The weakness in this cartilage leads to arthritis of the back.

Then, I wrote C-R-U-S-H and started explaining the cancer and cholesterol and drew pictures to explain it.

8

S-Skin

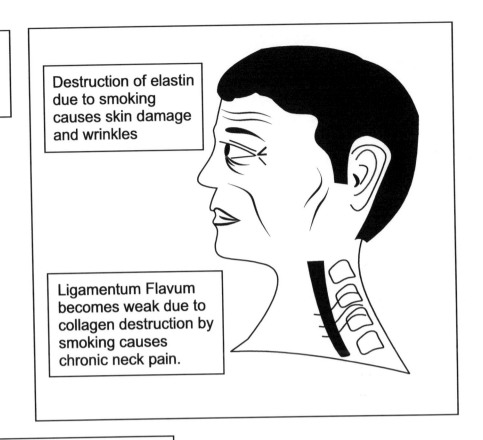

Destruction of elastin due to smoking causes skin damage and wrinkles

Ligamentum Flavum becomes weak due to collagen destruction by smoking causes chronic neck pain.

C-Cholesterol

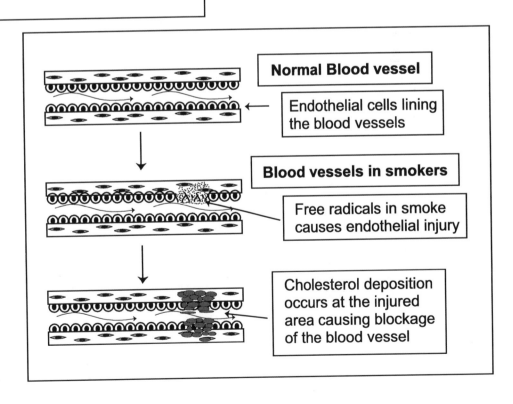

Normal Blood vessel

Endothelial cells lining the blood vessels

Blood vessels in smokers

Free radicals in smoke causes endothelial injury

Cholesterol deposition occurs at the injured area causing blockage of the blood vessel

C-Cancer: I told her smoking can cause colon cancer and a variety of other cancers.

C-Cancer

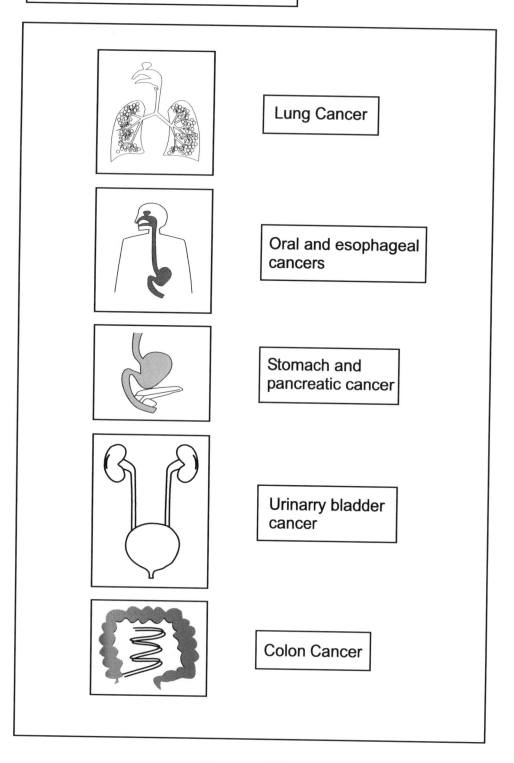

Lung Cancer

Oral and esophageal cancers

Stomach and pancreatic cancer

Urinarry bladder cancer

Colon Cancer

R-Reproduction and sexual health

Erectile dysfunction and decreasd libido in men

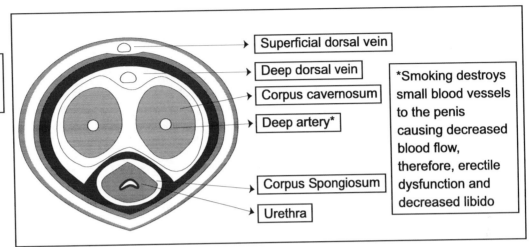

Superficial dorsal vein

Deep dorsal vein

Corpus cavernosum

Deep artery*

Corpus Spongiosum

Urethra

*Smoking destroys small blood vessels to the penis causing decreased blood flow, therefore, erectile dysfunction and decreased libido

Increased risk of abortions in women

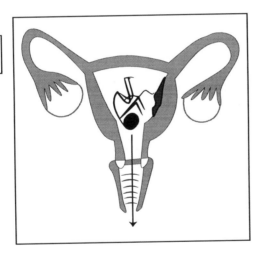

R-Reproductive issues: Women who smoke during pregnancy can develop placental abruption, a condition that causes the placenta to peel away from the inner wall of the uterus before delivery and placenta previa, in which the placenta covers the opening of the mother's cervix. Both conditions can cause serious complications for both mom and baby.

U-Urinary Incontinence: I explained to her that since smoking causes the muscles in the bladder to weaken, it can lead to incontinence or the urgent need to urinate. The muscle weakness can also cause the bladder to leak small amounts of urine.

Urinary Incontinence

A

Stress Incotinence-
Pelvic floor muscles become weak, thereby unable to maintain an angle between the urethra and urinary bladder. Increased intra-abdominal pressure (cough, sneeze,laughing, running) causes leakage of urine

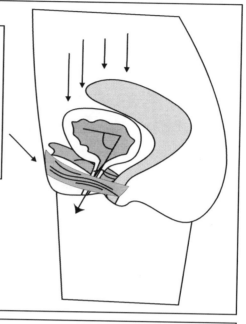

B

Urge Incontinence-
Smoking causes irritation of the urinary bladder leading to overactivity and sudden urge to urinate, leading to leakage of urine before the patient makes it to the bathroom

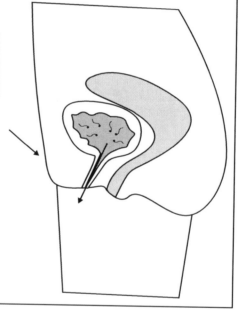

When I mentioned urinary incontinence, my patient had a concerned look. I knew I had hit a nerve but kept on going anyway with my checklist, since I didn't want to appear judgemental.

S-Stroke: Since smoking can increase the amount of cholesterol that is deposited in the walls of the arteries, smokers are at an increased risk for stroke.

Stroke

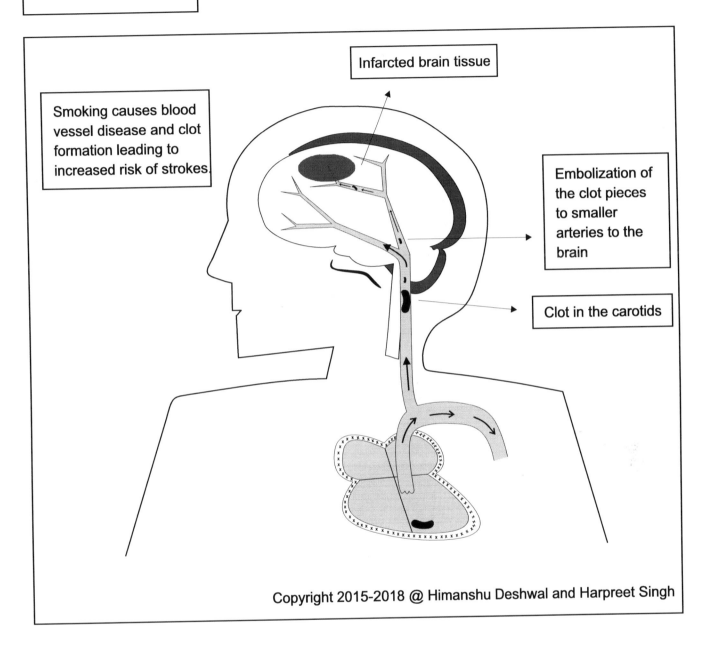

Infarcted brain tissue

Smoking causes blood vessel disease and clot formation leading to increased risk of strokes.

Embolization of the clot pieces to smaller arteries to the brain

Clot in the carotids

H-Heart Disease: Increased cholesterol deposits in the arteries also leads to heart disease.

Heart and Hypertension

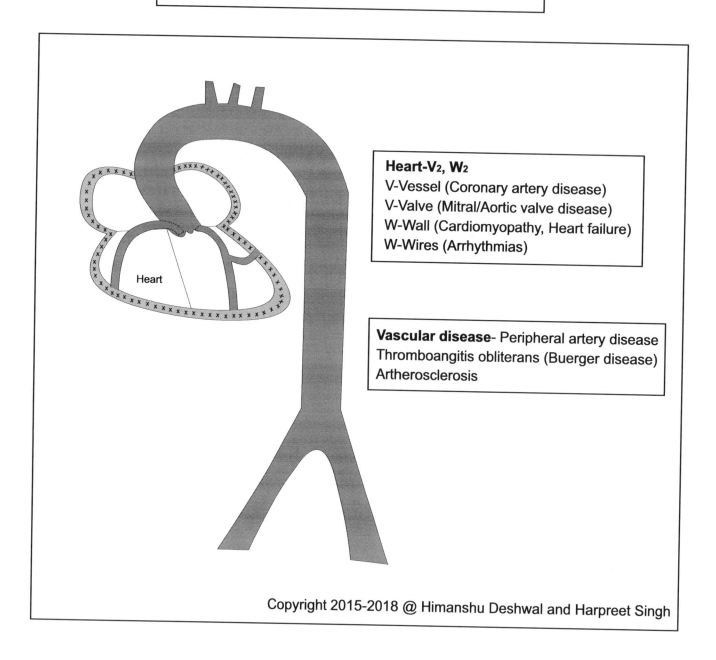

Heart

Heart-V$_2$, W$_2$
V-Vessel (Coronary artery disease)
V-Valve (Mitral/Aortic valve disease)
W-Wall (Cardiomyopathy, Heart failure)
W-Wires (Arrhythmias)

Vascular disease- Peripheral artery disease
Thromboangitis obliterans (Buerger disease)
Artherosclerosis

O-Osteoporosis: I continued on with the checklist and drew the diagram of a hip to demonstrate the increased incidence of osteoporosis in smokers.

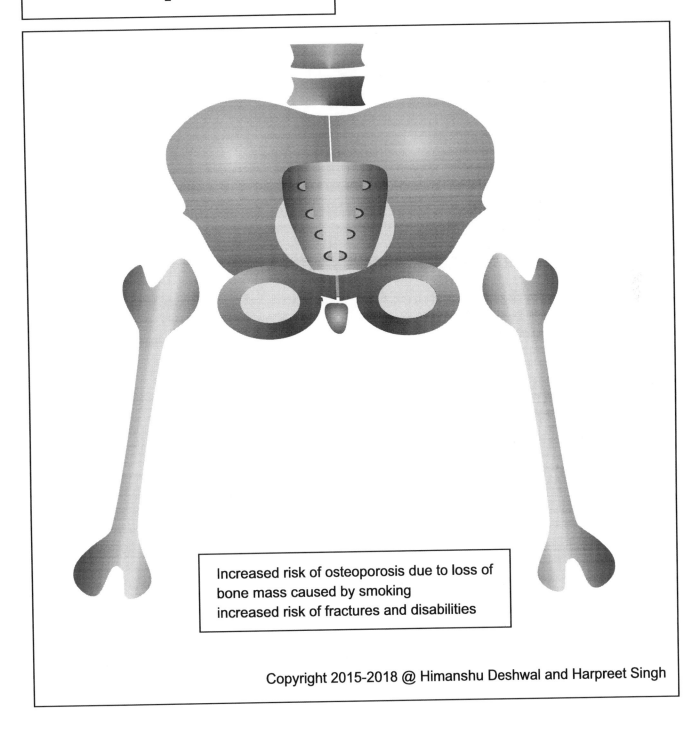

Increased risk of osteoporosis due to loss of
bone mass caused by smoking
increased risk of fractures and disabilities

K-Kidney: Kidney cancers are also more common in smokers than in non-smokers.

Kidney

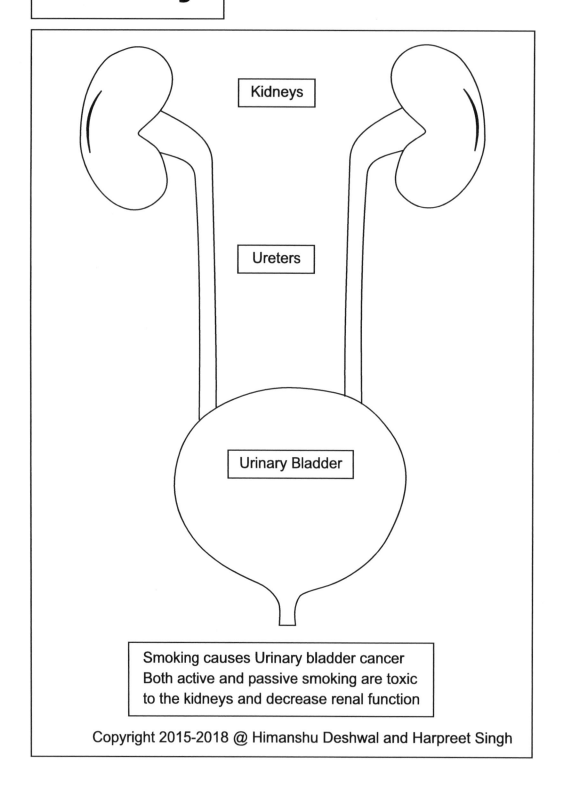

Kidneys

Ureters

Urinary Bladder

Smoking causes Urinary bladder cancer
Both active and passive smoking are toxic
to the kidneys and decrease renal function

A-Arterial Disease: Deposits of cholesterol can also lead to peripheral artery disease, a condition in which narrowed blood vessels reduce blood flow to the limbs.

Artery

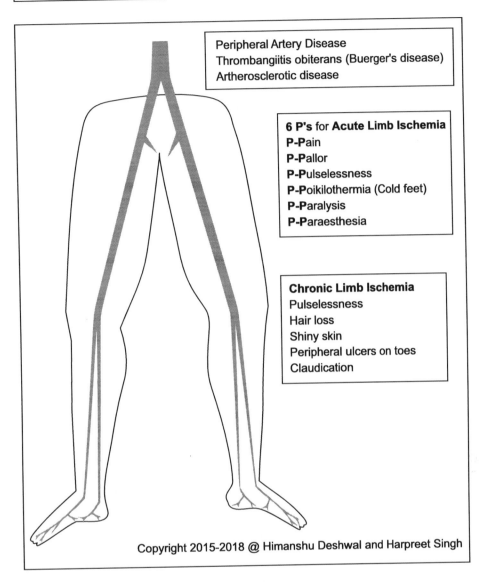

Peripheral Artery Disease
Thrombangiitis obiterans (Buerger's disease)
Artherosclerotic disease

6 P's for **Acute Limb Ischemia**
P-Pain
P-Pallor
P-Pulselessness
P-Poikilothermia (Cold feet)
P-Paralysis
P-Paraesthesia

Chronic Limb Ischemia
Pulselessness
Hair loss
Shiny skin
Peripheral ulcers on toes
Claudication

Y-Yearly expenses: If an average person spends $7 on cigarettesevery day, that averages out to $210 per month or $2,520 a year. In ten years, that is a whopping $25,200!

After I had completed my checklist, I asked my patient if she had urinary incontinence and she hesitantly admitted that she did. "Is this really due to my smoking?" she asked, concerned. I once again confirmed that it might be, and I warned her that if she did not quit now, she'd probably have to wear adult diapers, not something a 27-year-old wants to hear.

Yet the next question she asked not only shocked me, but it has forever changed the way I view my patients.

"That means eventually I won't be able to wear Victoria's Secret either?" she said.

I could not believe it. Here I was explaining how smoking causes cancer and my millennial patient was more concerned about her ability to wear sexy underwear.

I conduct USMLE Step 2 Clinical Skills workshop for medical students where I teach them how to draw simple two dimensional pictures to explain to their standardized patients and score high marks on communication interpersonal skills (CIS) and integrated clinical encounter (ICE). After this experience with my patient,I want help physician assistants, nurse practitioners, nurses, fellows, residents, doctors and other health caregivers how to improve their communication skills and patient experience score. This one question changed the trajectory of Vital Checklist from a USMLE Step 2 CS training company to a patient experience company.

Coincidentally, I had been reading "The Power of Habit" a book by Charles Duhigg that talks about the cue, routine and reward model.

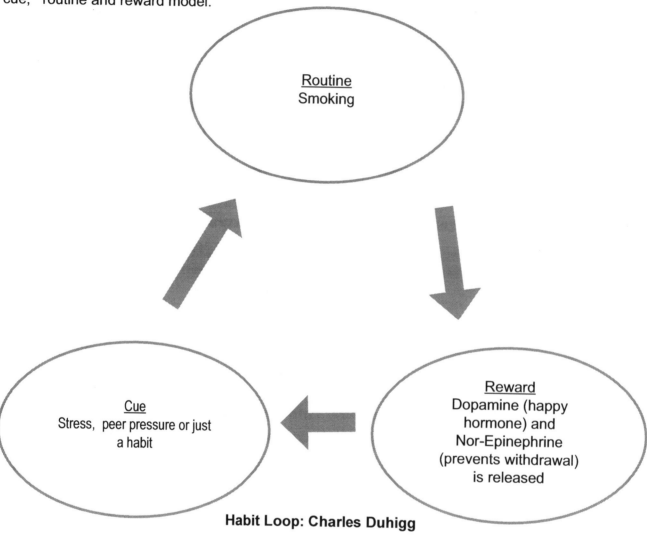

Habit Loop: Charles Duhigg

Duhigg successfully explains how habits work. At first, we have the cue, or the reason we do what we do. Then we have the established routine and the reward. To break a habit, one must break the chain of any of the cycles.

For this patient, I knew the reward was Victoria's Secret. To my male patients, however,it might be libido. For a few, it might simply be a healthy, long life.Some people may worry about heart disease or wrinkles, while othersmight worry about pregnancy-related side-effects.

I learned a few valuable lessons after the talk with my patient. Everybody has a variable reward system. Basically, if I want to help my patients I need to get into their limbic systems. I need to chalk out the details of their habit loops. However,how can this be simplified?

The approach should be made in the following manner. The routine should be teaching **"LET'S CRUSH SMOKING, OKAY!"** Plan and hope patient will connect with one of the side effects of the smoking and remember it when they get an urge to smoke or are pressured by their peers. The routine would be not to use tobacco. The cue or trigger can be classified under time, place, person or emotion and this can be due to their peers, at lunch break, in the office or the car. The routine of 'not smoking' should overpower the routine of moking. This transformation in the habit loop can only be achieved if a health caregiver can make patients understand the reward which matters most to them and in my patient it was Victoria Secret.

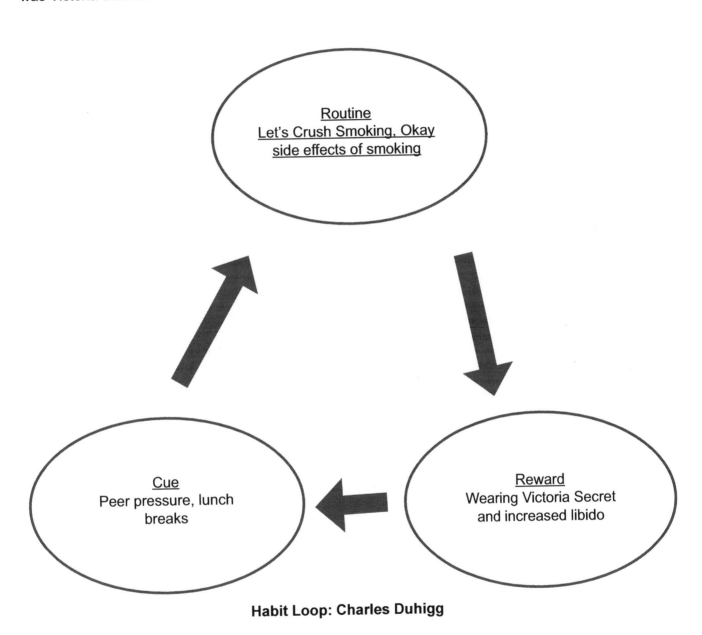

Habit Loop: Charles Duhigg

Every doctor can be a transformational coach and help patients in changing their old habits. In this book, I have provided checklists and two-dimensional pictures for caregivers and hope they can also become successful in improving their patient experience score by educating patients with this simple approach. At first, it will appear daunting to learn the checklists and then draw pictures, but once you start doing this, it will become easier with practice. This Vital Checklist will proactively assist patients by asking/answering doctors' questions resulting in patient empowerment.

4. How to improve HCAHPS?

HCAHPS: Hospital Consumer Assessment of Healthcare Providers and Systems clinic

Present Day Scenario

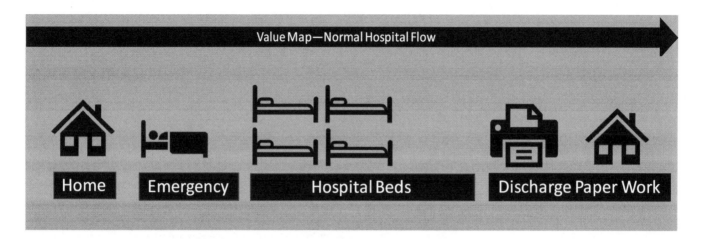

Value Map—Normal Hospital Flow

Home   Emergency   Hospital Beds   Discharge Paper Work

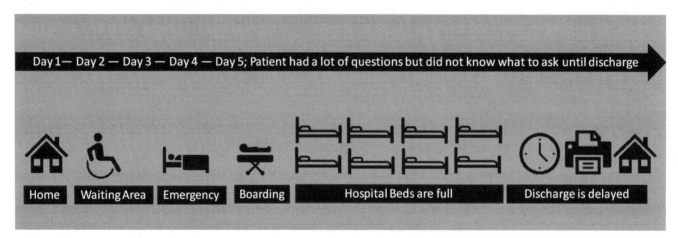

Day 1— Day 2 — Day 3 — Day 4 — Day 5; Patient had a lot of questions but did not know what to ask until discharge

Home   Waiting Area   Emergency   Boarding   Hospital Beds are full   Discharge is delayed

Hospital Process with Vital Checklist

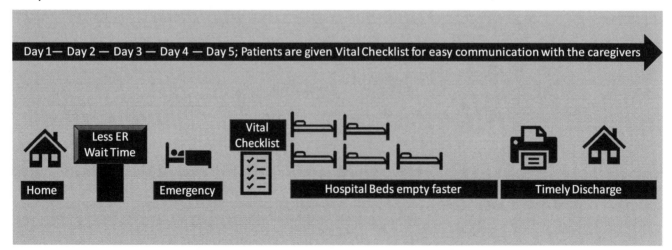

Day 1— Day 2 — Day 3 — Day 4 — Day 5; Patients are given Vital Checklist for easy communication with the caregivers

Home   Less ER Wait Time   Emergency   Vital Checklist   Hospital Beds empty faster   Timely Discharge

5. How to improve CG-CAHPS?

The Clinician and Group Consumer Assessment of Healthcare Providers and Systems

Present Day Outpatient Process

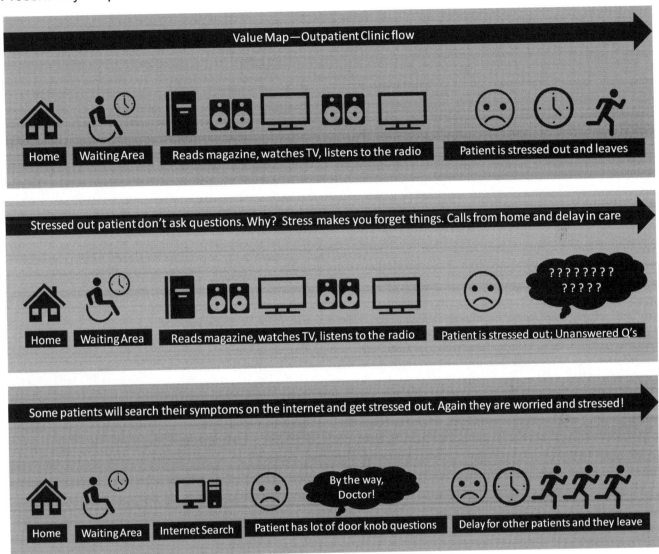

Outpatient Process with Vital Checklist

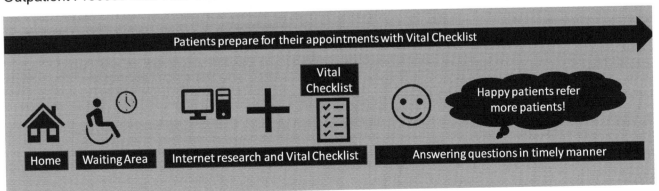

6. How to improve health and wellness of your team members?

Present day Health and Wellness Process

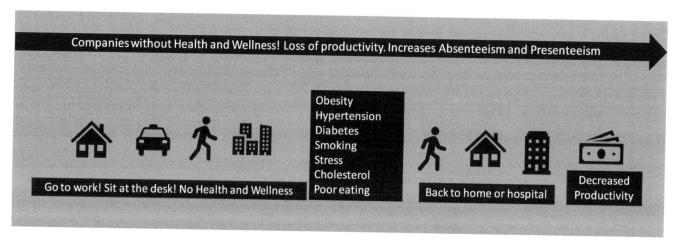

Health and Wellness Process with Vital Checklist

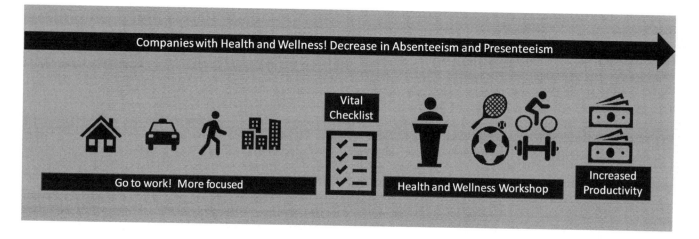

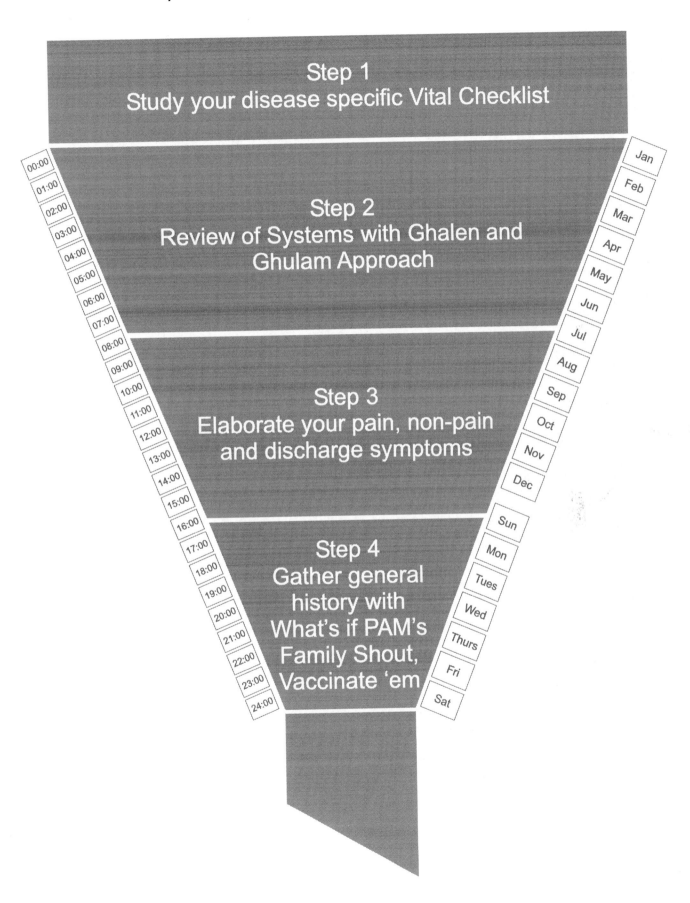

Step 1
Study your disease specific Vital Checklist

Step 2
Review of Systems with Ghalen and
Ghulam Approach

Step 3
Elaborate your pain, non-pain
and discharge symptoms

Step 4
Gather general
history with
What's if PAM's
Family Shout,
Vaccinate 'em

00:00
01:00
02:00
03:00
04:00
05:00
06:00
07:00
08:00
09:00
10:00
11:00
12:00
13:00
14:00
15:00
16:00
17:00
18:00
19:00
20:00
21:00
22:00
23:00
24:00

Jan
Feb
Mar
Apr
May
Jun
Jul
Aug
Sep
Oct
Nov
Dec
Sun
Mon
Tues
Wed
Thurs
Fri
Sat

Health history alone can yield 76%of diagnosis,it is because of this that health care providers ask many questions before they examine and get to the assessment and treatment plan. (1)With the advent of telehealth, health caregivers are going to depend on the history even more. To make sure they can make a correct diagnosis, they will need to collect a good history about disease symptoms, review of symptoms, disease prevention procedures, family history, social history, travel history, exposure to sick contacts, hospitalization history,and sexual history. Filtering negative history from the positive history is an art which health caregivers have mastered over the years in their medical schools, residencies,and fellowships and this is what helps them with the diagnosis. Health caregivers use this universal method of history taking to come to the diagnosis or generate differential diagnosis. We call this concept the Diagnostic Funnel.

All this focus on perfecting health caregivers has left patients in the lurch. This has led patients to search their own symptoms on the symptom checker provided by various healthcare portals. In the clinic or the hospitals, patients are usually stressed out and may forget to ask appropriate questions or they may not recall them because they have been inundated by medical jargon on the internet. Questions are the answers; patients who are ready with their questions provide a good history and facilitate the right diagnosis and treatment plan. In this book, we attempt to bring doctors and patients on the same page by providing easy-to-remember and difficult-to-forget checklists and two-dimensional pictures.

Section 1-Vital Checklist

In this chapter, we have provided a step-by-step approach for patients so they can better utilize this book.We already know that patients search their symptoms on the internet and will have some idea about the disease process. These symptoms may be a part of the numerous disease processes. This causes the patients stress as the first words that come to their minds are cancer or death. The 'C' word often creates anxiety and depression. In our book, we have compiled these symptoms in the form of Vital Checklist which we have divided in sections. Once the patients have gone through these checklists, they will move to the section 2 of the diagnostic funnel where they will check their associated symptoms.

Section 2-Review of Systems

After patients have gone through the symptom checker on the internet and studied the corresponding Vital Checklist, now is the time to gather associated symptoms.

Review of Systems

Skin- Remember skin is the largest organ. Document moles, skin cancer and scars.
Be RESPECTFUL (Signs of Inflammation)
R- Redness; ES-Excessive Swelling; P-Pain; EC-Excessive Calor; (T); FUL-Functional Loss

G	General Examination	G	Glands
H	Heart (Cardiovascular)	H	HEENT/ Hematology
A	Abdomen	U	Urogenital-Bowel and Bladder
L	Lungs	L	Lumbosacral
E	Extremities	A	Anal bleeding, Buttocks/Prostate
N	Neurological	M	Musculoskeletal-Muscles and Joints

Psychiatric-SAD
S-Sad (Depression)
A-Anxiety
D-Day time somnolence; Fatigue

Table:Review of Symptoms—An easy to remember and hard to forget Vital Checklist for Review of Systems

Section 3—Elaborating pain and non-pain symptoms

Symptom: PAIN Life isn't Good, DOCTOR AID @ PM©		Symptom: Non-Pain DOCTOR AID @ PM
Life isn't	Location	
Good	Grade	
D	Duration (Including frequency)	Duration (Including frequency)
O	Onset	Onset
C	Characteristic	Characteristic
T	Time of the Day	Time of the Day
O	Occasion	Occasion
R	Radiation	Rate of Progression
A	Associated Symptoms	Associated Symptoms
I	Increasing factors	Increasing factors
D @	Decreasing factors	Decreasing factors
P	Past Medical History for this symptom	Past Medical History for this symptom
M	Medications	Medications

Section 4—Gather general history

After reviewing the Vital Checklist, discussing areview of systems and elaborating on pain, non-pain and discharge symptoms, patients must focus on general history. It is essential to have a list of worries documented so that you can discuss with your health caregiver what is bothering you.

Make sure to document your past medical history and when it started. Always check your allergies and types of allergic reaction it causes. Bring your medication bottles, this includes all over the counter medications. If you have had any surgeries, document their date, type of surgery, and most importantly, who did the surgery. The family history of diabetes, heart disease, stroke, and/or cancer is critical to record as they will determine your predisposition to get the disease. Always mention if you were admitted overnight to the hospital and stayed for more than two midnights or you went to the emergency room alone. If you are women, remember your obstetric and gynecological history. Always talk to your doctor about urogenital and bowel issues. Travel to other places may expose you to diseases endemic to that area. Write your travel history and document any sickness while visiting there. Have you been exposed to sick people? Discussing your sexual history and yourpartners with your doctor is appropriate. Vaccinations are essential and talk about them.

What IF PAM'S FAMILY SHOUTS? Vaccinate 'em!	
What	Worries
I	Insomnia
F	Fever with or without chills and rigors, Fatigue
P	Past medical history (Blood pressure, Sugar)
A	Allergies and manifestations
M	Medications
S	Surgeries
Family	Family history (Blood pressure, Sugar, Heart disease)
S	Social history (Tobacco, Alcohol, Recreational drugs)
H	Hospitalization
O	Obstetric and gynecological history
U	Urogenital and bowel problems
T	Travel
S	Sick contacts and sexual history
Vaccinate	Vaccination history
em	Empathy to be shown

Always remember to document the time of onset of your symptoms.

The Vital Checklist Workshop started as a USMLE Step 2 Clinical Skills training workshop, where I taught medical students about empathy and patient experience. I used to portray a standardized patient and gave difficult scenarios to the medical students. This was when I had an epiphany of writing a book for patients. As a doctor, we have spent years in training and still have to go through the exams, CME, recertifications exams, guidelines, and protocols but when it comes to patients we have limited training material, and this is my attempt to make patients smarter, healthier and wiser.

1. Peterson MC, Holbrook JH, Von Hales D, Smith NL, Staker LV. Contributions of the history, physical examination, and laboratory investigation in making medical diagnoses. West J Med. 1992;156(2):163-5.

Section B

How to prepare for a doctor's
visit and plan a discharge
process from the hospital or a clinic

Patient Notes_____
Patient Drawings_____

Vital Checklist for Pain Symptoms: Life isn't Good, Doctor AID @PM

If you are in pain, use this Vital Checklist—Life isn't Good, Doctor aid @PM, to develop the story of your problems. Read the questions on the adjoining page and write the answers next to it and if you need to write more or like to draw, use the space below.

Patient Name_____
Caregiver Initials_____

Answer | Patient Initials

L Life | **Location**[1, 2]
Where is your pain located?
Can you point to where your pain is?

☐

G Good | **Grade**
Can you grade your pain on a scale of 0 to 10?
☐0 ☐1 ☐2 ☐3 ☐4 ☐5 ☐6 ☐7 ☐8 ☐9 ☐10

☐

D | **Duration**[3]
How long have you experienced this pain?

☐

O | **Onset**
When did your pain start?
Did it start all of a sudden or did it develop, slowly over a period of time?

☐

C | **Character/ Quality**
Can you describe your pain?

☐

T | **Time of the day**[4]
Any variation in pain in morning or evening?

☐

O | **Occasion**[5]
What were you doing when the pain started?

☐

R | **Radiation**[6]
Does your pain stay there or does it travel anywhere else?

☐

A | **Associated**[7]
Any other symptoms associated with pain?

☐

I **Increasing factors[2]**
What makes your pain worse?

☐

D **Decreasing factors[8, 9]**
What makes pain better?

☐

P **Previous episode**
Any similar episode in the past?

☐

M **Medications[10]**
Any medications that helped you with the pain in the past?

☐

Caregiver Initials_____

Bibliography

1. Marcus, G.M., et al., The utility of gestures in patients with chest discomfort. Am J Med, 2007. 120(1): p. 83-9.

2. Davies, H.A., et al., Angina-like esophageal pain: differentiation from cardiac pain by history. J Clin Gastroenterol, 1985. 7(6): p. 477-81.

3. Swap, C.J. and J.T. Nagurney, Value and limitations of chest pain history in the evaluation of patients with suspected acute coronary syndromes. Jama, 2005. 294(20): p. 2623-9.

4. Fu, L.W., Z.L. Guo, and J.C. Longhurst, Undiscovered role of endogenous thromboxane A2 in activation of cardiac sympathetic afferents during ischaemia. J Physiol, 2008. 586(13): p. 3287-300.

5. Lee, T.H., et al., Acute chest pain in the emergency room. Identification and examination of low-risk patients. Arch Intern Med, 1985. 145(1): p. 65-9.

6. Berger, J.P., et al., Right arm involvement and pain extension can help to differentiate coronary diseases from chest pain of other origin: a prospective emergency ward study of 278 consecutive patients admitted for chest pain. J Intern Med, 1990. 227(3): p. 165-72.

7. Kreiner, M., et al., Craniofacial pain as the sole symptom of cardiac ischemia: a prospective multicenter study. J Am Dent Assoc, 2007. 138(1): p. 74-9.

8. Chan, S., et al., The use of gastrointestinal cocktail for differentiating gastro-oesophageal reflux disease and acute coronary syndrome in the emergency setting: a systematic review. Heart Lung Circ, 2014. 23(10): p. 913-23.

9. Henrikson, C.A., et al., Chest pain relief by nitroglycerin does not predict active coronary artery disease. Ann Intern Med, 2003. 139(12): p. 979-86.

10. Mason, L., et al., Systematic review of topical capsaicin for the treatment of chronic pain. Bmj, 2004. 328(7446): p. 991.

Patient Notes_____
Patient Drawings_____

Patient Notes_____
Patient Drawings_____

Vital Checklist for the symptoms other than pain—Doctor AID @ PM

If you are not in pain, but have symptoms of dizziness, ringing in the ears, shortness of breath, palpitations (heart making funny sounds, loss of appetite, tremors, slurring of speech, hearing loss, blurring of vision, use the Vital Checklist—Doctor aid @PM. Read the questions on the adjoining page and write the answers next to it and if you need to write more or like to draw, use the space below.

DOCTOR AID @ PM™

Patient Name_____
Caregiver Initials_____

Answer

Patient
Initials

Duration[1]
How long have you experienced these symptoms?

☐

Onset
When did this start?

☐

Character/ Quality
Can you describe your symptoms?

☐

Time of onset
Diurnal variation[2]
Did it start all of a sudden or build up slowly over a period of time?
Any variation in the symptoms in the morning or evening?

☐

Occasion
What were you doing when the symptoms started?

☐

Rate of progression[3]
Have your symptoms become worse since they started?

☐

Associated features[4]
Any other symptoms associated with it?

☐

Increasing factors[5]
What makes it worse?

☐

Decreasing factors[6]
What makes it better?

☐

		Answer	Patient Initials

P **Previous episode**[7]

Any similar episodes in the past?

☐

M **Medications**[8]

Any medications that helped you with in the past?

☐

Caregiver Initials_____

Bibliography

1. Baloh, R.W., Vertebrobasilar insufficiency and stroke. Otolaryngol Head Neck Surg, 1995. 112(1): p. 114-7.

2. von Brevern, M., et al., Epidemiology of benign paroxysmal positional vertigo: a population based study. J Neurol Neurosurg Psychiatry, 2007. 78(7): p. 710-5.

3. Furman, J.M. and S.P. Cass, Benign paroxysmal positional vertigo. N Engl J Med, 1999. 341(21): p. 1590-6.

4. Kerber, K.A., et al., Stroke among patients with dizziness, vertigo, and imbalance in the emergency department: a population-based study. Stroke, 2006. 37(10): p. 2484-7.

5. Marzo, S.J., et al., Diagnosis and management of post-traumatic vertigo. Laryngoscope, 2004. 114(10): p. 1720-3.

6. Watson, S.R., G.M. Halmagyi, and J.G. Colebatch, Vestibular hypersensitivity to sound (Tullio phenomenon): structural and functional assessment. Neurology, 2000. 54(3): p. 722-8.

7. Knox, G.W. and A. McPherson, Meniere's disease: differential diagnosis and treatment. Am Fam Physician, 1997. 55(4): p. 1185-90, 1193-4.

8. Guneri, E.A. and O. Kustutan, The effects of betahistine in addition to epley maneuver in posterior canal benign paroxysmal positional vertigo. Otolaryngol Head Neck Surg, 2012. 146(1): p. 104-8.

Patient Notes_____
Patient Drawings_____

Patient Notes_____
Patient Drawings_____

Checklist for secretions or Discharge from the Body: ABCDEF

If you have diarrhea, phlegm or sputum, vomiting, discharge or any secretions use the Vital Checklist—ABCDEF, to elaborate your problems. Read the questions on the adjoining page and write the answers next to it or in the space provided below.

VitalChecklist™

ABCDEF[TM]

Patient Name_____
Caregiver Initials_____

Answer | Patient Initials

A **Amount**[1]
What is the amount of discharge?
_____Teaspoon/s; _____Tablespoon/s; _____Cup/s
☐

B **Blood/ No blood**[2]
Is there any blood in your discharge?
What is the color of discharge- bright red/ coffee colored or black colored?
☐

C **Color, Consistency**[3]
What is the color of your discharge?
What is the consistency of your discharge?
☐

D **Duration**[4]
How long have you been having this discharge?
☐

E **Episodes**[5]
How often do you have this discharge?
☐

F **Foul odor, ever**[6]
Does it have any foul smell?
Did you experience a fever with it?
☐

Bibliography

1. Hussain, A.N., C. Policarpio, and M.T. Vincent, Evaluating nipple discharge. Obstet Gynecol Surv, 2006. 61(4): p. 278-83.

2. Isaacs, J.H., Other nipple discharge. Clin Obstet Gynecol, 1994. 37(4): p. 898-902.

3. Murad, T.M., G. Contesso, and H. Mouriesse, Nipple discharge from the breast. Ann Surg, 1982. 195(3): p. 259-64.

4. Jardines, L., Management of nipple discharge. Am Surg, 1996. 62(2): p. 119-22.

5. King, T.A., et al., A simple approach to nipple discharge. Am Surg, 2000. 66(10): p. 960-5; discussion 965-6.

6. Dixon, J.M., et al., Periductal mastitis and duct ectasia: different conditions with different aetiologies. Br J Surg, 1996. 83(6): p. 820-2.

37

Patient Notes_____
Patient Drawings_____

Checklist for Medication Prescription: Drugs at Pharmacy

Always carry a medication list when you go to your doctor's office. If you do not remember a list of medications, how will your health caregiver match your medications with their electronic health records? Your health caregivers would prefer if you can carry your medications in their original containers as it is vital for them to have correct names of your drugs, doses, and number of times you take these medicines. An easy way to recall questions regarding your medications is if you remember this Vital Checklist—Drugs at Pharmacy.

Patient Name_____
Caregiver Initials_____

	Answer	Patient Initials

Drug Name, Dose, Duration[1]

What is the name of the prescription drug?
What is the dose?
How long it should be taken?

☐

Route, Refills[2]

How do you take this medication?
How many refills do you have?

☐

Use or Underuse

What is the purpose of this medicine?
Do you take medications regularly?

☐

Generic[3]

Do you have generic medications?

☐

Side effects, Schedule[4]

What are the side effects of the medicine?
How often should you take the medicine?

☐

Allergies, Alternative medication[5, 6]

Are you allergic to any of the medicines?
If yes, is there an alternative medication?

☐

Pharmacy name

What is the name and address of the pharmacy to where the prescription is sent?

☐

Bibliography

1. Wang, D.D., et al., Fixed dosing versus body size-based dosing of monoclonal antibodies in adult clinical trials. J Clin Pharmacol, 2009. 49(9): p. 1012-24.

2. Preskorn, S.H. and C.R. Hatt, How pharmacogenomics (PG) are changing practice: implications for prescribers, their patients, and the healthcare system (PG series part I). J Psychiatr Pract, 2013. 19(2): p. 142-9.

3. Krauss, G.L., et al., Assessing bioequivalence of generic antiepilepsy drugs. Ann Neurol, 2011. 70(2): p. 221-8.

4. Anderson, I.M., et al., Evidence-based guidelines for treating depressive disorders with antidepressants: a revision of the 2000 British Association for Psychopharmacology guidelines. J Psychopharmacol, 2008. 22(4): p. 343-96.

5. Messaad, D., et al., Drug provocation tests in patients with a history suggesting an immediate drug hypersensitivity reaction. Ann Intern Med, 2004. 140(12): p. 1001-6.

6. Aberer, W., et al., Drug provocation testing in the diagnosis of drug hypersensitivity reactions: general considerations. Allergy, 2003. 58(9): p. 854-63.

Patient Notes_____
Patient Drawings_____

Patient Notes_____
Patient Drawings_____

Checklist for High-Risk Medications: Dr. Was 3 MD

Every medication has side effects and discussing about side effects with your health caregivers is the most critical aspect of your clinical encounter with your health caregiver. Drugs are essential but their interactions with the other medications are important, and this is the reason, you must take all the pills—over the counter, homeopathy, vitamins, natural supplements and prescribed medications to the doctor's office. Remember the acronym—Dr. Was 3 MD, to remember the significant high-risk medications. This is not a complete list and always consult your doctor regarding this.

Write your medications here	Draw or doodle

VitalChecklist™

Patient Name_____

Caregiver Initials_____

	Answer	Patient Initials

D Digoxin[1]

Do you take Digoxin?
If yes, it is associated with risk of arrhythmias and heart failure in high doses.

☐

R Renin Angiotensin inhibitors[2]

Do you take blood pressure medications like Lisinopril or Losartan?
If yes, they are associated with producing birth defects in the baby, if used during pregnancy.

☐

W Warfarin[3]

Do you take Warfarin?
If yes, it is associated with risk of bleeding and birth defects in the baby, if used during pregnancy.

☐

A Anti-seizure, Anti-cancer[4, 5]

Do you take any anti-epileptic medications?
If yes, they are associated with risk of respiratory failure.
Do you take anti-cancer medications?
If yes, they are associated with increased risk of infections, bleeding and anemias.

☐

S Steroids[6]

Do you take Steroids like Prednisone or Dexamethasone?
If yes, they are associated with risk of high blood pressure, high blood sugar levels, infections, osteoporosis and cataracts.

☐

S **(Sugar medications) Anti-Diabetic drugs:Oral hypoglycemic Agents, Insulin** [7]

Do you take any medications for Diabetes?
If yes, they are associated with risk of low blood sugar levels in high doses.

☐

S **Sedatives or hypnotic agents**[8]

Do you take any medications for insomnia? If yes, it can result in heart and respiratory failure in high doses.

☐

M **Morphine and other opioid analgesics like Oxycodone**[9]

Do you take any opioid medications?
If yes, it they can result in respiratory failure in high doses and cause constipation with regular doses.

☐

D **Diuretics like Furosemide**[10]

Do you take Furosemide?
If yes, it can cause dehydration and electrolyte abnormalities.

☐

Bibliography

Caregiver Initials_____

1. Lip, G.Y., M.J. Metcalfe, and F.G. Dunn, Diagnosis and treatment of digoxin toxicity. Postgrad Med J, 1993. 69(811): p. 337-9.

2. Izzo, J.L., Jr. and M.R. Weir, Angiotensin-converting enzyme inhibitors. J Clin Hypertens (Greenwich), 2011. 13(9): p. 667-75.

3. Fitzmaurice, D.A., A.D. Blann, and G.Y. Lip, Bleeding risks of antithrombotic therapy. Bmj, 2002. 325(7368): p. 828-31.

4. Schiff, D., P.Y. Wen, and M.J. van den Bent, Neurological adverse effects caused by cytotoxic and targeted therapies. Nat Rev Clin Oncol, 2009. 6(10): p. 596-603.

5. Bronstein, A.C., et al., 2008 Annual Report of the American Association of Poison Control Centers' National Poison Data System (NPDS): 26th Annual Report. Clin Toxicol (Phila), 2009. 47(10): p. 911-1084.

6. Schacke, H., W.D. Docke, and K. Asadullah, Mechanisms involved in the side effects of glucocorticoids. Pharmacol Ther, 2002. 96(1): p. 23-43.

7. Murad, M.H., et al., Clinical review: Drug-induced hypoglycemia: a systematic review.J Clin Endocrinol Metab, 2009. 94(3): p.741-5.

8. Hojer, J., S. Baehrendtz, and L. Gustafsson, Benzodiazepine poisoning: experience of 702 admissions to an intensive care unit during a 14-year period. J Intern Med, 1989. 226(2): p. 117-22.

9. Dart, R.C., et al., Trends in opioid analgesic abuse and mortality in the United States. N Engl J Med, 2015. 372(3): p. 241-8.

10. Strom, B.L., et al., Absence of cross-reactivity between sulfonamide antibiotics and sulfonamide nonantibiotics. N Engl J Med, 2003. 349(17): p. 1628-35.

Ready→Set→(iCrush)

Before you go to next section, try to answer these questions. Have you received pamphlets, booklets or discharge paperwork from the hospital? Now, do you wish there was an easy way to remember so much information?

- Name of the doctor who will follow up: Primary Care Doctor _____
- Name of the doctor who will follow up: Cardiologist _____
- Name of the doctor who will follow up: Pulmonologist _____
- Name of the doctor who will follow up: Other doctors _____
- Name of the doctor who will follow up: Other doctors _____

Follow up on the test results: Complete Metabolic Profile, Complete Blood Count, Thyroid function test, liver function test, kidney function test, blood cultures, urine cultures, PT/INR

Follow up on the radiological studies: X-rays, CT-Scan, MRI, Nuclear studies, PET-Scan and more

Do you need any help with home health, nursing, and therapy? Yes or No

Do you need help with your activities of daily living?

Activities of daily living: Do you need assistance or can you manage on your own	Need some help	Able to do this without help	Name of the person or the company which helps you with this
Using toilet			
Bathing			
Dressing			
Eating			
Getting in and out of the bed or chairs			
Walking			
Managing money			
Taking medications			
Preparing meals			
Shopping and running errands			
Housekeeping chores			
Using the telephone			

Need additional resources	Yes	No	Name of the company or individual
Physical, occupational, speech therapy at home			
Home health aide			
Social worker			
Adult day care center			
Assistance with transportation			
Home health nurse			

Do you need any equipment?	Yes	No	Name of the person or the company which helps you with this
T.P.N or nutrition therapy			
Feeding tube			
Oxygen			
Colostomy care			
Cathetor care			
Help with insulin pump			
Help with taking blood pressure			
Wound dressing			
Wound vaccum			
Injections			
Wheelchair			
Walker or cane			

Are you expert in management	Yes	No	Comments
Blood pressure log book			
Blood sugar log book			
Wound management			
Diet Management log book			
Input and output log book			
Weight log book			

Talk about your diet

Are you on dialysis? Talk to your nurse about this, and your dialysis schedule.

Ask if you can drive.

Now try to remember all this. Can you remember and repeat?

An easy-to-remember and difficult-to-forget Vital Checklist is Dr. Saw3 MD

Remember this with our Mascot.

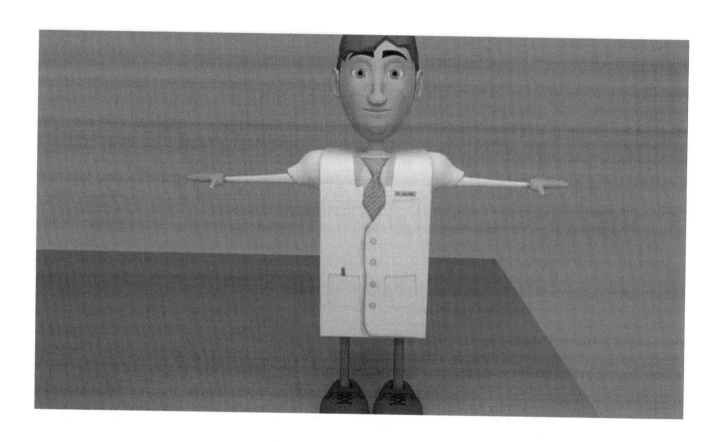

Patient Notes_____
Patient Drawings_____

Checklist for Discharge Instructions: Dr. Saw 3 MD

Draw your own Dr. Saw 3 MD

VitalChecklist™

Dr. (SAW)THREE MD™

Patient Name_____

Caregiver Initials_____

	Answer	Patient Initials

D Dr.

Doctor[1, 2]

Go see your doctor right away, if there is no improvement of symptoms.

Name of the doctor who will follow up:
Primary Care Doctor_____

Name of the doctor who will follow up:
Cardiologist_____

Name of the doctor who will follow up:
Pulmonologist _____

Name of the doctor who will follow up:
Other doctors _____

□

S

Symptom worsening[3]

Call 911 or go to the ER right away, if there is worsening of these symptoms.

□

A

Activity[4]

Lifestyle modification to prevent the incidence of cardiovascular events in the future. Ask your doctor about the lifestyle modifications.

□

W

Weight gain (more than 2 pounds/day or 5 pounds/week)[5]

Prevent weight gain, eat healthy diet, do regular exercise.

□

S

Smoking[6]

Quit smoking.

□

A

Alcohol[7]

Restrict Alcohol.

□

W **Wine[8]**
Restrict Wine.

☐

S **Sodium restrictions[9-11]**
Consume a sodium restricted diet as advised by a dietitian
or your doctor.

☐

A **And**

☐

W **Water/Fluid restriction[12]**
Fluid restriction as advised by a dietician or your doctor.

☐

T **Transport for follow up appointments[13]**
Transport facilities for regular follow up visits.

☐

H **Home health care nurse[14]**
Home health nurse helps to take care of patients with
activities of daily living, compliance with medications
and follow up visits, ER visits if needed.

☐

R **Return to work[15]**
Return to work depends upon the asymptomatic state
and job satisfaction.
Ask your doctor when can you retrun to work.

☐

E **Equipment[16]**
Equipment like walker, cane, nasal cannula and oxygen
are provided for the aid of the patient.

☐

E **Expert in wound care[17]**
Take care of the wound with regular change of wound
dressing.
Watch for signs of infection like fever, pain, discharge,
redness, and swelling at the site.

☐

Caregiver Initials_____

M Medications[18, 19]

Take medications regularly as advised by the physician.
See the doctor right away if you experience any side effects
or allergic reactions to any of the medicines

☐

D Diet[20]

Consume a diet as advised by dietician.
D: Driving When can you drive.
D: Dialysis : Are you on dialysis? Has your dialysis been scheduled?

☐

Caregiver Initials_____

Bibliography

1. Kuo, Y.F. and J.S. Goodwin, Association of hospitalist care with medical utilization after discharge: evidence of cost shift from a cohort study. Ann Intern Med, 2011. 155(3): p. 152-9.

2. Halasyamani, L., et al., Transition of care for hospitalized elderly patients—development of a discharge checklist for hospitalists. J Hosp Med, 2006. 1(6): p. 354-60.

3. Jha, A.K., E.J. Orav, and A.M. Epstein, Public reporting of discharge planning and rates of readmissions. N Engl J Med, 2009. 361(27): p. 2637-45.

4. LeFevre, M.L., Behavioral counseling to promote a healthful diet and physical activity for cardiovascular disease prevention in adults with cardiovascular risk factors: U.S. Preventive Services Task Force Recommendation Statement. Ann Intern Med, 2014. 161(8): p. 587-93.

5. Leslie, W.S., C.R. Hankey, and M.E. Lean, Weight gain as an adverse effect of some commonly prescribed drugs: a systematic review. Qjm, 2007. 100(7): p. 395-404.

6. Kotz, D., J. Brown, and R. West, Prospective cohort study of the effectiveness of smoking cessation treatments used in the "real world". Mayo Clin Proc, 2014. 89(10): p. 1360-7.

7. Rebholz, C.E., et al., Alcohol consumption and binge drinking in young adult childhood cancer survivors. Pediatr Blood Cancer, 2012. 58(2): p. 256-64.

8. La Vecchia, C., et al., Prevalence of chronic diseases in alcohol abstainers. Epidemiology, 1995. 6(4): p. 436-8.

9. Mente, A., et al., Association of urinary sodium and potassium excretion with blood pressure. N Engl J Med, 2014. 371(7): p. 601-11.

10. He, F.J., J. Li, and G.A. Macgregor, Effect of longer term modest salt reduction on blood pressure: Cochrane systematic review and meta-analysis of randomised trials. Bmj, 2013. 346: p. f1325.

11. Stolarz-Skrzypek, K., et al., Fatal and nonfatal outcomes, incidence of hypertension, and blood pressure changes in relation to urinary sodium excretion. Jama, 2011. 305(17): p. 1777-85.

12. Yancy, C.W., et al., 2013 ACCF/AHA guideline for the management of heart failure: a report of the American College of Cardiology Foundation/American Heart Association Task Force on practice guidelines. Circulation, 2013. 128(16): p. e240-327.

13. Siebens, H., Applying the domain management model in treating patients with chronic diseases. Jt Comm J Qual Improv, 2001. 27(6): p. 302-14.

14. Shepperd, S., et al., Discharge planning from hospital to home. Cochrane Database Syst Rev, 2010(1): p. Cd000313.

15. Mark, D.B., et al., Identification of acute myocardial infarction patients suitable for early hospital discharge after aggressive interventional therapy. Results from the Thrombolysis and Angioplasty in Acute Myocardial Infarction Registry. Circulation, 1991. 83(4): p. 1186-93.

16. Doherty, D.E., et al., Recommendations of the 6th long-term oxygen therapy consensus conference. Respir Care, 2006. 51(5): p. 519-25.

17. Paddle-Ledinek, J.E., Z. Nasa, and H.J. Cleland, Effect of different wound dressings on cell viability and proliferation. Plast Reconstr Surg, 2006. 117(7 Suppl): p. 110S-118S; discussion 119S-120S.

18. Cullen, D.J., et al., Preventable adverse drug events in hospitalized patients: a comparative study of intensive care and general care units. Crit Care Med, 1997. 25(8): p. 1289-97.

19. Sarkar, U., et al., Adverse drug events in U.S. adult ambulatory medical care. Health Serv Res, 2011. 46(5): p. 1517-33.

20. Diet, nutrition and the prevention of chronic diseases. World Health Organ Tech Rep Ser, 2003. 916: p. i-viii, 1-149, backcover.

Checklist for Post-Discharge Warning Symptoms: (iCrush)

You will receive truckloads of paperwork regarding the discharge instructions which you must read and implement in your daily life. Health caregivers will explain the discharge instructions to patients at the time of discharge. Giving health literacy booklets, pamphlets and discharge paperwork to the patients is a mandate as doctors have to check the box in the electronic health system, therefore, printing this paperwork is a must and makes the doctor accountable. Whether this communication between patients and doctors happen or not, checking of the box is an essential element of electronic health records.

As a caregiver, have you ever asked a patient if they remembered all discharge instructions after 24 hours? We forget things, and so do your patients. We have checklist, protocols, and guidelines but why don't we give these lists to the patients. We need to focus on the meaningful use and meaningful communications rather than just handing papers and assuming we talked to the patients.

Let's focus on simplifying healthcare with acronyms, mnemonics, and Vital Checklist.

Remember to repeat, repeat to remember—John Medina

iCRUSH™

Patient Name_____
Caregiver Initials_____

| | Answer | Patient Initials |

I — IV Lines and Catheters, Incisions, Intestinal Symptoms[1, 2]

Look for any discharge or redness.
Keep the area dry and clean.
If you have a fever, abdominal pain, nausea, vomiting or diarrhea, immediately see the doctor or come to ER urgently or call 911.

☐

C — Chest Pain[3]

If you have chest pain, call 911.

☐

R — ReSPeCTFul

Look for redness (Re), swelling (S), pain (Pe), warmth (Callor), fever (t) and difficulty in using the affected part (Full-functional loss).

☐

U — Urine Problems[4, 5]

If you have any burning in urine/ inability to control bladder/ increased frequency or urge to pass urine/ unable to pass urine, come to ER urgently or call 911.

☐

S — Shortness of breath[6]

If you are short of breath, call 911.

☐

H — Headache[7]

If you experience a worse headache, call 911.

☐

Bibliography

1. Mermel, L.A., et al., Clinical practice guidelines for the diagnosis and management of intravascular catheter-related infection: 2009 Update by the Infectious Diseases Society of America. Clin Infect Dis, 2009. 49(1): p. 1-45.

2. Mermel, L.A., Prevention of intravascular catheter-related infections. Ann Intern Med, 2000. 132(5): p. 391-402.

3. Lindsell, C.J., et al., The Internet Tracking Registry of Acute Coronary Syndromes (i*trACS): a multicenter registry of patients with suspicion of acute coronary syndromes reported using the standardized reporting guidelines for emergency department chest pain studies. Ann Emerg Med, 2006. 48(6): p. 666-77, 677.e1-9.

4. Abrams, P., et al., The standardisation of terminology of lower urinary tract function: report from the Standardisation Sub-committee of the International Continence Society. Neurourol Urodyn, 2002. 21(2): p. 167-78.

5. Mardon, R.E., et al., Management of urinary incontinence in Medicare managed care beneficiaries: results from the 2004 Medicare Health Outcomes Survey. Arch Intern Med, 2006. 166(10): p. 1128-33.

6. Parshall, M.B., et al., An official American Thoracic Society statement: update on the mechanisms, assessment, and management of dyspnea. Am J Respir Crit Care Med, 2012. 185(4): p. 435-52.

7. Gorelick, P.B., et al., Headache in acute cerebrovascular disease. Neurology, 1986. 36(11): p. 1445-50.

Patient Notes_____
Patient Drawings_____

Checklist for health, wellness and chronic disease prevention: Vital Compass

R U Logged in!

Vitalcompass.com

L--Lungs (Chest X Ray); Lower limb examination (It is not a mandate, but should be checked)
O--Obesity and BMI documentation
G--Gait testing
G--Glaucoma testing
E--EKG
D--Depression and Dementia Screening; Advance Directives

VitalChecklist™

ViTAL COMPASS™

Patient Name_____
Caregiver Initials_____

Answer | Patient Initials

V | ## Vaccination and Immunization:
T- Tetanus
I – Influenza(Flu shot)
P- Pneumococcal
C- Cervical cancer (HPV)[1, 2]

☐

Do you get Tetanus vaccine every 10 yrs.?
Did you get Flu shot every year after the age of 50 yrs.?
Did you get Pneumococcal vaccine after the age of 65 yrs.?
Did you get HPV vaccine between 9 to 23 yrs. of age?

I | ## Incontinence
Do you have problems with urine leakage when you cough or sneeze?

☐

Do you have to run to the bathroom to pee?
Do you pee in your underwear?

T | ## Tobacco use, Thyroid tests, Testosterone level[3, 4]

☐

Do you have thyroid problems?
Do you use tobacco in any form?

A | ## Alcohol, A1C, Albuminuria[5, 6]

☐

If Diabetic, how often you get HbA1C checked?
If Diabetic, how often you follow up with the physician for regular blood and urine tests?
Do you use alcohol in any form?

L — Labs, Radiology

When was the last time you had blood and urine tests done?
When was the last time you had X-Ray or CT scan or MRI done?

☐

C — Colonoscopy, Cholesterol[7]

Did you get colonoscopy done every 10 yrs. after 50 yrs. of age?
Do you have high cholesterol?

☐

O — Osteoporosis[8]

For females, did you get DEXA scan done after 65yrs. of age?
If you are on steroids talk to your doctor about osteoporosis screening

☐

M — Mammography

For females, did you get Mammography done every 2 years after the age of 40 years?

☐

P — PAP Smear and PSA[9]

For females, did you get PAP smear done regularly after 21 yrs. of age?
PSA= Prostate Specific Antigen in men

☐

A — Abdominal USG[10]

If you are a smoker, did you get an abdominal ultrasound done after 65 yrs. of age?

☐

S — Sexual Partners, Sexual Orientation and Sexually Transmitted Infections

Are you sexually active?
How many sexual partners do you have?
What is your sexual orientation?
Have you ever had sexually transmitted infections like chlamydia, gonorrhea, syphilis, HIV, Hepatitis B, and Hepatitis C?

☐

S Sugar and Diabetes

Do you urinate a lot at night?
Do you eat a lot?
Did you get your blood sugars checked?

Caregiver Initials_____

Bibliography

1. Kim, D.K., C.B. Bridges, and K.H. Harriman, Advisory Committee on Immunization Practices Recommended Immunization Schedule for Adults Aged 19 Years or Older: United States, 2016. Ann Intern Med, 2016. 164(3): p. 184-94.

2. Pickering, L.K., et al., Immunization programs for infants, children, adolescents, and adults: clinical practice guidelines by the Infectious Diseases Society of America. Clin Infect Dis, 2009. 49(6): p. 817-40.

3. de los Santos, E.T., G.H. Starich, and E.L. Mazzaferri, Sensitivity, specificity, and cost-effectiveness of the sensitive thyrotropin assay in the diagnosis of thyroid disease in ambulatory patients. Arch Intern Med, 1989. 149(3): p. 526-32.

4. Surks, M.I., et al., American Thyroid Association guidelines for use of laboratory tests in thyroid disorders. Jama, 1990. 263(11): p. 1529-32.

5. Nathan, D.M., et al., The clinical information value of the glycosylated hemoglobin assay. N Engl J Med, 1984. 310(6): p. 341-6.

6. Goldstein, D.E., Is glycosylated hemoglobin clinically useful? N Engl J Med, 1984. 310(6): p. 384-5.

7. Rex, D.K., et al., Quality indicators for colonoscopy. Gastrointest Endosc, 2015. 81(1): p. 31-53.

8. Marin, F., et al., Bone mineral density referral for dual-energy X-ray absorptiometry using quantitative ultrasound as a prescreening tool in postmenopausal women from the general population: a cost-effectiveness analysis. Calcif Tissue Int, 2004. 74(3): p. 277-83.

9. Wilt, T.J., R.P. Harris, and A. Qaseem, Screening for cancer: advice for high-value care from the American College of Physicians. Ann Intern Med, 2015. 162(10): p. 718-25.

10. Screening for abdominal aortic aneurysm: recommendation statement. Ann Intern Med, 2005. 142(3): p. 198-202.

11. Workowski, K.A. and G.A. Bolan, Sexually transmitted diseases treatment guidelines, 2015. MMWR Recomm Rep, 2015. 64(Rr-03): p. 1-137.

Patient Name_____
Caregiver Initials_____

Answer   Patient Initials

S   Surgical Clearance[1]

Do you need a clearance for this surgery?

☐

U   Urgency or Emergency[2]

Do you need to get an urgent surgery done?
What will be the duration of surgery?

☐

R   Risks[3]

What are the risks with this surgery?

☐

G   General or Epidural Anesthesia[4]

What kind of anesthesia will you require for this surgery?

☐

E   EKG, Blood work, PT, INR[5, 6]

Do you need to get an EKG and blood tests done?
What are the reports of your blood work and EKG?

☐

R   Recovery Time[7]

How much time will it take to recover from this surgery?

☐

Y   Y (WHY) of the surgery

Why do you need surgery?
How long will the surgery last?
Where will you have surgery done?
How long will be the surgery?
Who will do the surgery?

☐

Bibliography

1. Hilditch, W.G., et al., Validation of a pre-anaesthetic screening questionnaire. Anaesthesia, 2003. 58(9): p. 874-7.

2. Fleisher, L.A., et al., 2009 ACCF/AHA focused update on perioperative beta blockade incorporated into the ACC/AHA 2007 guidelines on perioperative cardiovascular evaluation and care for noncardiac surgery: a report of the American college of cardiology foundation/American heart association task force on practice guidelines. Circulation, 2009. 120(21): p. e169-276.

3. Devereaux, P.J., et al., Association between postoperative troponin levels and 30-day mortality among patients undergoing noncardiac surgery. Jama, 2012. 307(21): p. 2295-304.

4. Gan, T.J., et al., Consensus guidelines for the management of postoperative nausea and vomiting. Anesth Analg, 2014. 118(1): p. 85-113.

5. Goldberger, A.L. and M. O'Konski, Utility of the routine electrocardiogram before surgery and on general hospital admission. Critical review and new guidelines. Ann Intern Med, 1986. 105(4): p. 552-7.

6. Becker, A., K. Niehaus, and A. Puhler, Low-molecular-weight succinoglycan is predominantly produced by Rhizobium meliloti strains carrying a mutated ExoP protein characterized by a periplasmic N-terminal domain and a missing C-terminal domain. Mol Microbiol, 1995. 16(2): p. 191-203.

7. Hines, R., et al., Complications occurring in the postanesthesia care unit: a survey. Anesth Analg, 1992. 74(4): p. 503-9.

Checklist for questions to be asked about your surgery: SURGERY

Patient Note

Patient Notes_____
Patient Drawings_____

No Bumper to Bumper Driving

VitalChecklist™

No Bumper to Bumper Driving™

Patient Name_____
Caregiver Initials_____

	Answer	Patient Initials

N (No) Sign the narcotic contract[1] ☐

B Blood-work: Liver function test, Kidney function test [2] ☐

U Urine Drug Screen[2] ☐

M Monitor automated prescription dispensing system[2, 3] ☐

P Pill Count[2-4] ☐

E EKG and effects of methadone[5] ☐

R Recreational drugs[6] ☐

T (To) Testosterone level (if more than a year)[7] ☐

Bumper

D (Driving) No driving while on narcotics[8] ☐

Bibliography

1. Rager JB, Schwartz PH. Defending Opioid Treatment Agreements: Disclosure, Not Promises. Hastings Cent Rep. 2017;47(3):24-33.

2. Dowell D, Division of Unintentional Injury Prevention NCfIPaC, Centers for Disease Control and Prevention, Atlanta, Georgia, Haegerich TM, Division of Unintentional Injury Prevention NCfIPaC, Centers for Disease Control and Prevention, Atlanta, Georgia, Chou R, Division of Unintentional Injury Prevention NCfIPaC, Centers for Disease Control and Prevention, Atlanta, Georgia. CDC Guideline for Prescribing Opioids for Chronic Pain—United States, 2016. JAMA. 2017;315(15):1624-45.

3. Edlund MJ, Martin BC, Russo JE, DeVries A, Braden JB, Sullivan MD. The role of opioid prescription in incident opioid abuse and dependence among individuals with chronic noncancer pain: the role of opioid prescription. Clin J Pain. 2014;30(7):557-64.

4. Jamison RN, Sheehan KA, Scanlan E, Matthews M, Ross EL. Beliefs and attitudes about opioid prescribing and chronic pain management: survey of primary care providers. J Opioid Manag. 2014;10(6):375-82.

5. Stringer J, Welsh C, Tommasello A. Methadone-associated Q-T interval prolongation and torsades de pointes. Am J Health Syst Pharm. 2009;66(9):825-33.

6. McCall Jones C, Baldwin GT, Compton WM. Recent Increases in Cocaine-Related Overdose Deaths and the Role of Opioids. Am J Public Health. 2017;107(3):430-2.

7. Smith HS, Elliott JA. Opioid-induced androgen deficiency (OPIAD). Pain Physician. 2012;15(3 Suppl):Es145-56.

8. Pollini RA, Waehrer G, Kelley-Baker T. Receipt of Warnings Regarding Potentially Impairing Prescription Medications and Associated Risk Perceptions in a National Sample of U.S. Drivers. J Stud Alcohol Drugs. 2017;78(6):805-13.

Patient Notes_____
Patient Drawings_____

Section C

Brain

Patient Notes_____
Patient Drawings_____

Checklist for Stroke: (iCrush) Stroke

Do you have risk factors for stroke?

1. Irregular heartbeat
2. Cholesterol problems
3. Recreational drugs and alcohol
4. Uncontrolled diabetes mellitus
5. Using tobacco in any form
6. High blood pressure

If you have above-mentioned risk factors, educate yourself on the symptoms and signs of S.T.R.O.K.E as time saved is brain saved.

Do you know any other acronyms to remember stroke?

F	Face
A	Arm
S	Speech
T	Time to call 911

Patient Name_____
Caregiver Initials_____

Answer | Patient Initials

I Irregular heartbeat[1]
Did you ever experience an irregular heart beat?

☐

C Cholesterol problems[2]
Do you have high cholesterol?

☐

R Recreational Drugs and alcohol[3]
Do you use recreational drugs?
Do you drink alcohol?

☐

U Uncontrolled diabetes mellitus[4]
Do you have diabetes?
In what range are your blood sugar levels usually?
What was your last HbA1c?

☐

S Smoking or tobacco in any form[5]
Do you smoke?
Do you chew tobacco?

☐

H Hypertension (high blood pressure) or heart disease[6]
Do you have high blood pressure?
Do you have a heart disease?

☐

Did you experience any of the following symptoms of stroke?

S **Sudden onset severe headache,
Slurred speech**[7]

☐

Did you ever have a sudden onset severe headache?
Do you notice a change in your speech?

T **Topple over (Dizziness)
Trouble walking (imbalance)**[8]

☐

Did you feel dizzy?
Did you ever black-out?
Did you ever tend to lose balance while walking?
Time to call 9-1-1

R **Raise your arms.
Raise your legs**[9]

☐

Do you have weakness in your arms or legs?

O **Orientation to time, place, and person.
Change in behavior**[10]

☐

What is your name?
Where are you now (country/state/city/building)?
What is the year/ month/ day/ time of the day?
Did any family members notice any change of
behavior in you?

K **(K) Confusion.
(K) Coordination**[11]

☐

Did your family members or home support notice any
confusion and difficulties with balance in you?

E **Examine for vision changes, facial
droop**[12, 13]

☐

Do you have blurring of vision or changes in vision?
Did you notice any facial droop or numbness of face?

Caregiver Initials_____

Bibliography

1. Caplan, L.R., Brain embolism, revisited. Neurology, 1993. 43(7): p. 1281-7.

2. Yaghi, S. and M.S. Elkind, Lipids and Cerebrovascular Disease: Research and Practice. Stroke, 2015. 46(11): p. 3322-8.

3. Hankey, G.J., Potential new risk factors for ischemic stroke: what is their potential? Stroke, 2006. 37(8): p. 2181-8.

4. Luitse, M.J., et al., Diabetes, hyperglycaemia, and acute ischaemic stroke. Lancet Neurol, 2012. 11(3): p. 261-71.

5. Kurth, T., et al., Smoking and risk of hemorrhagic stroke in women. Stroke, 2003. 34(12): p. 2792-5.

6. Lewington, S., et al., Age-specific relevance of usual blood pressure to vascular mortality: a meta-analysis of individual data for one million adults in 61 prospective studies. Lancet, 2002. 360(9349): p. 1903-13.

7. Gorelick, P.B., et al., Headache in acute cerebrovascular disease. Neurology, 1986. 36(11): p. 1445-50.

8. Hemphill, J.C., 3rd, et al., Guidelines for the Management of Spontaneous Intracerebral Hemorrhage: A Guideline for Healthcare Professionals From the American Heart Association/American Stroke Association. Stroke, 2015. 46(7): p. 2032-60.

9. Kothari, R., et al., Early stroke recognition: developing an out-of-hospital NIH Stroke Scale. Acad Emerg Med, 1997. 4(10): p. 986-90.

10. Connolly, E.S., Jr., et al., Guidelines for the management of aneurysmal subarachnoid hemorrhage: a guideline for healthcare professionals from the American Heart Association/american Stroke Association. Stroke, 2012. 43(6): p. 1711-37.

11. Goldstein, L.B. and D.L. Simel, Is this patient having a stroke? Jama, 2005. 293(19): p. 2391-402.

12. Adams, H.P., Jr., et al., Baseline NIH Stroke Scale score strongly predicts outcome after stroke: A report of the Trial of Org 10172 in Acute Stroke Treatment (TOAST). Neurology, 1999. 53(1): p. 126-31.

13. Generalized efficacy of t-PA for acute stroke. Subgroup analysis of the NINDS t-PA Stroke Trial. Stroke, 1997. 28(11): p. 2119-25.

Patient Notes_____
Patient Drawings_____

Checklist for headache: New Pie Headache

19. Checklist for Headache

New Pie Headache™

Patient Name_____
Caregiver Initials_____

	Answer	Patient Initials

N **Neurological signs (headache with focal neurological deficit/loss of consciousness)[1]**

Did you ever have weakness or altered sensations in any parts of body?
Did you ever black-out?

☐

E **Early morning headaches or sleep disturbance due to headache (tumor/ COPD/ Obstructive Sleep Apnea)[2, 3]**

Do you experience early morning headaches?
Do you have COPD?
Do you have sleep apnea?

☐

W **"Worst headache of my life", seen in Subarachnoid hemorrhage (SAH)[4]**

Do you have a severe headache that you have never had before?

☐

P **Increased pressure on bending. Does your headache becomes worse with bending forward.
Pseudo-tumor cerebri/ raised intracranial pressure**

Does the headache become worse with bending forward?

☐

I **Infection (meningitis/ encephalitis/ brain abscess)[6]**

☐

Do you have headache with fever, with neck rigidity and photophobia?
Do you have headache with fever and confusion?

E **Elderly (risk of neoplasm increases after age of 55yrs)[7]**

☐

Do you have headache severe in morning, worse with bending and associated with weakness or numbness in limbs?

H Head **Headache with blurring of vision in elderly. (Giant cell arteritis/ carotid atherosclerosis)[8, 9]**

☐

Do you have headache with tenderness on the temples and blurring/loss of vision?

A Ache **Cluster headache: awakens patient at night.**
Migraine: unilateral headache in sun[10]

☐

Do you have headache on one side of head at night?
Do you have headache on one side of the head during the day, associated with photophobia, nausea and vomiting?

Caregiver Initials_____

Bibliography

1. Johnson, W., M.L. Nguyen, and R. Patel, Hypertension crisis in the emergency department. Cardiol Clin, 2012. 30(4): p. 533-43.

2. Forsyth, P.A. and J.B. Posner, Headaches in patients with brain tumors: a study of 111 patients. Neurology, 1993. 43(9): p. 1678-83.

3. Russell, M.B., H.A. Kristiansen, and K.J. Kvaerner, Headache in sleep apnea syndrome: epidemiology and pathophysiology. Cephalalgia, 2014. 34(10): p. 752-5.

4. Gorelick, P.B., et al., Headache in acute cerebrovascular disease. Neurology, 1986. 36(11): p. 1445-50.

5. Evans, R.W., New daily persistent headache. Curr Pain Headache Rep, 2003. 7(4): p. 303-7.

6. Brouwer, M.C., J.M. Coutinho, and D. van de Beek, Clinical characteristics and outcome of brain abscess: systematic review and meta-analysis. Neurology, 2014. 82(9): p. 806-13.

7. Pfund, Z., et al., Headache in intracranial tumors. Cephalalgia, 1999. 19(9): p. 787-90; discussion 765.

8. Gonzalez-Gay, M.A., et al., Giant cell arteritis: disease patterns of clinical presentation in a series of 240 patients. Medicine (Baltimore), 2005. 84(5): p. 269-76.

9. Jonas, P., et al., A unique combination of congenital genitourinary anomalies in a child. J Urol, 1977. 118(2): p. 349-50.

10. The International Classification of Headache Disorders, 3rd edition (beta version). Cephalalgia, 2013. 33(9): p. 629-808.

- Do you know how migraine headaches present? What is the difference between a common and classical migraine?

- Do you know how cluster headaches present?

- Do you know how tension headaches present?

- Do you know how temporal arteritis presents?

- Do you know how trigeminal neuralgia presents?

- Can glaucoma present with headaches? How does glaucoma present?

Patient Notes_____
Patient Drawings_____

Checklist for Multiple Sclerosis: (iCrush) MS

VitalChecklist™

Patient Name_____
Caregiver Initials_____

	Answer	Patient Initials

i — **INO (Internal Nuclear Ophthalmoplegia)[1-3]** ☐

Do you see double?
Did you notice that your one eye is jumpy?

C — **Color Blindness Optic neuritis[4]** ☐

Do you see things black and white only?
Did you ever had pain in eye along with blurred vision?

R — **Raise your arms[5]** ☐

Do you have any difficulty raising your arms or legs?

U — **Urine problems[6]** ☐

Do you have problems in controlling your bladder?

S — **Sexual dysfunction/ Spasms[7-10]** ☐

Do you have erectile dysfunction?
Do you have tightness in your arms and legs?

H — **Heat[11]** ☐

Are your symptoms made worse by hot temperature like hot shower or hot weather?

M — **Motor Weakness[12]** ☐

Do you have weakness in your arms and legs?

S — **Speech; Sensory deficit[13, 14]** ☐

Did you notice any change in your speech?
Did you notice any altered sensations?

Bibliography

1. Rice, C.M., et al., Primary progressive multiple sclerosis: progress and challenges. J Neurol Neurosurg Psychiatry, 2013. 84(10): p. 1100-6.

2. Sakaie, K., et al., Diffusion tensor imaging the medial longitudinal fasciculus in INO: opportunities and challenges. Ann N Y Acad Sci, 2011. 1233: p. 307-12.

3. Sakaie, K., et al., Injury to a specific neural pathway detected by ultra-high-field MRI. Neurology, 2014. 82(2): p. 182-3.

4. Balcer, L.J., Clinical practice. Optic neuritis. N Engl J Med, 2006. 354(12): p. 1273-80.

5. Schurks, M. and P. Bussfeld, Multiple sclerosis and restless legs syndrome: a systematic review and meta-analysis. Eur J Neurol, 2013. 20(4): p. 605-15.

6. DasGupta, R. and C.J. Fowler, Bladder, bowel and sexual dysfunction in multiple sclerosis: management strategies. Drugs, 2003. 63(2): p. 153-66.

7. Rizzo, M.A., et al., Prevalence and treatment of spasticity reported by multiple sclerosis patients. Mult Scler, 2004. 10(5): p. 589-95.

8. Thompson, A.J., et al., Clinical management of spasticity. J Neurol Neurosurg Psychiatry, 2005. 76(4): p. 459-63.

9. Trompetto, C., et al., Pathophysiology of spasticity: implications for neurorehabilitation. Biomed Res Int, 2014. 2014: p. 354906.

10. Zivadinov, R., et al., Sexual dysfunction in multiple sclerosis: II. Correlation analysis. Mult Scler, 1999. 5(6): p. 428-31.

11. Davis, S.L., et al., Thermoregulation in multiple sclerosis. J Appl Physiol (1985), 2010. 109(5): p. 1531-7.

12. Rinker, J.R., 2nd, et al., Prevalence and characteristics of tremor in the NARCOMS multiple sclerosis registry: a cross-sectional survey. BMJ Open, 2015. 5(1): p. e006714.

13. Kanchandani, R. and J.G. Howe, Lhermitte's sign in multiple sclerosis: a clinical survey and review of the literature. J Neurol Neurosurg Psychiatry, 1982. 45(4): p. 308-12.

14. Carnicka, Z., et al., Sleep disorders in patients with multiple sclerosis. J Clin Sleep Med, 2015. 11(5): p. 553-7.

Patient Notes_____
Patient Drawings_____

Checklist for Depression: Digest P Capsule

DIGEST P CAPsule™

Patient Name_____
Caregiver Initials_____

	Answer	Patient Initials

D | **Depression[1]** | ☐
Do you feel sad or depressed?

I | **Insomnia or hypersomnia[2]** | ☐
Did you notice any changes in your sleep?

G | **Guilt[3]** | ☐
Do you feel guilty about something in life?

E | **Energy loss[4]** | ☐
Do you feel loss of energy at all times?

S | **Suicidal ideation[5]** | ☐
Do you have any thoughts about hurting yourself?
Did you ever plan about hurting yourself?

T | **Time more than 2 weeks (symptoms of depression for at least 2 weeks)[6]** | ☐
Since how long do you feel depressed or sad?

P | **Pleasure loss[7]** | ☐
Do you think you have lost interest in all the activities that you used to love earlier?

C | **Concentration lapses[8]** | ☐
Do you have difficulty in concentrating in your work?

A | **Appetite change or weight loss/gain[9]** | ☐
Any changes in your appetite?
Did you notice any changes in your weight?

Psychotic symptoms, Somatic symptoms[10]

Did you see or hear things that others denied?
Did you feel that your limbs were heavy?

Caregiver Initials_____

Bibliography

1. Ansseau, M., et al., High prevalence of mental disorders in primary care. J Affect Disord, 2004. 78(1): p. 49-55.

2. McCullough, J.P., Jr., et al., Comparison of DSM-III-R chronic major depression and major depression superimposed on dysthymia (double depression): validity of the distinction. J Abnorm Psychol, 2000. 109(3): p. 419-27.

3. Yang, T. and D.L. Dunner, Differential subtyping of depression. Depress Anxiety, 2001. 13(1): p. 11-7.

4. Zimmerman, M., et al., Diagnosing major depressive disorder X: can the utility of the DSM-IV symptom criteria be improved? J Nerv Ment Dis, 2006. 194(12): p. 893-7.

5. Tidemalm, D., et al., Risk of suicide after suicide attempt according to coexisting psychiatric disorder: Swedish cohort study with long term follow-up. Bmj, 2008. 337: p. a2205.

6. Zimmerman, M., et al., A simpler definition of major depressive disorder. Psychol Med, 2010. 40(3): p. 451-7.

7. Andrews, G., et al., Issues for DSM-V: simplifying DSM-IV to enhance utility: the case of major depressive disorder. Am J Psychiatry, 2007. 164(12): p. 1784-5.

8. Zimmerman, M., et al., Validity of a simpler definition of major depressive disorder. Depress Anxiety, 2010. 27(10): p. 977-81.

9. Regier, D.A., et al., DSM-5 field trials in the United States and Canada, Part II: test-retest reliability of selected categorical diagnoses. Am J Psychiatry, 2013. 170(1): p. 59-70.

10. Tylee, A. and P. Gandhi, The importance of somatic symptoms in depression in primary care. Prim Care Companion J Clin Psychiatry, 2005. 7(4): p. 167-76.

Patient Name_____
Caregiver Initials_____

	Answer	Patient Initials

Impaired recent short term memory[1]
What did you have for breakfast this morning?
Confirm the answer with family member or support at home.

☐

Challenges with event planning or problem solving/ managing finances/ driving around. Challenge with Check book. Challenge with controlling bowel and bladder functions[2]

Who manages your bills?
Do you have difficulty in remembering things?
Do you often get lost when you are driving by yourself?
Any changes in bladder and bowel habits? Have you lost control over your bowel and bladder?

☐

Rush and rash judgment and poor decisions[3]
Have your family members noticed you make a rash decision?

☐

Speech problems[4]
Do you have problems in communicating?

☐

Eyes- Visual hallucinations (Delirium or Lewy Body Dementia)[5]
Do you see things that others deny seeing?

☐

Nose-smell altered[6]
Do you smell weird odors that others deny smelling?

☐

I Impaired behavior & personality changes[1]

Do your family members or support at home tell you about a change in your behavior or change in your personality?

□

O Or Orientation to time, place, and person[7]

What is your name?
Where are you right now (which country/ state/ city/ building)?
Which year/ month/ day is it today?

□

M Mo Motor incoordination[8]

Did you notice any changes in your balance or increase in number of falls?

□

M Me Memory loss[9]

Can you tell me your date of birth?
When is your wedding anniversary?
Confirm the answer with a family member or support at home.

□

N Neglect activities of daily living

Do you have difficulties in moving around your house/ taking shower/ getting dressed/ cooking for yourself/ feeding yourself?

□

T Thoughts of depression[10]

Do you feel depressed?

□

S Stroke[10]

Do you have a past h/o stroke or weakness or numbness in any parts of your body?

□

Caregiver Initials_____

Bibliography

1. Pfeiffer, E., A short portable mental status questionnaire for the assessment of organic brain deficit in elderly patients. J Am Geriatr Soc, 1975. 23(10): p. 433-41.

2. Tangalos, E.G., et al., The Mini-Mental State Examination in general medical practice: clinical utility and acceptance. Mayo Clin Proc, 1996. 71(9): p. 829-37.

3. Grisso, T. and P.S. Appelbaum, Comparison of standards for assessing patients' capacities to make treatment decisions. Am J Psychiatry, 1995. 152(7): p. 1033-7.

4. Anthony, J.C., et al., Limits of the 'Mini-Mental State' as a screening test for dementia and delirium among hospital patients. Psychol Med, 1982. 12(2): p. 397-408.

5. Crum, R.M., et al., Population-based norms for the Mini-Mental State Examination by age and educational level. Jama, 1993. 269(18): p. 2386-91.

6. Freidl, W., et al., Mini mental state examination: influence of sociodemographic, environmental and behavioral factors and vascular risk factors. J Clin Epidemiol, 1996. 49(1): p. 73-8.

7. Folstein, M.F., S.E. Folstein, and P.R. McHugh, "Mini-mental state". A practical method for grading the cognitive state of patients for the clinician. J Psychiatr Res, 1975. 12(3): p. 189-98.

8. Royall, D.R., J.A. Cordes, and M. Polk, CLOX: an executive clock drawing task. J Neurol Neurosurg Psychiatry, 1998. 64(5): p. 588-94.

9. Borson, S., et al., The mini-cog: a cognitive 'vital signs' measure for dementia screening in multi-lingual elderly. Int J Geriatr Psychiatry, 2000. 15(11): p. 1021-7.

10. Jorm, A.F., L. Fratiglioni, and B. Winblad, Differential diagnosis in dementia. Principal components analysis of clinical data from a population survey. Arch Neurol, 1993. 50(1): p. 72-7.

Vital Checklist for Dementia: (iCrush) Senior Moments

Patient Notes

VitalChecklist™

Cover all the B.A.S.E.S. First! Then Walk™

Patient Name_____
Caregiver Initials_____

Red Flag Signs for Cauda Equina Syndrome

		Answer	Patient Initials

B

Bilateral[1]

If the patient has bilateral loss of motor strength, bilateral loss of sensation, bilateral loss of reflexes, bilateral radicular pain they are at high risk of cauda equina syndrome[2]

☐

B Base

Cannot feel your base[3]

Do you feel the toilet paper when you wipe your bottom?

☐

B

Bowel and Bladder Incontinence[1]

Are you able to feel when your bladder or bowel are full? No! If you have painless retention of urine with overflow incontinence, check for complete cauda equina syndrome
Do you have sense of full bladder and then leak urine?[2]

☐

A

Anesthesia[1]

Are you able to feel in between the legs? Do you have any numbness around the anus and genitalia?

☐

S

Sciatica[4]

Does the pain radiate from the back into one leg or both legs?

☐

E

Erection[4]

Are you able to achieve erection? Are you able to ejaculate?

☐

S **Sensory disturbance[1]**
Do you have numbness, tingling, loss of sensation in both legs?

☐

F **Fracture[5]**
Evaluate for compression fracture and osteoporosis

☐

I **Infection or IV Drug USE[6]**
Signs of infection, Inflammation and IV Drug Use

☐

R **Ruptured AAA[7]**
History of smoking, ruptured AAA

☐

S **Sciatica[4]**
Pain starts in the back and goes into the legs

☐

T **Trauma or Tumor[8, 9]**
Any history of trauma or tumor

☐

W Walk **If you cannot even walk, Admit![9]**
Can you walk? If you can't then admit the patient. Can you get on the scale to measure your weight? If you have any unintentional weight loss, please report it to your doctor

☐

Caregiver Initials_____

Bibliography

1. Spector LR, Madigan L, Rhyne A, Darden B, 2nd, Kim D. Cauda equina syndrome. J Am Acad Orthop Surg. 2008;16(8):471-9.

2. Todd NV. An algorithm for suspected cauda equina syndrome. Ann R Coll Surg Engl. 2009;91(4):358-9; author reply 9-60.

3. Fairbank J, Mallen C. Cauda equina syndrome: implications for primary care. Br J Gen Pract. 2014;64(619):67-8.

4. Gardner A, Gardner E, Morley T. Cauda equina syndrome: a review of the current clinical and medico-legal position. Eur Spine J. 2011;20(5):690-7.

5. Aresti N, Murugachandran G, Shetty R. Cauda equina syndrome following sacral fractures: a report of three cases. J Orthop Surg (Hong Kong). 2012;20(2):250-3.

6. Panos G, Watson DC, Karydis I, Velissaris D, Andreou M, Karamouzos V, et al. Differential diagnosis and treatment of acute cauda equina syndrome in the human immunodeficiency virus positive patient: a case report and review of the literature. J Med Case Rep. 2016;10:165.

7. Engamba SA, Garaleviciene D, Baldry J. Contained ruptured abdominal aortic aneurysm presenting as cauda equina syndrome. BMJ Case Rep. 2017;2017.

8. Singh H, Rao VS, Mangla R, Laheri VJ. Traumatic transverse fracture of sacrum with cauda equina injury--a case report and review of literature. J Postgrad Med. 1998;44(1):14-5.

9. Wada S, Matsuo R, Matsushita T, Fukushima Y, Ago T, Kitazono T. [Intravascular Large B Cell Lymphoma with Cauda Equina Syndrome: A Case Report and Review of the Literature]. Brain Nerve. 2016;68(1):97-101.

Section D

Endocrine

Patient Notes_____
Patient Drawings_____

Checklist for Diabetes: (iCrush) Diabetes

Do you know the complications of diabetes? Write it here.

24. Checklist for Diabetes

(iCRUSH) DIABETES™

Patient Name_____
Caregiver Initials_____

Answer   Patient Initials

i   **Infection of the feet or other skin issues**[1, 2]

Do you pay regular visits to your foot doctor?

☐

C   **Cholesterol(checked every 3-6 months if uncontrolled)**[3]

Do you get blood cholesterol levels checked regularly?

☐

R   **Record of low and high blood sugars**[4]

Do you check blood glucose levels regularly at home?
Do you maintain a log book with the readings of low and high blood glucose levels?

☐

U   **Urine protein and kidney function**[5]

Do you go for regular follow-ups to your Primary Care Physician?
Do you get blood and urine tests done regularly?

☐

S   **Sleep apnea**[6]
Stroke

Do you snore while you sleep?
Do you feel that you did not have a good sleep at night?
Do you feel sleepy and fatigued during the day?
Do you know symptoms of stroke?

☐

H   **Heart disease**[7, 8]

Do you have heart disease?

☐

D   **Depression**[9]

Do you feel sad or depressed?

☐

I   **Impotence[10]**

Do you have erectile dysfunction?

☐

A   **A1C[11, 12]**

Do you get HbA1C checked regularly?
What was the last HbA1C levels?

☐

B   **Blood pressure[13]**

Do you have high blood pressure?

☐

E   **Eye: Diabetic retinopathy[14, 15]**

Do you go for regular eye exams to the eye doctor?

☐

T   **Tingling/ numbness in limbs: Diabetic Peripheral Neuropathy[16]**

Do you have any tingling and numbness in any parts of body?
Did you notice any weakness in your arms or legs?

☐

E   **Ear check-up[17]**

Did you notice any changes in your hearing?
Did you notice any problems with your balance?

☐

S   **Stomach problems (Gastroparesis, constipation)[18-20]**

Do you experience early satiety, nausea, bloating sensation after meals?
Do you have constipation?

☐

Caregiver Initials_____

Bibliography

1. Chirillo, F., et al., Infective endocarditis in patients with diabetes mellitus. J Heart Valve Dis, 2010. 19(3): p. 312-20.

2. Kanafani, Z.A., et al., Clinical characteristics and outcomes of diabetic patients with Staphylococcus aureus bacteremia and endocarditis. Eur J Clin Microbiol Infect Dis, 2009. 28(12): p. 1477-82.

3. Standards of medical care in diabetes--2014. Diabetes Care, 2014. 37 Suppl 1: p. S14-80.

4. Nathan, D.M., et al., Intensive diabetes treatment and cardiovascular disease in patients with type 1 diabetes. N Engl J Med, 2005. 353(25): p. 2643-53.

5. Mogensen, C.E., et al., Microalbuminuria and potential confounders. A review and some observations on variability of urinary albumin excretion. Diabetes Care, 1995. 18(4): p. 572-81.

6. Kuna, S.T., et al., Long-term effect of weight loss on obstructive sleep apnea severity in obese patients with type 2 diabetes. Sleep, 2013. 36(5): p. 641-649a.

7. Wackers, F.J., et al., Detection of silent myocardial ischemia in asymptomatic diabetic subjects: the DIAD study. Diabetes Care, 2004. 27(8): p. 1954-61.

8. Scognamiglio, R., et al., Detection of coronary artery disease in asymptomatic patients with type 2 diabetes mellitus. J Am Coll Cardiol, 2006. 47(1): p. 65-71.

9. Pillay, J., et al., Behavioral Programs for Type 1 Diabetes Mellitus: A Systematic Review and Meta-analysis. Ann Intern Med, 2015. 163(11): p. 836-47.

10. Kalter-Leibovici, O., et al., Clinical, socioeconomic, and lifestyle parameters associated with erectile dysfunction among diabetic men. Diabetes Care, 2005. 28(7): p. 1739-44.

11. Jakicic, J.M., et al., Four-year change in cardiorespiratory fitness and influence on glycemic control in adults with type 2 diabetes in a randomized trial: the Look AHEAD Trial. Diabetes Care, 2013. 36(5): p. 1297-303.

12. Ohkubo, Y., et al., Intensive insulin therapy prevents the progression of diabetic microvascular complications in Japanese patients with non-insulin-dependent diabetes mellitus: a randomized prospective 6-year study. Diabetes Res Clin Pract, 1995. 28(2): p. 103-17.

13. Buse, J.B., et al., Primary prevention of cardiovascular diseases in people with diabetes mellitus: a scientific statement from the American Heart Association and the American Diabetes Association. Circulation, 2007. 115(1): p. 114-26.

14. Pasquale, L.R., et al., Prospective study of type 2 diabetes mellitus and risk of primary open-angle glaucoma in women. Ophthalmology, 2006. 113(7): p. 1081-6.

15. Obrosova, I.G., S.S. Chung, and P.F. Kador, Diabetic cataracts: mechanisms and management. Diabetes Metab Res Rev, 2010. 26(3): p. 172-80.

16. Standards of Medical Care in Diabetes-2016: Summary of Revisions. Diabetes Care, 2016. 39 Suppl 1: p. S4-5.

17. Rubin, J. and V.L. Yu, Malignant external otitis: insights into pathogenesis, clinical manifestations, diagnosis, and therapy. Am J Med, 1988. 85(3): p. 391-8.

18. Horowitz, M., et al., Disordered gastric motor function in diabetes mellitus. Recent insights into prevalence, pathophysiology, clinical relevance, and treatment. Scand J Gastroenterol, 1991. 26(7): p. 673-84.

19. Mearin, F. and J.R. Malagelada, Gastroparesis and dyspepsia in patients with diabetes mellitus. Eur J Gastroenterol Hepatol, 1995. 7(8): p. 717-23.

20. Buysschaert, M., et al., Impaired gastric emptying in diabetic patients with cardiac autonomic neuropathy. Diabetes Care, 1987. 10(4): p. 448-52.

Patient Notes_____
Patient Drawings_____

Checklist for Hypothyroidism: Less Thyroid

Do you know where is your thyroid gland?

Do you know the pituitary gland in your brain releases thyroid stimulating hormone?

25. Checklist for Hypothyroidism

LESS THYROID™

Patient Name_____
Caregiver Initials_____

	Answer	Patient Initials

☐ (Patient Initials)

L | **Lower lung function- decreased respiratory capacity.**
Lower heart function- decreased cardiac output and contractility.
Libido is decreased in men[1-5]

Do you have cough/ chest pain/ shortness of breath?
Do you have light-headedness/ black-outs/ swelling of feet?
Did you experience a decrease in libido?

☐

E | **Energy loss Eye Swelling[6]**

Do you feel loss of energy at all times?
Did you notice any swelling around your eyes?

☐

S | **Skin is dry and thin.**
Sweating is decreased[7]

Did you notice any dryness of your skin?

☐

S | **Sensory loss.**
Carpal tunnel syndrome
+ Other neurological findings[8]

Do you have tingling/ numbness/ weakness in any parts of your body?

☐

T | **Temperature- cold intolerance,**
Tired and fatigued

Have you ever noticed that you feel cold when others in the room are comfortable?
Do you feel tired and fatigued at all times?

95

H

Hypertension[9, 10]
Hair loss

Were you diagnosed to have high blood pressure at the same time when these symptoms (tired & fatigue) started?
Do you have hair loss?

☐

Y

"Y" are you Dull (Memory loss), Down (Menorrhagia), Depressed (Depression)[11]

Have you become forgetful recently?
Do you have increased bleeding during your menstrual cycles?
Do you feel sad or depressed?

☐

R

Reproductive issues[12]

Are you having problems with conceiving?
Do you have irregular menstrual cycles with heavy bleeding?

☐

O

Obesity[13]

Did you notice any unintentional weight gain, without any changes in your diet?

☐

I

Insomnia (sleep apnea, as patients may have enlarged gland, tongue) Or Increased sleepiness[14]

Did you notice any changes in your sleep?
Do you snore while sleeping?

☐

D

Digestive system- Constipation[15, 16]

Do you have constipation?

☐

Caregiver Initials_____

Bibliography

1. Laroche, C.M., et al., Hypothyroidism presenting with respiratory muscle weakness. Am Rev Respir Dis, 1988. 138(2): p. 472-4.

2. Zhou, K.R., [X-ray diagnosis of the downward displacement of the tricuspid valve (author's transl)]. Zhonghua Fang She Xue Za Zhi, 1979. 13(2): p. 69-71.

3. Siafakas, N.M., et al., Respiratory muscle strength in hypothyroidism. Chest, 1992. 102(1): p. 189-94.

4. Ladenson, P.W., P.D. Goldenheim, and E.C. Ridgway, Prediction and reversal of blunted ventilatory responsiveness in patients with hypothyroidism. Am J Med, 1988. 84(5): p. 877-83.

5. Klein, I. and K. Ojamaa, Thyroid hormone and the cardiovascular system: from theory to practice. J Clin Endocrinol Metab, 1994. 78(5): p. 1026-7.

6. Smith, T.J., R.S. Bahn, and C.A. Gorman, Connective tissue, glycosaminoglycans, and diseases of the thyroid. Endocr Rev, 1989. 10(3): p. 366-91.

7. Heymann, W.R., Cutaneous manifestations of thyroid disease. J Am Acad Dermatol, 1992. 26(6): p. 885-902.

8. Duyff, R.F., et al., Neuromuscular findings in thyroid dysfunction: a prospective clinical and electrodiagnostic study. J Neurol Neurosurg Psychiatry, 2000. 68(6): p. 750-5.

9. Klein, I. and S. Danzi, Thyroid disease and the heart. Circulation, 2007. 116(15): p. 1725-35.

10. Fommei, E. and G. Iervasi, The role of thyroid hormone in blood pressure homeostasis: evidence from short-term hypothyroidism in humans. J Clin Endocrinol Metab, 2002. 87(5): p. 1996-2000.

11. Osterweil, D., et al., Cognitive function in non-demented older adults with hypothyroidism. J Am Geriatr Soc, 1992. 40(4): p. 325-35.

12. Krassas, G.E., et al., Disturbances of menstruation in hypothyroidism. Clin Endocrinol (Oxf), 1999. 50(5): p. 655-9.

13. Diekman, T., et al., Prevalence and correction of hypothyroidism in a large cohort of patients referred for dyslipidemia. Arch Intern Med, 1995. 155(14): p. 1490-5.

14. Haupt, M. and A. Kurz, Reversibility of dementia in hypothyroidism. J Neurol, 1993. 240(6): p. 333-5.

15. Shafer, R.B., R.A. Prentiss, and J.H. Bond, Gastrointestinal transit in thyroid disease. Gastroenterology, 1984. 86(5 Pt 1): p. 852-5.

16. Lauritano, E.C., et al., Association between hypothyroidism and small intestinal bacterial overgrowth. J Clin Endocrinol Metab, 2007. 92(11): p. 4180-4.

26. Checklist for Complications of Obesity

(iCrush) Obesity[TM]

Patient Name_____
Caregiver Initials_____

Answer   Patient Initials

i **Insulin resistance[1, 2]**
Impaired glucose tolerance[3]

Do you have high sugars? Do you have diabetes mellitus?

☐

C **Cholesterol[4]**
Cardiovascular[5]

Do you have heart disease? Do you have cholesterol issues?

☐

R **Respiratory**

Do you have shortness of breath? Do you wheeze? Do you have asthma?

☐

U **Urinary and Kidneys**

Do you leak when you cough or sneeze? Check for proteinuria in the urine. May have kidney disease (glomerulosclerosis)

☐

S **Sleep Apnea[6]**

Do you snore? Do you have night time gasps? Do you doze off while driving or watching television?

☐

H **Hypertension[4]**
Headaches[7]

Do you have headaches? Do you have high blood pressure? Check for pseudotumor cerebri.

☐

O **Orthopedic and arthritis[8]**

Do you have any joint pain? Do you have any arthritis? Check for blount disease.

☐

B ## Body image
Do you have depression? Do you have anxiety?

☐

E ## Endocrine[9]
Ask questions about menstrual cycle and polycystic
ovarian disease?

☐

S ## Social Isolation[10, 11]
Teasing, Bullying, poor self-esteem

☐

I ## Inflammation and Cancer
Inflammation in the body may result in cancer
O:Ovarian; B: Breast; Es: Esophagus; I: Intestine:
T: Thyroid;

☐

T ## Thyroid and Obesity: How are they related?[12]
Is obesity cause or complication of hypothyroidism?
Check for complete thyroid panel--TSH, Free t4, t3,
reverse t3, thyroid peroxidase antibodies and
thyroglobulin

☐

Y ## Y are you dull, down and depressed[13]
Are you depressed or sad because of Obesity?

☐

Caregiver Initials_____

Bibliography

1. Chiarelli F, Marcovecchio ML. Insulin resistance and obesity in childhood. Eur J Endocrinol. 2008;159 Suppl 1:S67-74.

2. Ebbeling CB, Pawlak DB, Ludwig DS. Childhood obesity: public-health crisis, common sense cure. Lancet. 2002;360(9331):473-82.

3. Sinha R, Fisch G, Teague B, Tamborlane WV, Banyas B, Allen K, et al. Prevalence of impaired glucose tolerance among children and adolescents with marked obesity. N Engl J Med. 2002;346(11):802-10.

4. McMurray RG, Harrell JS, Levine AA, Gansky SA. Childhood obesity elevates blood pressure and total cholesterol independent of physical activity. Int J Obes Relat Metab Disord. 1995;19(12):881-6.

5. Freedman DS, Khan LK, Dietz WH, Srinivasan SR, Berenson GS. Relationship of childhood obesity to coronary heart disease risk factors in adulthood: the Bogalusa Heart Study. Pediatrics. 2001;108(3):712-8.

6. Dietz WH. Health consequences of obesity in youth: childhood predictors of adult disease. Pediatrics. 1998;101(3 Pt 2):518-25.

7. Paley G, Sheldon CA, Burrows EK, Chilutti MR, Liu GT, McCormack SE. Overweight and Obesity in Pediatric Secondary Pseudotumor Cerebri Syndrome. Am J Ophthalmol. 2015;159(2):344-52 e1.

8. Wills M. Orthopedic complications of childhood obesity. Pediatr Phys Ther. 2004;16(4):230-5.

9. Anderson AD, Solorzano CM, McCartney CR. Childhood obesity and its impact on the development of adolescent PCOS. Semin Reprod Med. 2014;32(3):202-13.

10. Janssen I, Craig WM, Boyce WF, Pickett W. Associations between overweight and obesity with bullying behaviors in school-aged children. Pediatrics. 2004;113(5):1187-94.

11. Srabstein JC, McCarter RJ, Shao C, Huang ZJ. Morbidities associated with bullying behaviors in adolescents. School based study of American adolescents. Int J Adolesc Med Health. 2006;18(4):587-96.

12. Marzullo P, Minocci A, Tagliaferri MA, Guzzaloni G, Di Blasio A, De Medici C, et al. Investigations of thyroid hormones and antibodies in obesity: leptin levels are associated with thyroid autoimmunity independent of bioanthropometric, hormonal, and weight-related determinants. J Clin Endocrinol Metab. 2010;95(8):3965-72.

13. Reeves GM, Postolache TT, Snitker S. Childhood Obesity and Depression: Connection between these Growing Problems in Growing Children. Int J Child Health Hum Dev. 2008;1(2):103-14.

VitalChecklist™

HI SWEPT™

Patient Name_____
Caregiver Initials_____

Answer

Patient Initials

H | HDL
(less than 40mg/dl in men)
(less than 50mg/dl in woman)[1, 2]

Were you found to have low HDL levels in blood tests?

☐

I | Insulin resistance[1, 3, 4]

Do you have high blood glucose levels?

☐

S | Sugars Above 100mg/dl or drug treatment of elevated blood sugars[3, 4]

Do you take medicines for Diabetes?

☐

W | Waist circumference
(more than 40inches in men)
(more than 35 inches in woman)[3, 5, 6]

Were you found to have increased waist circumference during evaluation?

☐

E | Extra weight around the middle and upper parts of the body[5, 6]

Did you have any unintentional weight gain?

☐

P | Pressure(Blood Pressure) more than 130/85 mmHg[1]

Do you have high blood pressure?

☐

Answer | Patient Initials

 Triglycerides equal to or higher than 150mg/dl[2, 6]
Were you found to have high blood triglyceride levels in blood tests?

☐

Caregiver Initials_____

Bibliography

1. Dragsbaek, K., et al., Metabolic syndrome and subsequent risk of type 2 diabetes and cardiovascular disease in elderly women: Challenging the current definition. Medicine (Baltimore), 2016. 95(36): p. e4806.

2. Chen, Q., et al., Metabolic syndrome and its individual components with mortality among patients with coronary heart disease. Int J Cardiol, 2016. 224: p. 8-14.

3. Richelsen, B. and S.B. Pedersen, Associations between different anthropometric measurements of fatness and metabolic risk parameters in non-obese, healthy, middle-aged men. Int J Obes Relat Metab Disord, 1995. 19(3): p. 169-74.

4. Geragotou, T., et al., The Relationship of Metabolic Syndrome Traits with Beta-Cell Function and Insulin Sensitivity by Oral Minimal Model Assessment in South Asian and European Families Residing in the Netherlands. J Diabetes Res, 2016. 2016: p. 9286303.

5. Oh, E.J., et al., Body volume, body fatness, and metabolic syndrome. Women Health, 2016: p. 1-15.

6. Jean-Luc Gradidge, P., et al., Metabolic and Body Composition Risk Factors Associated with Metabolic Syndrome in a Cohort of Women with a High Prevalence of Cardiometabolic Disease. PLoS One, 2016. 11(9): p. e0162247.

Checklist for Metabolic Syndrome: HI SWEPT

Patient Note

Patient Notes_____
Patient Drawings_____

Section E

Heart

ABCDE of CHEST PAIN™

Patient Name_____
Caregiver Initials_____

	Answer	Patient Initials

A **Aspirin, ACE Inhibitors, ARBs, Aldosterone antagonists**[1] ☐

Did you take Aspirin?
Did you take Lisinopril?
Did you take Losartan?
Did you take Spironolactone?

B **Beta blockers, Blood thinners, BP control**[2-7] ☐

Did you take Metoprolol?
Did you take Blood thinners like Plavix?
Did you take any drugs for blood pressure control?

C **Cessation of smoking**[8] ☐

Did you quit smoking?

D **Diuretics**[9] ☐

Did you take any water pill like Furosemide?

E **Exercise & Rehabilitation**[1] ☐

Were you advised to join an exercise program after your recovery from heart attack?
Did you go to rehab facilities after you recovered from heart attack?

C **Call 911**[10] ☐

Did you call 911 right away, when you had symptoms of chest pain, chest discomfort, shortness of breath or sweating?

H **Head dizziness, Heart Heaviness, Hand Numbness, Lightheadedness**[11]

Did you feel dizzy or light-headed?
Did you feel chest discomfort associated with pain or numbness in arms?

☐

E **Elephant Sitting on the Chest**[12-14]

Did you have heaviness in your chest region?

☐

S **Shortness of Breath**[15]

Were you short of breath?

☐

T **Tiredness, Tingling over the left arm**[16]

Did you feel fatigued?
Did you feel pain or numbness in your arms?

☐

P **Palpitations**[14]

Did you feel any palpitations?

☐

A **Acid reflux & heart burn**[14]

Was your chest discomfort of burning type?

☐

I **Irregular heartbeat**[15, 17, 18]

Did you experience any palpitations or irregular heartbeats as if your heart skips a beat?

☐

N **Neck/Jaw discomfort, Nausea, Nitrates, Nitroglycerin**[19, 20]

Was your chest discomfort associated with pain in the neck or jaw region?
Did you experience nausea when you had chest pain?
Did you take nitrates when you had chest pain?
Did the nitrates help you with the chest pain?
Were you given Nitroglycerine in the hospital?

☐

Caregiver Initials_____

Bibliography

1. Smith, S.C., Jr., et al., AHA/ACCF Secondary Prevention and Risk Reduction Therapy for Patients with Coronary and other Atherosclerotic Vascular Disease: 2011 update: a guideline from the American Heart Association and American College of Cardiology Foundation. Circulation, 2011. 124(22): p. 2458-73.

2. Ryden, L., et al., A double-blind trial of metoprolol in acute myocardial infarction. Effects on ventricular tachyarrhythmias. N Engl J Med, 1983. 308(11): p. 614-8.

3. Nuttall, S.L., V. Toescu, and M.J. Kendall, beta Blockade after myocardial infarction. Beta blockers have key role in reducing morbidity and mortality after infarction. Bmj, 2000. 320(7234): p. 581.

4. Friedman, L.M., et al., Effect of propranolol in patients with myocardial infarction and ventricular arrhythmia. J Am Coll Cardiol, 1986. 7(1): p. 1-8.

5. Clark, A.M., et al., Meta-analysis: secondary prevention programs for patients with coronary artery disease. Ann Intern Med, 2005. 143(9): p. 659-72.

6. Bhatt, D.L., et al., Clopidogrel and aspirin versus aspirin alone for the prevention of atherothrombotic events. N Engl J Med, 2006. 354(16): p. 1706-17.

7. Chobanian, A.V., et al., The Seventh Report of the Joint National Committee on Prevention, Detection, Evaluation, and Treatment of High Blood Pressure: the JNC 7 report. Jama, 2003. 289(19): p. 2560-72.

8. Rea, T.D., et al., Smoking status and risk for recurrent coronary events after myocardial infarction. Ann Intern Med, 2002. 137(6): p. 494-500.

9. Brater, D.C., et al., Bumetanide and furosemide in heart failure. Kidney Int, 1984. 26(2): p. 183-9.

10. Lindsell, C.J., et al., The Internet Tracking Registry of Acute Coronary Syndromes (i*trACS): a multicenter registry of patients with suspicion of acute coronary syndromes reported using the standardized reporting guidelines for emergency department chest pain studies. Ann Emerg Med, 2006. 48(6): p. 666-77, 677.e1-9.

11. Kakouros, N. and D.V. Cokkinos, Right ventricular myocardial infarction: pathophysiology, diagnosis, and management. Postgrad Med J, 2010. 86(1022): p. 719-28.

12. Anderson, J.L., et al., 2012 ACCF/AHA focused update incorporated into the ACCF/AHA 2007 guidelines for the management of patients with unstable angina/non-ST-elevation myocardial infarction: a report of the American College of Cardiology Foundation/ American Heart Association Task Force on Practice Guidelines. J Am Coll Cardiol, 2013. 61(23): p. e179-347.

13. Kushner, F.G., et al., 2009 focused updates: ACC/AHA guidelines for the management of patients with ST-elevation myocardial infarction (updating the 2004 guideline and 2007 focused update) and ACC/AHA/SCAI guidelines on percutaneous coronary intervention (updating the 2005 guideline and 2007 focused update) a report of the American College of Cardiology Foundation/American Heart Association Task Force on Practice Guidelines. J Am Coll Cardiol, 2009. 54(23): p. 2205-41.

14. Swap, C.J. and J.T. Nagurney, Value and limitations of chest pain history in the evaluation of patients with suspected acute coronary syndromes. Jama, 2005. 294(20): p. 2623-9.

15. Canto, J.G., et al., Prevalence, clinical characteristics, and mortality among patients with myocardial infarction presenting without chest pain. Jama, 2000. 283(24): p. 3223-9.

16. Fanaroff, A.C., et al., Does This Patient With Chest Pain Have Acute Coronary Syndrome?: The Rational Clinical Examination Systematic Review. Jama, 2015. 314(18): p. 1955-65.

17. Pope, J.H., et al., Missed diagnoses of acute cardiac ischemia in the emergency department. N Engl J Med, 2000. 342(16): p. 1163-70.

18. Brieger, D., et al., Acute coronary syndromes without chest pain, an underdiagnosed and undertreated high-risk group: insights from the Global Registry of Acute Coronary Events. Chest, 2004. 126(2): p. 461-9.

19. Goodacre, S., et al., How useful are clinical features in the diagnosis of acute, undifferentiated chest pain? Acad Emerg Med, 2002. 9(3): p. 203-8.

20. Panju, A.A., et al., The rational clinical examination. Is this patient having a myocardial infarction? Jama, 1998. 280(14): p. 1256-63.

Patient Notes_____
Patient Drawings_____

Checklist for Heart Attack: Heart Attack ABCD

HEART ATTACK ABCD[TM]

Patient Name_____
Caregiver Initials_____

Answer | Patient Initials

H — Head to the Hospital or call 911

Do you have any chest pain with shortness of breath, sweating, nausea?
If yes, rush to the ER.

☐

E — EKG[1]

Get an EKG done urgently.

☐

A — Aspirin, Antiplatelet Agents[2]

Did you take any aspirin or blood thinning drugs like Plavix?

☐

R — Radiology[3]

Did you get an X-Ray Chest done?

☐

T — Troponin[4]

Did you get your blood work done to check for levels of cardiac enzymes like Troponin?

☐

A — Activate Cath Lab Team

After you were diagnosed with heart attack, did you get cardiac stenting done to re-open the blocked blood vessels?

☐

T — Thrombolytic Therapy[5]

After you were diagnosed with heart attack, did you receive drugs to dissolve the thrombus blocking the blood vessels?

☐

T | **Time less than 90 minutes from the door to balloon**[6-8]

When you entered the hospital, after how long were to taken to Cardiac lab to re-open the blocked blood vessels?

☐

A | **Anti-thrombin therapy**[9]

Did you receive Heparin?

☐

C | **Call 911**[10]

Did you call 911 right away once you had the symptoms?
Did you receive any CPR or Chest compressions?

☐

K | **Know the symptoms**

Alarming symptoms of heart attack include: chest pain on rest or exertion, shortness of breath, sweating, nausea, light-headedness, palpitations.

☐

Medications after Heart Attack

A | **Aspirin, ACE inhibitors or ARBs**

Do you take Aspirin?
Do you take Lisinopril?
Do you take Losartan?

☐

B | **Beta blockers Blood Thinners**

Do you take Metoprolol?
Do you take any blood thinners?

☐

C | **Cholesterol lowering medications**

Do you take cholesterol lowering drugs like statins?

☐

D | **Diuretics (in selected patients)**

Do you take diuretics like furosemide?

☐

Caregiver Initials_____

Bibliography

1. Pope, J.H., et al., Missed diagnoses of acute cardiac ischemia in the emergency department. N Engl J Med, 2000. 342(16): p. 1163-70.

2. Amsterdam, E.A., et al., 2014 AHA/ACC guideline for the management of patients with non-ST-elevation acute coronary syndromes: executive summary: a report of the American College of Cardiology/American Heart Association Task Force on Practice Guidelines. Circulation, 2014. 130(25): p. 2354-94.

3. Goodacre, S., et al., How useful are clinical features in the diagnosis of acute, undifferentiated chest pain? Acad Emerg Med, 2002. 9(3): p. 203-8.

4. Brieger, D., et al., Acute coronary syndromes without chest pain, an underdiagnosed and undertreated high-risk group: insights from the Global Registry of Acute Coronary Events. Chest, 2004. 126(2): p. 461-9.

5. Eikelboom, J.W., et al., Unfractionated heparin and low-molecular-weight heparin in acute coronary syndrome without ST elevation: a meta-analysis. Lancet, 2000. 355(9219): p. 1936-42.

6. Thygesen, K., et al., Third universal definition of myocardial infarction. Circulation, 2012. 126(16): p. 2020-35.

7. Lambert, L., et al., Association between timeliness of reperfusion therapy and clinical outcomes in ST-elevation myocardial infarction. Jama, 2010. 303(21): p. 2148-55.

8. Brodie, B.R., et al., Importance of time to reperfusion for 30-day and late survival and recovery of left ventricular function after primary angioplasty for acute myocardial infarction. J Am Coll Cardiol, 1998. 32(5): p. 1312-9.

9. Wright, R.S., et al., 2011 ACCF/AHA Focused Update of the Guidelines for the Management of Patients With Unstable Angina/Non-ST-Elevation Myocardial Infarction (Updating the 2007 Guideline): a report of the American College of Cardiology Foundation/American Heart Association Task Force on Practice Guidelines. Circulation, 2011. 123(18): p. 2022-60.

10. Rea, T.D., et al., Temporal trends in sudden cardiac arrest: a 25-year emergency medical services perspective. Circulation, 2003. 107(22): p. 2780-5.

Patient Notes_____
Patient Drawings_____

Checklist for Heart Failure: Special Cows

VitalChecklist™

Patient Name_____
Caregiver Initials_____

	Answer	Patient Initials

S | **Shortness of breath**[1, 2]
Do you have shortness of breath? | ☐

P | **Pillows**[3, 4]
How many pillows do you use to sleep? | ☐

E | **Exhaustion**[5]
Do you feel tired and fatigued? | ☐

C | **Chest pain. Confusion**[6, 7]
Do you have chest pain?
Did you have any episodes of confusion? | ☐

I | **Irregular heartbeat**[8]
Did you feel your heart racing?
Did you ever notice your heart skipped a beat? | ☐

A | **Appetite is lost**
Any changes in your appetite? | ☐

L | **Light headedness**[9]
Do you feel light headed? | ☐

C Co | **Cough**[10]
Do you have any cough? | ☐

W | **Weight gain**[11]
Any unintentional weight gain? | ☐

S Swelling in the legs[12]

Do you have any swelling in your legs?

Bibliography

1. Jorge, S., et al., Cardiac asthma in elderly patients: incidence, clinical presentation and outcome. BMC Cardiovasc Disord, 2007. 7: p. 16.

2. Scano, G., L. Stendardi, and M. Grazzini, Understanding dyspnoea by its language. Eur Respir J, 2005. 25(2): p. 380-5.

3. Mahler, D.A. and C.K. Wells, Evaluation of clinical methods for rating dyspnea. Chest, 1988. 93(3): p. 580-6.

4. Dzau, V.J., Renal and circulatory mechanisms in congestive heart failure. Kidney Int, 1987. 31(6): p. 1402-15.

5. Francis, G.S., et al., The neurohumoral axis in congestive heart failure. Ann Intern Med, 1984. 101(3): p. 370-7.

6. Ware, L.B. and M.A. Matthay, Clinical practice. Acute pulmonary edema. N Engl J Med, 2005. 353(26): p. 2788-96.

7. Flaherty, J.D., et al., Acute heart failure syndromes in patients with coronary artery disease early assessment and treatment. J Am Coll Cardiol, 2009. 53(3): p. 254-63.

8. Wang, T.J., et al., Temporal relations of atrial fibrillation and congestive heart failure and their joint influence on mortality: the Framingham Heart Study. Circulation, 2003. 107(23): p. 2920-5.

9. Schwartzenberg, S., et al., Effects of vasodilation in heart failure with preserved or reduced ejection fraction implications of distinct pathophysiologies on response to therapy. J Am Coll Cardiol, 2012. 59(5): p. 442-51.

10. Mant, J., et al., Systematic review and individual patient data meta-analysis of diagnosis of heart failure, with modelling of implications of different diagnostic strategies in primary care. Health Technol Assess, 2009. 13(32): p. 1-207, iii.

11. O'Reilly, R.A., Splenomegaly in 2,505 patients at a large university medical center from 1913 to 1995. 1963 to 1995: 449 patients. West J Med, 1998. 169(2): p. 88-97.

12. Kitzman, D.W., et al., Pathophysiological characterization of isolated diastolic heart failure in comparison to systolic heart failure. Jama, 2002. 288(17): p. 2144-50.

Patient Notes_____
Patient Drawings_____

Patient Notes_____
Patient Drawings_____

Checklist for Heart Failure Log Book: (iCrush) Heart Failure

VitalChecklist™

31. Checklist for Heart Failure

(iCRUSH) Heart Failure™

Patient Name_____
Caregiver Initials_____

	Answer	Patient Initials

I

Input[1]
How much fluids do you drink in a day?

☐

C

Cough with pink phlegm[2]
Do you have a cough that brings up pink phlegm?
If yes, how many teaspoons?

☐

R

Record of daily weight[3]
Do you measure your weight daily and maintain a log book?
If the weight gain is more than 2lbs a day or more than 5lbs
a week, please call your physician.

☐

U

Urine Output
How much is your urine output in a day?

☐

S

Sodium intake
(restrict to less than 1500mg/day)[2, 3]
How much sodium you take in a day?

☐

H

H²O intake (Water intake)
(restrict to less than 1500ml/day)[3]
How much water you take in a day?

☐

Bibliography

1. J. Lindenfeld et al., "HFSA 2010 Comprehensive Heart Failure Practice Guideline," (in eng), J Card Fail, vol. 16, no. 6, pp. e1-194, Jun 2010.

2. C. W. Yancy et al., "2013 ACCF/AHA guideline for the management of heart failure: a report of the American College of Cardiology Foundation/American Heart Association Task Force on practice guidelines," (in eng), Circulation, vol. 128, no. 16, pp. e240-327, Oct 2013.

3.
    J. J. McMurray et al., "ESC Guidelines for the diagnosis and treatment of acute and chronic heart failure 2012: The Task Force for the Diagnosis and Treatment of Acute and Chronic Heart Failure 2012 of the European Society of Cardiology. Developed in collaboration with the Heart Failure Association (HFA) of the ESC," (in eng), Eur Heart J, vol. 33, no. 14, pp. 1787-847, Jul 2012.

Checklist for Enzyme Inducers: PERCCS

Why should you tell your healthcare provider about all the medications you are on?

You need to mention prescription medications, over the counter medications, homeopathy, and Ayurvedic medications. Medications interact with each other, and their bioavailability (concentration in the blood) can vary depending on whether they are metabolized (processed) by liver or kidneys

PERCCS™

Patient Name_____
Caregiver Initials_____

Answer

Patient Initials

P **Phenytoin[1]**
Do you take Phenytoin?

☐

E **Ethanol (chronic intake)[2]**
Do you drink alcohol?
How much do you drink in a day?
Since how long you have been drinking?
What do you drink?

☐

R **Rifampin[3]**
Do you take Rifampin?

☐

C **Carbamazepine (Tegretol)**
Do you take Carbamazepine (Tegretol)?

☐

C **(Carba and Barba) Barbiturates (Phenobarbital)**
Do you take Phenobarbital or any other barbiturates?

☐

S **Steroids (Dexamethasone)**
Do you take Dexamethasone or any other steroids?

☐

Perk up! If you are getting PERCCS, You will stimulate the enzyme and warfarin will be
metabolized sooner leading to a fall in INR which increases risk of thrombotic events.

Bibliography

1. Flockhart, D.A. and J.R. Oesterheld, Cytochrome P450-mediated drug interactions. Child Adolesc Psychiatr Clin N Am, 2000. 9(1): p. 43-76.

2. Kalgutkar, A.S., R.S. Obach, and T.S. Maurer, Mechanism-based inactivation of cytochrome P450 enzymes: chemical mechanisms, structure-activity relationships and relationship to clinical drug-drug interactions and idiosyncratic adverse drug reactions. Curr Drug Metab, 2007. 8(5): p. 407-47.

3. Stepan, A.F., et al., Structural alert/reactive metabolite concept as applied in medicinal chemistry to mitigate the risk of idiosyncratic drug toxicity: a perspective based on the critical examination of trends in the top 200 drugs marketed in the United States. Chem Res Toxicol, 2011. 24(9): p. 1345-410.

Patient Notes_____
Patient Drawings_____

Checklist for Enzyme Inhibitors: PQRS in EKG or ECG

33. Checklist for Enzyme Inhibitors

PQRS In EKG Or ECG™

Patient Name_____

Caregiver Initials_____

Answer | Patient Initials

P | Paroxetine[1]
Do you take Paroxetine? ☐

Q | Quinolones, Quinidine[2]
Do you take Quinolones like Ciprofloxacin?
Do you take Quinidine? ☐

R | Ritonavir[3]
Do you take Ritonavir? ☐

S | Sertraline[4]
Do you take Sertraline? ☐

I (In) | Indinavir[5]
Do you take Indinavir? ☐

E | Ethanol (acute intake)[6]
Did you take alcohol recently?
How much alcohol did you drink? ☐

K | Ketoconazole or Itraconazole[7]
Do you take Ketoconazole or Itraconazole? ☐

G | Grape Fruit Juice[8]
Do you take grape fruit juice? ☐

O (Or) | Omeprazole
Do you take anti-acid drugs like Omeprazole? ☐

		Answer	Patient Initials

E **Erythromycin**[9]

Do you take Erythromycin?

☐

C **Cimetidine, Cymbalta**[10]

Do you take Cimetidine?
Do you take Cymbalta (Duloxetine)?

☐

G **Gemfibrozil**[11]

Do you take Gemfibrozil?

☐

The P.Q.R.S In EKG or ECG will inhibit P450 and thus warfarin will not be metabolized leading to an increase in INR, which increases the risk of bleeding.

Caregiver Initials_____

Bibliography

1. Gu, L., et al., Biotransformation of caffeine, paraxanthine, theobromine and theophylline by cDNA-expressed human CYP1A2 and CYP2E1. Pharmacogenetics, 1992. 2(2): p. 73-7.

2. Peterson, J.A. and S.E. Graham, A close family resemblance: the importance of structure in understanding cytochromes P450. Structure, 1998. 6(9): p. 1079-85.

3. Smith, G., et al., Molecular genetics of the human cytochrome P450 monooxygenase superfamily. Xenobiotica, 1998. 28(12): p. 1129-65.

4. Werck-Reichhart, D. and R. Feyereisen, Cytochromes P450: a success story. Genome Biol, 2000. 1(6): p. Reviews3003.

5. Danielson, P.B., The cytochrome P450 superfamily: biochemistry, evolution and drug metabolism in humans. Curr Drug Metab, 2002. 3(6): p. 561-97.

6. Watkins, P.B., Drug metabolism by cytochromes P450 in the liver and small bowel. Gastroenterol Clin North Am, 1992. 21(3): p. 511-26.

7. Wrighton, S.A., M. VandenBranden, and B.J. Ring, The human drug metabolizing cytochromes P450. J Pharmacokinet Biopharm, 1996. 24(5): p. 461-73.

8. Wilkinson, G.R., Cytochrome P4503A (CYP3A) metabolism: prediction of in vivo activity in humans. J Pharmacokinet Biopharm, 1996. 24(5): p. 475-90.

9. Ketter, T.A., et al., The emerging role of cytochrome P450 3A in psychopharmacology. J Clin Psychopharmacol, 1995. 15(6): p. 387-98.

10. Murray, M., Mechanisms and significance of inhibitory drug interactions involving cytochrome P450 enzymes (review). Int J Mol Med, 1999. 3(3): p. 227-38.

11. Nelson, D.R., et al., The P450 superfamily: update on new sequences, gene mapping, accession numbers, early trivial names of enzymes, and nomenclature. DNA Cell Biol, 1993. 12(1): p. 1-51.

Patient Notes_____
Patient Drawings_____

Checklist for Post Catheterization complications: eye BLINCC

We are using catheters in the groin and the arm, and therefore we need to look for the blood clots, swelling, redness, pain, and infections at the site of catheters.

If you see any discharge or any pus coming from the site, call your doctor.

Don't blink your eyes after procedures with catheters!

34. Post Catheterization Checklist

eye BLINCC[TM]

Patient Name_____
Caregiver Initials_____

	Answer	Patient Initials

VitalChecklist[TM]

B — Blue legs or toes[1]
Did you notice blue color of your legs or toes?
☐

L — Large lumps[2]
Did you notice any large lumps?
☐

I — Infection[3, 4]
Did you experience any fever after your stenting?
☐

N — Numbness in legs[5]
Did you feel any numbness in your legs?
☐

C — Cold legs[6]
Did you feel as if your legs have become cold?
☐

C — Caution! Do not lift weights of more than 10lbs for 4-5 days.
Did you lift any heavy weights immediately after the procedure?
☐

Bibliography

1. Muller, D.W., et al., Peripheral vascular complications after conventional and complex percutaneous coronary interventional procedures. Am J Cardiol, 1992. 69(1): p. 63-8.

2. Carrozza, J.P., Jr. and D.S. Baim, Complications of directional coronary atherectomy: incidence, causes, and management. Am J Cardiol, 1993. 72(13): p. 47e-54e.

3. Samore, M.H., et al., Frequency, risk factors, and outcome for bacteremia after percutaneous transluminal coronary angioplasty. Am J Cardiol, 1997. 79(7): p. 873-7.

4. Cleveland, K.O. and M.S. Gelfand, Invasive staphylococcal infections complicating percutaneous transluminal coronary angioplasty: three cases and review. Clin Infect Dis, 1995. 21(1): p. 93-6.

5. Popma, J.J., et al., Vascular complications after balloon and new device angioplasty. Circulation, 1993. 88(4 Pt 1): p. 1569-78.

6. Keeley, E.C. and C.L. Grines, Scraping of aortic debris by coronary guiding catheters: a prospective evaluation of 1,000 cases. J Am Coll Cardiol, 1998. 32(7): p. 1861-5.

Checklist for Varicose Veins Staging: Save Legs

VitalChecklist™

Patient Name_____
Caregiver Initials_____

Answer

Patient Initials

S Spider-like Veins[1-3] (Stage 1)

Do you notice any thin prominent spider like veins on your legs?

☐

A Asymptomatic Varicose Veins

Do you notice any large prominent swollen veins on your legs but have no pain in the legs?

☐

V Varicose Veins[3, 4] (Stage 2)

Do you notice any large prominent swollen veins on your legs and have pain in the legs?

☐

E Edema of legs[4-6] (Stage 3)

Any swelling in your legs?
No Skin changes

☐

L Legs looks pigmented[7, 8] (Stage 4)

Any change in the color of the skin near your ankles?
(Skin changes +)

☐

E Eczema (Stage 4)

Legs look pigmented, has eczema or looks like inverted champagne like bottle or Lipodermatosclerosis

☐

	Answer	Patient Initials

G **Got healed ulcers**[3, 9, 11]
(Stage 5)

Any healed ulcers near the ankles?
(Skin changes + healed ulcers)

☐

S **Skin sores**
(Stage 6)

Any active ulcers near the ankles?
(Skin changes + Active Ulcers)

☐

Caregiver Initials_____

Bibliography

1. Yiannakopoulou, E., Safety Concerns for Sclerotherapy of Telangiectases, Reticular and Varicose Veins. Pharmacology, 2016. 98(1-2): p. 62-9.

2. Smith, P.C., Management of reticular veins and telangiectases. Phlebology, 2015. 30(2 Suppl): p. 46-52.

3. Fuessl, H.S., [Spider-bust, varicosis, crural ulcer - problems of the legs]. MMW Fortschr Med, 2014. 156(18): p. 40.

4. Fox, J.D., et al., Ankle Range of Motion, Leg Pain, and Leg Edema Improvement in Patients With Venous Leg Ulcers. JAMA Dermatol, 2016. 152(4): p. 472-4.

5. Smyth, R.M., N. Aflaifel, and A.A. Bamigboye, Interventions for varicose veins and leg oedema in pregnancy. Cochrane Database Syst Rev, 2015(10): p. Cd001066.

6. Todd, M., Venous disease and chronic oedema: treatment and patient concordance. Br J Nurs, 2014. 23(9): p. 466, 468-70.

7. Caggiati, A., et al., The nature of skin pigmentations in chronic venous insufficiency: a preliminary report. Eur J Vasc Endovasc Surg, 2008. 35(1): p. 111-8.

8. Priollet, P., [Chronic venous insufficiency: clinical aspects]. Presse Med, 1994. 23(5): p. 229-35.

9. Vivas, A., H. Lev-Tov, and R.S. Kirsner, Venous Leg Ulcers. Ann Intern Med, 2016. 165(3): p. Itc17-itc32.

10. Abelyan, G., L. Abrahamyan, and G. Yenokyan, A case-control study of risk factors of chronic venous ulceration in patients with varicose veins. Phlebology, 2017: p. 268355516687677.

11. Hammerle, G., Case 3: chronic venous leg ulcer. J Wound Care, 2016. 25(3 Suppl): p. S12.

Checklist for Peripheral Artery Disease: Take your Shoes and Socks Off in the clinic

Patient Note

VitalChecklist™

Take your SHOES and SOCKS off in the clinic™

Patient Name_____
Caregiver Initials_____

Answer | Patient Initials

S

Smoking[1-4]
Sugar[5, 6]

Do you use tobacco in any form?
Have you ever smoked in the past?
Do you have diabetes?

☐

H

Hair loss[7]

Have you noticed any hair loss on your legs?

☐

O

Okay, if you have above problems[8, 9]

If you use tobacco in any form or have high blood sugars (diabetes), please check your nails and skin for any changes. If you notice any changes, please see your doctor. Do you have any pain in legs?

☐

E

Erectile dysfunction[10, 11]

Did you notice any erectile dysfunction?

☐

S

Skin changes[12]

Have you noticed any skin changes of your legs?
Any change in the color of the skin of legs?

☐

S

Sensation[13-15]
Strength of muscles is decreased[13]

Any change in the sensation in your legs?
(pain, touch, temperature)
Do you notice any weakness in your legs?

☐

O

On: pain on walking[8, 16]

Do you notice any cramp like pain in your legs while walking that goes away with rest?

☐

C Cramp like pain[8, 16]

Do you notice any cramp like pain in your legs while walking that goes away with rest?

☐

K Keep calm and go to your doctor and ask them to check your pulse.
Risk of cardiovascular disease[17, 18]

With these symptoms, keep calm and go visit your doctor. If you have peripheral arterial disease, it increases your risk of having heart disease.

☐

S Sores on legs or feet[19]

Did you notice any sores or ulcers on your feet? Ulcers or sores due to peripheral artery disease are usually at the tip of the toes.

☐

O Off: pain off walking or at rest[16]

Do you get pain at rest or while sleeping? Do you have to get up from the bed in the middle of the night because of the cramps?

☐

Caregiver Initials_____

Bibliography

1. Gerhard-Herman, M.D., et al., 2016 AHA/ACC Guideline on the Management of Patients with Lower Extremity Peripheral Artery Disease: Executive Summary. Vasc Med, 2017. 22(3): p. Np1-np43.

2. Faulkner, K.W., A.K. House, and W.M. Castleden, The effect of cessation of smoking on the accumulative survival rates of patients with symptomatic peripheral vascular disease. Med J Aust, 1983. 1(5): p. 217-9.

3. Ponte, E. and D. Battigelli, [Clinico-statistical evaluation of the effects of cigarette smoke on the blood vessels of the lower extremities]. Minerva Med, 1983. 74(22-23): p. 1325-32.

4. Myers, K.A., Relationship of smoking to peripheral arterial disease. Aust Fam Physician, 1979. 8(7): p. 765-8.

5. Abtan, J., et al., Geographic variation and risk factors for systemic and limb ischemic events in patients with symptomatic peripheral artery disease: Insights from the REACH Registry. Clin Cardiol, 2017.

6. Maric-Bilkan, C., Sex differences in micro- and macro-vascular complications of diabetes mellitus. Clin Sci (Lond), 2017. 131(9): p. 833-846.

7. Brueseke, T.J., S. Macrino, and J.J. Miller, Lack of lower extremity hair not a predictor for peripheral arterial disease. Arch Dermatol, 2009. 145(12): p. 1456-7.

8. Venkatesh, B.A., et al., Baseline assessment and comparison of arterial anatomy, hyperemic flow, and skeletal muscle perfusion in peripheral artery disease: The Cardiovascular Cell Therapy Research

9. Grozinger, G., et al., Perfusion measurements of the calf in patients with peripheral arterial occlusive disease before and after percutaneous transluminal angioplasty using MR arterial spin labeling. J Magn Reson Imaging, 2014. 40(4): p. 980-7.

10. Spessoto, L.C., et al., Association of Hypertension With Erectile Function in Chronic Peripheral Arterial Insufficiency Patients. J Clin Med Res, 2016. 8(8): p. 582-4.

11. Lahoz, C., et al., Peripheral Atherosclerosis in Patients With Erectile Dysfunction: A Population-Based Study. J Sex Med, 2016. 13(1): p. 63-9.

12. Weragoda, J., et al., Risk factors of peripheral arterial disease: a case control study in Sri Lanka. BMC Res Notes, 2016. 9(1): p. 508.

13. McDermott, M.M., et al., Leg symptom categories and rates of mobility decline in peripheral arterial disease. J Am Geriatr Soc, 2010. 58(7): p. 1256-62.

14. Lang, P.M., et al., [Correlation between quantitative sensory testing and questionnaires on neuropathic pain for chronic ischemic pain in peripheral arterial disease]. Schmerz, 2009. 23(3): p. 251-4, 256-8.

15. Ruger, L.J., et al., Characteristics of chronic ischemic pain in patients with peripheral arterial disease. Pain, 2008. 139(1): p. 201-8.

16. Hamburg, N.M. and M.A. Creager, Pathophysiology of Intermittent Claudication in Peripheral Artery Disease. Circ J, 2017. 81(3): p. 281-289.

17. Rada, C., et al., [Ankle-brachial index screening for peripheral artery disease in high cardiovascular risk patients. Prospective observational study of 370 asymptomatic patients at high cardiovascular risk]. J Mal Vasc, 2016. 41(6): p. 353-357.

18. Fores, R., et al., Evolution and degree of control of cardiovascular risk factors after 5 years of follow-up and their relationship with the incidence of peripheral arterial disease: ARTPER cohort. Med Clin (Barc), 2017. 148(3): p. 107-113.

19. Scholl, L., M. Dorler, and M. Stucker, [Ulcers in obesity-associated chronic venous insufficiency]. Hautarzt, 2017.

Is it difficult for you to remember "5 P's" of Acute Limb Ischemia?

P- Pain

P- Pulselessness (arteries and circulation)

P- Pallor (mottled coloration)

P- Paraesthesias (numbness and tingling)

P- Paralysis (moving the legs is impossible)

Some authorities have added poikilothermia (cold legs) or difficult to thermo-regulate. Many caregivers will overlap the signs of acute limb ischemia with acute compartment syndrome, however, this is inaccurate. Although the signs don't overlap between the two conditions but to remember Acute Limb Ischemia, you may chunk the word compartment like this "Co-m-p-art-me-nt" to remember the "5 P's" or "6 P's" of Acute Limb Ischemia.

37. Checklist for Acute Limb Ischemia

CO-M-P-ART-ME-NT™

Patient Name_____
Caregiver Initials_____

Answer | Patient Initials

C CO — Cold legs (Poikilothermia)[1]
Are your legs cold to touch?
Is your one leg colder than the other?
Record the level of coldness.

☐

M — Mottled discoloration (Pallor)[2]
Have you noticed any change in the color of your legs
Are your legs pale?
Are your legs blue or cyanotic looking?
Record the level of pallor

☐

P — Pain[3]
Do you have pain on walking?
Do you have stop because of the pain in the legs
Do you have rest pain?

☐

A ART — Artery and circulation (Pulselessness)[4]
Can you or your doctor feel the pulse in your legs?

☐

M ME — Not able to Move legs (Paralysis)[5]
Are you able to move your legs?
Do you feel heaviness in your legs?

☐

N NT — Numbness and Tingling (Paresthesia)[4]
Do you feel pin-prick sensation in the legs?

☐

Bibliography

1. Acar RD, Sahin M, Kirma C. One of the most urgent vascular circumstances: Acute limb ischemia. SAGE Open Med. 2013;1:2050312113516110.

2. Callum K, Bradbury A. ABC of arterial and venous disease: Acute limb ischaemia. BMJ. 2000;320(7237):764-7.

3. Creager MA, Kaufman JA, Conte MS. Clinical practice. Acute limb ischemia. N Engl J Med. 2012;366(23):2198-206.

4. Brooks M, Jenkins MP. Acute and chronic ischaemia of the limb. Surgery - Oxford International Edition.26(1):17-20.

5. Costantini V, Lenti M. Treatment of acute occlusion of peripheral arteries. Thromb Res. 2002;106(6):V285-94.

38. Nocturnal Leg Cramps

LEG CRAMPS[TM]

Patient Name_____
Caregiver Initials_____

Answer | Patient Initials

L Lumbosacral Stenosis[1]

Lumbar canal stenosis associated with leg cramps
Botulinum toxin injection may be beneficial
Do you have back pain, sciatica or pain in the buttocks?

☐

E End Stage Renal Disease[2]

End stage renal disease and hemodialysis associated
with increased prevalence of leg cramps
Do you have kidney disease?

☐

G Goiter[3]

Leg cramps associated with hypothyroidism
Hypothyroid myopathy
Do you have thyroid issues?

☐

C Cirrhosis[4]
Cancer[2]

Cramping associated with hepatic cirrhosis
Nerve damage from cancer treatment may cause leg
cramps
Do you have liver issues?

☐

R Restless Leg Syndrome[2,5]

Urge to move or shake legs relieved by movement
Occurs at rest, usually during evening or night
Sometimes painful and cramp-like sensation
Do you have restless legs at night?

☐

136

A Arteriovenous disease[6,7]

Peripheral vascular disease may cause claudication
Venous insufficiency associated with nocturnal leg cramps
Do you have cramps in the legs?

☐

M Medication/Myoclonus/Myositis[8,9]

LABAs, potassium sparing diuretics, thiazide-like diuretics
Nocturnal myoclonus –involuntary jerking during sleep and at night
Hypnic myoclonus –sudden jerking of limbs around time of sleep onset
Do your legs shake when you are about to sleep?

☐

P Pregnancy/Periodic Limb Movements[10, 12]

Pregnancy-related leg cramps associated with low magnesium levels
Periodic limb movements -involuntary jerking movements of the legs during sleep
Do your legs shake during sleep?

☐

S Sensory or peripheral neuropathy[2]

Dysesthesias
Muscle weakness
Nerve injury
Muscle pathology
Do you have numbness and tingling in the legs?

☐

Caregiver Initials_____

Bibliography

1. Park SJ, Yoon KB, Yoon DM, Kim SH. Botulinum Toxin Treatment for Nocturnal Calf Cramps in Patients With Lumbar Spinal Stenosis: A Randomized Clinical Trial. Arch Phys Med Rehabil. 2017;98(5):957-63.

2. Allen RE, Kirby KA. Nocturnal leg cramps. Am Fam Physician. 2012;86(4):350-5.

3. Maquirriain J, Merello M. The athlete with muscular cramps: clinical approach. J Am Acad Orthop Surg. 2007;15(7):425-31.

4. Baskol M, Ozbakir O, Coşkun R, Baskol G, Saraymen R, Yucesoy M. The role of serum zinc and other factors on the prevalence of muscle cramps in non-alcoholic cirrhotic patients. J Clin Gastroenterol. 2004;38(6):524-9.

5. Rana AQ, Khan F, Mosabbir A, Ondo W. Differentiating nocturnal leg cramps and restless legs syndrome. Expert Rev Neurother. 2014;14(7):813-8.

6. Naylor JR, Young JB. A general population survey of rest cramps. Age Ageing. 1994;23(5):418-20.

7. Atreja A, Abacan C, Licata A. A 51-year-old woman with debilitating cramps 12 years after bariatric surgery. Cleve Clin J Med. 2003;70(5):417-8, 20, 23-6.

8. Walters AS. Clinical identification of the simple sleep-related movement disorders. Chest. 2007;131(4):1260-6.

9. Garrison SR, Dormuth CR, Morrow RL, Carney GA, Khan KM. Nocturnal leg cramps and prescription use that precedes them: a sequence symmetry analysis. Arch Intern Med. 2012;172(2):120-6.

10. Nygaard IH, Valbø A, Pethick SV, Bøhmer T. Does oral magnesium substitution relieve pregnancy-induced leg cramps? Eur J Obstet Gynecol Reprod Biol. 2008;141(1):23-6.

11. Sohrabvand F, Shariat M, Haghollahi F. Vitamin B supplementation for leg cramps during pregnancy. Int J Gynaecol Obstet. 2006;95(1):48-9.

12. Sebo P, Cerutti B, Haller DM. Effect of magnesium therapy on nocturnal leg cramps: a systematic review of randomized controlled trials with meta-analysis using simulations. Fam Pract. 2014;31(1):7-19.

Section F

Lungs

Patient Notes_____
Patient Drawings_____

39. Checklist for Obstructive Sleep Apnea

Snoring Nap[TM]

Patient Name_____
Caregiver Initials_____

	Answer	Patient Initials

S Snoring[1]

Do you snore? Have you been told that you snore when you sleep?

☐

N Night-time gasps[2]

Do you choke at night? Do you have night time gasps?
Do you have any interruptions in breathing?
Most useful individual finding on clinical examination

☐

O Oxygen[3,4]

Reduction in blood oxygen saturation and hypoxia
Increase in blood carbon dioxide

☐

R Restless legs[5]

High prevalence of restless leg syndrome in those with OSA
Do you have restless legs?

☐

I Impotence[6]

Do you have problem with erection?

☐

N Nocturia[7]

Do you wake up to pee at least two times per night?

☐

G Gender[8]

Two to three times more common in males than females

☐

Doze [9]

Nap / Dozing off Dozing off while driving

Dozing off while driving

Dozing off while watching TV

Doze off during the day at work

Poor concentration

Doze off while Sitting and talking to someone

Doze off after lunch without alcohol

☐

Neck Circumference and Obesity[10, 11, 12]

Neck circumference 17 inches in male
Neck circumference 16 inches in females
BMI >35 Kg/meter square

☐

Age[10]

Are you above 50 years of age?

☐

Blood Pressure[1]

Do you have high blood pressure?

☐

Caregiver Initials_____

Bibliography

1. Chung F, Yegneswaran B, Liao P, Chung SA, Vairavanathan S, Islam S, et al. STOP questionnaire: a tool to screen patients for obstructive sleep apnea. Anesthesiology. 2008;108(5):812-21.

2. Myers KA, Mrkobrada M, Simel DL. Does this patient have obstructive sleep apnea?: The Rational Clinical Examination systematic review. JAMA. 2013;310(7):731-41.

3. Gale SD, Hopkins RO. Effects of hypoxia on the brain: neuroimaging and neuropsychological findings following carbon monoxide poisoning and obstructive sleep apnea. J Int Neuropsychol Soc. 2004;10(1):60-71.

4. Jennum P, Riha RL. Epidemiology of sleep apnoea/hypopnoea syndrome and sleep-disordered breathing. Eur Respir J. 2009;33(4):907-14.

5. Roux FJ. Restless legs syndrome: impact on sleep-related breathing disorders. Respirology. 2013;18(2):238-45.

6. Liu L, Kang R, Zhao S, Zhang T, Zhu W, Li E, et al. Sexual Dysfunction in Patients with Obstructive Sleep Apnea: A Systematic Review and Meta-Analysis. J Sex Med. 2015;12(10):1992-2003.

7. Raheem OA, Orosco RK, Davidson TM, Lakin C. Clinical predictors of nocturia in the sleep apnea population. Urol Ann. 2014;6(1):31-5.

8. Quintana-Gallego E, Carmona-Bernal C, Capote F, Sánchez-Armengol A, Botebol-Benhamou G, Polo-Padillo J, et al. Gender differences in obstructive sleep apnea syndrome: a clinical study of 1166 patients. Respir Med. 2004;98(10):984-9.

9. Johns MW. A new method for measuring daytime sleepiness: the Epworth sleepiness scale. Sleep. 1991;14(6):540-5.

10. Young T, Palta M, Dempsey J, Peppard PE, Nieto FJ, Hla KM. Burden of sleep apnea: rationale, design, and major findings of the Wisconsin Sleep Cohort study. WMJ. 2009;108(5):246-9.

11. Young T, Skatrud J, Peppard PE. Risk factors for obstructive sleep apnea in adults. JAMA. 2004;291(16):2013-6.

12. Tufik S, Santos-Silva R, Taddei JA, Bittencourt LR. Obstructive sleep apnea syndrome in the Sao Paulo Epidemiologic Sleep Study. Sleep Med. 2010;11(5):441-6.

Patient Notes_____
Patient Drawings_____

Checklist for COPD: (iCrush) COPD

VitalChecklist™

	Answer	Patient Initials

i — **Infection (chances of admission are increased if more than one infections in a year) ; Insomnia[1, 2]** ☐

Did you have fever?
Did you have worsening of shortness of breath/ productive cough?
How many infections you have in one year?
Do you have difficulty in sleeping?

C — **Chest tightness[3, 4]** ☐

Do you have chest tightness?

R — **Ratio (FEV1/FVC Ratio)[4-6]** ☐

When did you have a pulmonary function test done?
Has your lung function become worse over the years or has it improved?

U — **Uphill walk[7, 8]** ☐

Do you get short of breath while walking uphill or climbing a flight of stairs?

U — **Undernourished[1, 9, 10]** ☐

Any changes in weight, since you were diagnosed with COPD?

S — **Shortness of breath/ Dyspnea[9]** ☐

Do you have shortness of breath?

H — **Homebound[7, 11]** ☐

Do you have limitation of activities of daily living?

		Answer	Patient Initials

C **Co** **Cough**[12]

Do you have cough?

☐

P **Phlegm**[13]

Do you cough up phlegm?
What is the color of phlegm?
How much is phlegm in terms of teaspoons?

☐

D **Distance walked in 6 minutes (6min walk test/ Exercise testing)**[3]

Do you have difficulty in walking for 6 minutes due to breathlessness?

☐

Caregiver Initials_____

Bibliography

1. Rennard, S., et al., Impact of COPD in North America and Europe in 2000: subjects' perspective of Confronting COPD International Survey. Eur Respir J, 2002. 20(4): p. 799-805.

2. Vaz Fragoso, C.A., et al., Respiratory impairment in older persons: when less means more. Am J Med, 2013. 126(1): p. 49-57.

3. Kessler, R., et al., Symptom variability in patients with severe COPD: a pan-European cross-sectional study. Eur Respir J, 2011. 37(2): p. 264-72.

4. Puente-Maestu, L., et al., Abnormal mitochondrial function in locomotor and respiratory muscles of COPD patients. Eur Respir J, 2009. 33(5): p. 1045-52.

5. Shirtcliffe, P., et al., COPD prevalence in a random population survey: a matter of definition. Eur Respir J, 2007. 30(2): p. 232-9.

6. Vaz Fragoso, C.A., et al., Use of lambda-mu-sigma-derived Z score for evaluating respiratory impairment in middle-aged persons. Respir Care, 2011. 56(11): p. 1771-7.

7. Eisner, M.D., et al., COPD as a systemic disease: impact on physical functional limitations. Am J Med, 2008. 121(9): p. 789-96.

8. van Noord, J.A., et al., Effects of tiotropium with and without formoterol on airflow obstruction and resting hyperinflation in patients with COPD. Chest, 2006. 129(3): p. 509-17.

9. Sin, D.D., L. Wu, and S.F. Man, The relationship between reduced lung function and cardiovascular mortality: a population-based study and a systematic review of the literature. Chest, 2005. 127(6): p. 1952-9.

10. Weisberg, J., et al., Megestrol acetate stimulates weight gain and ventilation in underweight COPD patients. Chest, 2002. 121(4): p. 1070-8.

11. Vaz Fragoso, C.A., et al., Respiratory impairment and COPD hospitalisation in older persons: a competing risk analysis. Eur Respir J, 2012. 40(1): p. 37-44.

12. Rennard, S.I., et al., Use of a long-acting inhaled beta2-adrenergic agonist, salmeterol xinafoate, in patients with chronic obstructive pulmonary disease. Am J Respir Crit Care Med, 2001. 163(5): p. 1087-92.

13. Seemungal, T.A., et al., Long-term erythromycin therapy is associated with decreased chronic obstructive pulmonary disease exacerbations. Am J Respir Crit Care Med, 2008. 178(11): p. 1139-47.

Patient Notes_____
Patient Drawings_____

Checklist for Smoking Side Effects: Let's Crush Smoking, Okay!

LET'S CRUSH (Smoking) OKAY™

Patient Name_____
Caregiver Initials_____

Answer | Patient Initials

L Lungs: Risk of having COPD, Asthma, Lung Cancer[1-4]

Do you have productive cough/ shortness of breath/ blood in the phlegm/ weight loss?
Do you have COPD/ Asthma/ lung cancer?

☐

E Endocrine: Risk of Diabetes[5]

Do you have Diabetes?
Do you have increased frequency of urination/ increased appetite/ increased thirst?

☐

T Teeth & Oral Cavity: Risk of having: Gingivitis, Periodontitis, Tongue cancer, Cancer of floor of mouth Buccal cancer[6]

Do you have any pain or swelling or bleeding in your gums?
Do you have any whitish or red colored patches in your mouth?
Do you have any non-healing ulcer on your tongue or in mouth?
Do you have any tongue cancer or cancer of mouth?

☐

S Skin[7]

Do you have nicotine stains on your fingers or nails?
Do you have any wrinkles on the skin?

☐

C Cholesterol, Clots, Cancer (Colon/ Esophageal/ Bladder/ Cervix)[8-10]

Do you have high cholesterol?
Did you ever have blood clots?
Do you have anemia or blood in stools?
Do you have difficulty in swallowing?
Do you have any blood in urine?
Do you have foul smelling cervical discharge?
Do you have any cancer of colon/ bladder/ esophagus/ cervix?

R Reproductive organs[11]

Do you have erectile dysfunction?
Did you ever have complications during pregnancy like Abruptio placenta, Preterm premature rupture of membranes, Still birth, Low birth weight?

U Ulcer: Peptic ulcer disease[12-15] Urge Incontinence

Do you have peptic ulcer disease?
Do you have to run to the bathroom to pee?

S Stroke, Sleep apnea, Snoring[16-20]

Did you ever have stroke?
Do you snore during sleep?
Do you have an interrupted sleep at night?
Do you feel sleepy even after you wake up in the morning?

H Hypertension, Heart attack, Heart failure[21]

Do you have high blood pressure?
Do you have a heart disease?
Do you have shortness of breath, swelling of feet?

Caregiver Initials_____

O Osteoporosis[22-24]

Did you get a bone scan done?
Any history of fractures?

☐

K Kidney Cancer[14]

Did you ever have abdominal pain, blood in urine?
Do you have kidney cancer?

☐

A Artery: Risk of Peripheral artery disease[25]

Did you ever have abdominal pain, blood in urine?

☐

Y Yearly expense:
Approximately $7 per pack per day times 30 is $210, Multiply this with 12 months and this is equal to $2520

Are you aware of the yearly expense of smoking?

☐

Caregiver Initials_____

151

Bibliography

1. Smoking-attributable mortality, years of potential life lost, and productivity losses--United States, 2000-2004. MMWR Morb Mortal Wkly Rep, 2008. 57(45): p. 1226-8.

2. Doll, R. and A.B. Hill, Smoking and carcinoma of the lung; preliminary report. Br Med J, 1950. 2(4682): p. 739-48.

3. Wynder, E.L. and E.A. Graham, Etiologic factors in bronchiogenic carcinoma with special reference to industrial exposures; report of eight hundred fifty-seven proved cases. AMA Arch Ind Hyg Occup Med, 1951. 4(3): p. 221-35.

4. Willemse, B.W., et al., The impact of smoking cessation on respiratory symptoms, lung function, airway hyperresponsiveness and inflammation. Eur Respir J, 2004. 23(3): p. 464-76.

5. Willi, C., et al., Active smoking and the risk of type 2 diabetes: a systematic review and meta-analysis. Jama, 2007. 298(22): p. 2654-64.

6. Zee, K.Y., Smoking and periodontal disease. Aust Dent J, 2009. 54 Suppl 1: p. S44-50.

7. Rigotti, N.A., Clinical practice. Treatment of tobacco use and dependence. N Engl J Med, 2002. 346(7): p. 506-12.

8. Wyss, A., et al., Cigarette, cigar, and pipe smoking and the risk of head and neck cancers: pooled analysis in the International Head and Neck Cancer Epidemiology Consortium. Am J Epidemiol, 2013. 178(5): p. 679-90.

9. Blot, W.J., et al., Smoking and drinking in relation to oral and pharyngeal cancer. Cancer Res, 1988. 48(11): p. 3282-7.

10. Spitz, M.R., Epidemiology and risk factors for head and neck cancer. Semin Oncol, 1994. 21(3): p. 281-8.

11. Dillner, J., et al., Etiology of squamous cell carcinoma of the penis. Scand J Urol Nephrol Suppl, 2000(205): p. 189-93.

12. Ladeiras-Lopes, R., et al., Smoking and gastric cancer: systematic review and meta-analysis of cohort studies. Cancer Causes Control, 2008. 19(7): p. 689-701.

13. Lynch, S.M., et al., Cigarette smoking and pancreatic cancer: a pooled analysis from the pancreatic cancer cohort consortium. Am J Epidemiol, 2009. 170(4): p. 403-13.

14. Cumberbatch, M.G., et al., The Role of Tobacco Smoke in Bladder and Kidney Carcinogenesis: A Comparison of Exposures and Meta-analysis of Incidence and Mortality Risks. Eur Urol, 2016. 70(3): p. 458-66.

15. Parasher, G. and G.L. Eastwood, Smoking and peptic ulcer in the Helicobacter pylori era. Eur J Gastroenterol Hepatol, 2000. 12(8): p. 843-53.

16. Anthonisen, N.R., et al., The effects of a smoking cessation intervention on 14.5-year mortality: a randomized clinical trial. Ann Intern Med, 2005. 142(4): p. 233-9.

17. Vollset, S.E., A. Tverdal, and H.K. Gjessing, Smoking and deaths between 40 and 70 years of age in women and men. Ann Intern Med, 2006. 144(6): p. 381-9.

18. Kenfield, S.A., et al., Smoking and smoking cessation in relation to mortality in women. Jama, 2008. 299(17): p. 2037-47.

19. Ikeda, F., et al., Smoking cessation improves mortality in Japanese men: the Hisayama study. Tob Control, 2012. 21(4): p. 416-21.

20. Cao, Y., et al., Cigarette smoking cessation and total and cause-specific mortality: a 22-year follow-up study among US male physicians. Arch Intern Med, 2011. 171(21): p. 1956-9.

21. Ezzati, M., et al., Role of smoking in global and regional cardiovascular mortality. Circulation, 2005. 112(4): p. 489-97.

22. Kanis, J.A., et al., Smoking and fracture risk: a meta-analysis. Osteoporos Int, 2005. 16(2): p. 155-62.

23. Cornuz, J., et al., Smoking, smoking cessation, and risk of hip fracture in women. Am J Med, 1999. 106(3): p. 311-4.

24. Oncken, C., et al., Impact of smoking cessation on bone mineral density in postmenopausal women. J Womens Health (Larchmt), 2006. 15(10): p. 1141-50.

25. Conte, M.S., et al., Society for Vascular Surgery practice guidelines for atherosclerotic occlusive disease of the lower extremities: management of asymptomatic disease and claudication. J Vasc Surg, 2015. 61(3 Suppl): p. 2s-41s.

Patient Notes_____
Patient Drawings_____

Checklist for Side Effects of Passive Smoking: No ABC for Tobacco

42. Checklist for Side Effects of Passive Smoking

VitalChecklist™

No ABC For TOBACCO™

Patient Name_____
Caregiver Initials_____

	Answer	Patient Initials

N (No)

Nicotine[1-3]
Do you know inhaling nicotine via smoking puts you at risk of high blood pressure, blood clots and heart disease?
☐

A

Arsenic[4]
Do you know you inhale arsenic in smoke, which increases your risk of heart disease?
☐

B

Benzene[5]
Do you know you inhale benzene, which puts you at risk of blood cancers?
☐

C

Cadmium[6, 7]
Do you know you inhale cadmium which increases of risk of cancers and kidney failure?
☐

F (For)

Formaldehyde[8]
Do you know you inhale formaldehyde, which puts you at risk of lung diseases?
☐

T

Tar[3]
Do you know you inhale tar which causes staining of teeth, fingers and in long term causes lung problems?
☐

O

Oxide (Nitric Oxide)[9]
Do you know you inhale nitric oxide, which puts you at risk of heart diseases?
☐

B **Benzopyrene/ Butadiene[2]**

Do you know you inhale benzopyrene/ butadiene which increases your risk for cancers?

☐

A **Acrolein; Ammonia[10]**

Do you know inhaling acrolein or ammonia puts you at risk of lung cancer?

☐

C **Chromium**

Do you know you inhale chromium, which increases your risk of lung cancer?

☐

C **Carbon monoxide[11]**

Do you know you inhale carbon monoxide, which causes breathing problems?

☐

O **Other gases like Hydrogen cyanide[12]**

Do you know you also inhale many other toxic gases like hydrogen cyanide which increases your risk of heart disease?

☐

Caregiver Initials_____

Bibliography

1. Kannel, W.B., Hypertension, blood lipids, and cigarette smoking as co-risk factors for coronary heart disease. Ann N Y Acad Sci, 1978. 304: p. 128-39.

2. Wilhelmsen, L., Coronary heart disease: epidemiology of smoking and intervention studies of smoking. Am Heart J, 1988. 115(1 Pt 2): p. 242-9.

3. McBride, P.E., The health consequences of smoking. Cardiovascular diseases. Med Clin North Am, 1992. 76(2): p. 333-53.

4. Hirayama, T., Non-smoking wives of heavy smokers have a higher risk of lung cancer: a study from Japan. Br Med J (Clin Res Ed), 1981. 282(6259): p. 183-5.

5. Trichopoulos, D., et al., Lung cancer and passive smoking. Int J Cancer, 1981. 27(1): p. 1-4.

6. Friberg, L., Health hazards in the manufacture of alkaline accumulators with special reference to chronic cadmium poisoning; a clinical and experimental study. Acta Med Scand Suppl, 1950. 240: p. 1-124.

7. Butler, E.A. and F.V. Flynn, The proteinuria of renal tubular disorders. Lancet, 1958. 2(7054): p. 978-80.

8. Coggon, D., et al., Extended follow-up of a cohort of british chemical workers exposed to formaldehyde. J Natl Cancer Inst, 2003. 95(21): p. 1608-15.

9. Kharitonov, S.A., et al., Increased nitric oxide in exhaled air of asthmatic patients. Lancet, 1994. 343(8890): p. 133-5.

10. Philips, F.S., et al., Cyclophosphamide and urinary bladder toxicity. Cancer Res, 1961. 21: p. 1577-89.

11. Ernst, A. and J.D. Zibrak, Carbon monoxide poisoning. N Engl J Med, 1998. 339(22): p. 1603-8.

12. Rehberg, S., et al., Pathophysiology, management and treatment of smoke inhalation injury. Expert Rev Respir Med, 2009. 3(3): p. 283-297.

Patient Notes_____
Patient Drawings_____

Checklist for Side Effects of Smokeless Tobacco: TOBACCO

43. Checklist for Side Effects of Smokeless Tobacco

TOBACCO™

Patient Name_____
Caregiver Initials_____

Answer | Patient Initials

T

Throat and Esophagus[1-3]
Do you know chewing tobacco increases risk for throat cancer, laryngeal cancer and cancer of esophagus?

☐

O

Oral (mouth) cancer[4-7]
Do you know chewing tobacco puts you at risk of tongue cancer or cancer in any other part of mouth like floor of mouth?

☐

B

Bladder Cancer[8, 9]
Do you know chewing tobacco increases your risk of bladder cancer and kidney cancer?

☐

A

Acute Myeloid Leukemia (AML)[10, 11]
Do you know chewing tobacco increases your risk of blood cancer?

☐

C

Colon Cancer[12, 13]
Do you know chewing tobacco puts you at risk of colon cancer?

☐

C

Cervical Cancer[14-17]
Do you know chewing tobacco increases your risk for cervical cancer, cancer of ovaries or fallopian tubes?

☐

O

Other rare types of cancer[18-22]
Are you aware that chewing tobacco also increases your risk for cancer of the pancreas, anal cancer and cancer of the penis?

☐

Bibliography

1.   Mazurek, J.M., et al., Smokeless tobacco use among working adults - United States, 2005 and 2010. MMWR Morb Mortal Wkly Rep, 2014. 63(22): p. 477-82.

2.   Blot, W.J., et al., Smoking and drinking in relation to oral and pharyngeal cancer. Cancer Res, 1988. 48(11): p. 3282-7.

3.   Spitz, M.R., Epidemiology and risk factors for head and neck cancer. Semin Oncol, 1994. 21(3): p. 281-8.

4.   Christen, A.G., et al., Smokeless tobacco: the folklore and social history of snuffing, sneezing, dipping, and chewing. J Am Dent Assoc, 1982. 105(5): p. 821-9.

5.   Wyss, A., et al., Cigarette, cigar, and pipe smoking and the risk of head and neck cancers: pooled analysis in the International Head and Neck Cancer Epidemiology Consortium. Am J Epidemiol, 2013. 178(5): p. 679-90.

6.   Sapkota, A., et al., Smokeless tobacco and increased risk of hypopharyngeal and laryngeal cancers: a multicentric case-control study from India. Int J Cancer, 2007. 121(8): p. 1793-8.

7.   Proia, N.K., et al., Smoking and smokeless tobacco-associated human buccal cell mutations and their association with oral cancer--a review. Cancer Epidemiol Biomarkers Prev, 2006. 15(6): p. 1061-77.

8.   Djordjevic, M.V. and K.A. Doran, Nicotine content and delivery across tobacco products. Handb Exp Pharmacol, 2009(192): p. 61-82.

9.   Cumberbatch, M.G., et al., The Role of Tobacco Smoke in Bladder and Kidney Carcinogenesis: A Comparison of Exposures and Meta-analysis of Incidence and Mortality Risks. Eur Urol, 2016. 70(3): p. 458-66.

10. Sandler, D.P., et al., Cigarette smoking and risk of acute leukemia: associations with morphology and cytogenetic abnormalities in bone marrow. J Natl Cancer Inst, 1993. 85(24): p. 1994-2003.

11. Taylor, J.A., et al., ras oncogene activation and occupational exposures in acute myeloid leukemia. J Natl Cancer Inst, 1992. 84(21): p. 1626-32.

12. Boyle, T., et al., Lifestyle factors associated with survival after colorectal cancer diagnosis. Br J Cancer, 2013. 109(3): p. 814-22.

13. Ladeiras-Lopes, R., et al., Smoking and gastric cancer: systematic review and meta-analysis of cohort studies. Cancer Causes Control, 2008. 19(7): p. 689-701.

14. Appleby, P., et al., Carcinoma of the cervix and tobacco smoking: collaborative reanalysis of individual data on 13,541 women with carcinoma of the cervix and 23,017 women without carcinoma of the cervix from 23 epidemiological studies. Int J Cancer, 2006. 118(6): p. 1481-95.

15. Castellsague, X. and N. Munoz, Chapter 3: Cofactors in human papillomavirus carcinogenesis--role of parity, oral contraceptives, and tobacco smoking. J Natl Cancer Inst Monogr, 2003(31): p. 20-8.

16. Castle, P.E., et al., A prospective study of high-grade cervical neoplasia risk among human papillomavirus-infected women. J Natl Cancer Inst, 2002. 94(18): p. 1406-14.

17. Jordan, S.J., et al., Does smoking increase risk of ovarian cancer? A systematic review. Gynecol Oncol, 2006. 103(3): p. 1122-9.

18. Hatsukami, D.K., et al., Developing the science base for reducing tobacco harm. Nicotine Tob Res, 2007. 9 Suppl 4: p. S537-53.

19. Lowenfels, A.B., P. Maisonneuve, and D.C. Whitcomb, Risk factors for cancer in hereditary pancreatitis. International Hereditary Pancreatitis Study Group. Med Clin North Am, 2000. 84(3): p. 565-73.

20. Holly, E.A., et al., Anal cancer incidence: genital warts, anal fissure or fistula, hemorrhoids, and smoking. J Natl Cancer Inst, 1989. 81(22): p. 1726-31.

21. Daling, J.R., et al., Cigarette smoking and the risk of anogenital cancer. Am J Epidemiol, 1992. 135(2): p. 180-9.

22. Harish, K. and R. Ravi, The role of tobacco in penile carcinoma. Br J Urol, 1995. 75(3): p. 375-7.

Patient Notes_____
Patient Drawings_____

Checklist for Smoking Cessation Counselling: Dr. Spade

44. Checklist for Smoking Cessation Counselling

Dr. SPADE[TM]

Patient Name_____
Caregiver Initials_____

	Answer	Patient Initials

D Dr. Doctor or Caregiver
Doctor or caregiver should assess any triggers and risks of you going back to smoking. ☐

S Survey the routine and triggers[1]
Doctor should survey if patient smokes and document it. ☐

P Point out
Doctor should point out the risks of smoking with the patient. ☐

A Assess
Doctor should assess the willingness of patient to quit within 30 days. ☐

D Drugs, Device[2]
Doctor should discuss medications and devices that can help with quitting smoking. ☐

E Evaluate
Doctor should evaluate and follow up with the patient. ☐

Bibliography

1. Kenfield, S.A., et al., Smoking and smoking cessation in relation to mortality in women. Jama, 2008. 299(17): p. 2037-47.

2. Rigotti, N.A., Clinical practice. Treatment of tobacco use and dependence. N Engl J Med, 2002. 346(7): p. 506-12.

Patient Notes_____
Patient Drawings_____

Checklist for COPD Treatment: I GOOD Son

VitalChecklist™

I GOOD SON™

Patient Name_____
Caregiver Initials_____

Answer | Patient Initials

I — Influenza (Recommended for all COPD patients)[1-3]
Do you get a Flu shot every year?

☐

G — Glucocorticoids[4, 5]
Do you take steroids like Prednisone or Hydrocortisone?

☐

O — Oxygen Therapy (Goal to keep Oxygen sat >90%) (Used for at least 15 hrs. a day)[6-9]
Do you use home oxygen therapy?

☐

O — Open & Dilate (Bronchodilators: beta agonists, anticholinergics), (Oral glucocorticoids)[10-14]
What medications do you take for COPD?
Do you use inhalers like Albuterol or Tiotropium bromide?

☐

D — Dilate or bronchodilators.
As mentioned above

☐

S — Smoking Cessation[15]
Did you quit smoking?

☐

O — Other medications (Antibiotics)[16, 17]
How often do you take antibiotics for your lung infection?

☐

N — Nutrition[18]
Did you notice any changes in your weight since your diagnosis of COPD?

☐

Bibliography

1. Nichol, K.L., L. Baken, and A. Nelson, Relation between influenza vaccination and outpatient visits, hospitalization, and mortality in elderly persons with chronic lung disease. Ann Intern Med, 1999. 130(5): p. 397-403.

2. Poole, P.J., et al., Influenza vaccine for patients with chronic obstructive pulmonary disease. Cochrane Database Syst Rev, 2006(1): p. Cd002733.

3. Wongsurakiat, P., et al., Acute respiratory illness in patients with COPD and the effectiveness of influenza vaccination: a randomized controlled study. Chest, 2004. 125(6): p. 2011-20.

4. Calverley, P.M., et al., Salmeterol and fluticasone propionate and survival in chronic obstructive pulmonary disease. N Engl J Med, 2007. 356(8): p. 775-89.

5. Ferguson, G.T., et al., Effect of fluticasone propionate/salmeterol (250/50 microg) or salmeterol (50 microg) on COPD exacerbations. Respir Med, 2008. 102(8): p. 1099-108.

6. Man, S.F., et al., Contemporary management of chronic obstructive pulmonary disease: clinical applications. Jama, 2003. 290(17): p. 2313-6.

7. Qaseem, A., et al., Diagnosis and management of stable chronic obstructive pulmonary disease: a clinical practice guideline update from the American College of Physicians, American College of Chest Physicians, American Thoracic Society, and European Respiratory Society. Ann Intern Med, 2011. 155(3): p. 179-91.

8. Sin, D.D., et al., Contemporary management of chronic obstructive pulmonary disease: scientific review. Jama, 2003. 290(17): p. 2301-12.

9. Tarpy, S.P. and B.R. Celli, Long-term oxygen therapy. N Engl J Med, 1995. 333(11): p. 710-4.

10. Calderon-Larranaga, A., et al., Association of population and primary healthcare factors with hospital admission rates for chronic obstructive pulmonary disease in England: national cross-sectional study. Thorax, 2011. 66(3): p. 191-6.

11. Cazzola, M. and C.F. Donner, Long-acting beta2 agonists in the management of stable chronic obstructive pulmonary disease. Drugs, 2000. 60(2): p. 307-20.

12. Jones, P.W. and T.K. Bosh, Quality of life changes in COPD patients treated with salmeterol. Am J Respir Crit Care Med, 1997. 155(4): p. 1283-9.

13. Ramirez-Venegas, A., et al., Salmeterol reduces dyspnea and improves lung function in patients with COPD. Chest, 1997. 112(2): p. 336-40.

14. van Noord, J.A., et al., Effects of tiotropium with and without formoterol on airflow obstruction and resting hyperinflation in patients with COPD. Chest, 2006. 129(3): p. 509-17.

15. Celli, B.R. and W. MacNee, Standards for the diagnosis and treatment of patients with COPD: a summary of the ATS/ERS position paper. Eur Respir J, 2004. 23(6): p. 932-46.

16. Barnes, P.J. and B.R. Celli, Systemic manifestations and comorbidities of COPD. Eur Respir J, 2009. 33(5): p. 1165-85.

17. He, Z.Y., et al., Effect of 6 months of erythromycin treatment on inflammatory cells in induced sputum and exacerbations in chronic obstructive pulmonary disease. Respiration, 2010. 80(6): p. 445-52.

18. Kjensli, A., et al., High prevalence of vertebral deformities in COPD patients: relationship to disease severity. Eur Respir J, 2009. 33(5): p. 1018-24.

Do you have questions about COPD, Emphysema or Bronchitis for your health caregiver?

Patient Notes_____
Patient Drawings_____

Checklist for Asthma: We Can Rescue

What do you know about asthma? Write it here.

VitalChecklist™

Patient Name_____
Caregiver Initials_____

Answer

Patient
Initials

☐

Wheeze[1]
W
Have you noticed any wheezing when you breathe?

☐

Exercise induced asthma[2, 3]
E
Do your symptoms become worse with exercise?

☐

Cough[4]
C
Do you have cough?
Is it dry cough?

☐

Allergies[5-8]
A
Do you have any history of allergic rhinitis?
Do you have any history of eczema?
Is there history of asthma or allergies in your family?

☐

Nocturnal Symptoms[9]
N
Do your symptoms become worse at night and wake you up from sleep?

☐

Rescue Inhalers
R
Do your symptoms get better with inhalers?
How often do you take inhalers in a day for relief of symptoms?

☐

Exacerbations
Early morning symptoms
E
How often do you need to come to the ER for sudden worsening of symptoms?
Do you experience any early morning cough and wheezing?

S **Shortness of breath**[10]
Smoking tobacco[11, 12]

☐

Do you experience any shortness of breath?
Do you smoke?
Does anyone at your work or home smoke?

C **Cold exposure**[13]

☐

Do your symptoms worsen on exposure to cold?

U **Unable to perform activities of daily
living and/or household chores**

☐

Do your symptoms interfere with activities of daily living?
Do you have difficulty doing household chores? Call 911
if you are unable to breathe?

E **Evaluation with Pulmonary Function
Tests**[14-16]

☐

Have you had pulmonary function tests done to evaluate
your lung function?

If you have sudden onset, severe shortness of breath and are unable to
breathe, call 911 and go to the ER right away.

Caregiver Initials_____

Bibliography

1. Pratter, M.R., D.M. Hingston, and R.S. Irwin, Diagnosis of bronchial asthma by clinical evaluation. An unreliable method. Chest, 1983. 84(1): p. 42-7.

2. Parsons, J.P., et al., An official American Thoracic Society clinical practice guideline: exercise-induced bronchoconstriction. Am J Respir Crit Care Med, 2013. 187(9): p. 1016-27.

3. Anderson, S.D. and E. Daviskas, The mechanism of exercise-induced asthma is. J Allergy Clin Immunol, 2000. 106(3): p. 453-9.

4. Irwin, R.S., F.J. Curley, and C.L. French, Chronic cough. The spectrum and frequency of causes, key components of the diagnostic evaluation, and outcome of specific therapy. Am Rev Respir Dis, 1990. 141(3): p. 640-7.

5. Weinmayr, G., et al., Atopic sensitization and the international variation of asthma symptom prevalence in children. Am J Respir Crit Care Med, 2007. 176(6): p. 565-74.

6. Burrows, B., et al., Association of asthma with serum IgE levels and skin-test reactivity to allergens. N Engl J Med, 1989. 320(5): p. 271-7.

7. Platts-Mills, T.A., How environment affects patients with allergic disease: indoor allergens and asthma. Ann Allergy, 1994. 72(4): p. 381-4.

8. Dixon, A.E., et al., Allergic rhinitis and sinusitis in asthma: differential effects on symptoms and pulmonary function. Chest, 2006. 130(2): p. 429-35.

9. Tan, N.C., et al., Ten-year longitudinal study of factors influencing nocturnal asthma symptoms among Asian patients in primary care. NPJ Prim Care Respir Med, 2015. 25: p. 15064.

10. Pratter, M.R., et al., Cause and evaluation of chronic dyspnea in a pulmonary disease clinic. Arch Intern Med, 1989. 149(10): p. 2277-82.

11. Siroux, V., et al., Relationships of active smoking to asthma and asthma severity in the EGEA study. Epidemiological study on the Genetics and Environment of Asthma. Eur Respir J, 2000. 15(3): p. 470-7.

12. Althuis, M.D., M. Sexton, and D. Prybylski, Cigarette smoking and asthma symptom severity among adult asthmatics. J Asthma, 1999. 36(3): p. 257-64.

13. Barne, C., et al., Climate change and our environment: the effect on respiratory and allergic disease. J Allergy Clin Immunol Pract, 2013. 1(2): p. 137-41.

14. Brown, R.H., et al., The structural basis of airways hyperresponsiveness in asthma. J Appl Physiol (1985), 2006. 101(1): p. 30-9.

15. Mead, J., et al., Significance of the relationship between lung recoil and maximum expiratory flow. J Appl Physiol, 1967. 22(1): p. 95-108.

16. Kaminsky, D.A. and C.G. Irvin, What long-term changes in lung function can tell us about asthma control. Curr Allergy Asthma Rep, 2015. 15(3): p. 505.

Patient Notes_____
Patient Drawings_____

Section G

Infection

47. Checklist for Ebola Symptoms
(iCRUSH)™

Patient Name_____
Caregiver Initials_____

	Answer	Patient Initials

i | **Initial presentation[1-3]**
Did you have fever with chills and malaise?
Any sore throat? | ☐

C | **Conjunctival Injection[4, 5]**
Any redness of the eyes? | ☐

R | **Rash[6]**
Any rash over the face, trunk, arms and legs? | ☐

U | **Urine proteins[7]**
Any retention of urine, shortness of breath,
swelling of face and feet?
Any features of kidney failure on your blood tests? | ☐

S | **Stool, Seizure, Shock[8-10]**
Any pain abdomen with loose stools and vomiting?
Any episode of fits?
Any episode of feeling light-headed or black-out? | ☐

H | **Hemorrhage[11]**
Did you bleed from any parts of the body?
Any blood in urine or stools? | ☐

Bibliography

1. Bah, E.I., et al., Clinical presentation of patients with Ebola virus disease in Conakry, Guinea. N Engl J Med, 2015. 372(1): p. 40-7.

2. Schieffelin, J.S., et al., Clinical illness and outcomes in patients with Ebola in Sierra Leone. N Engl J Med, 2014. 371(22): p. 2092-100.

3. Uyeki, T.M., et al., Clinical Management of Ebola Virus Disease in the United States and Europe. N Engl J Med, 2016. 374(7): p. 636-46.

4. Bwaka, M.A., et al., Ebola hemorrhagic fever in Kikwit, Democratic Republic of the Congo: clinical observations in 103 patients. J Infect Dis, 1999. 179 Suppl 1: p. S1-7.

5. Kibadi, K., et al., Late ophthalmologic manifestations in survivors of the 1995 Ebola virus epidemic in Kikwit, Democratic Republic of the Congo. J Infect Dis, 1999. 179 Suppl 1: p. S13-4.

6. Chertow, D.S., et al., Ebola virus disease in West Africa--clinical manifestations and management. N Engl J Med, 2014. 371(22): p. 2054-7.

7. Formenty, P., et al., Human infection due to Ebola virus, subtype Cote d'Ivoire: clinical and biologic presentation. J Infect Dis, 1999. 179 Suppl 1: p. S48-53.

8. Kreuels, B., et al., A case of severe Ebola virus infection complicated by gram-negative septicemia. N Engl J Med, 2014. 371(25): p. 2394-401.

9. Martini, G.A., Marburg agent disease: in man. Trans R Soc Trop Med Hyg, 1969. 63(3): p. 295-302.

10. Parra, J.M., O.J. Salmeron, and M. Velasco, The first case of Ebola virus disease acquired outside Africa. N Engl J Med, 2014. 371(25): p. 2439-40.

11. Kortepeter, M.G., D.G. Bausch, and M. Bray, Basic clinical and laboratory features of filoviral hemorrhagic fever. J Infect Dis, 2011. 204 Suppl 3: p. S810-6.

Patient Notes_____
Patient Drawings_____

Checklist for Hygiene Precautions: What If You Fly, Remember ABCD

VitalChecklist™

48. Checklist for Hygiene Precautions for Ebola

WHAT IF U FLY Remember ABCD™

Patient Name_____
Caregiver Initials_____

	Answer	Patient Initials

W **Wash**[1]
Wash hands frequently. ☐

H (Hat) **Hand sanitizer**[2]
Use alcohol based hand sanitizer frequently. ☐

I **Isolate**[3]
Do not travel if you are ill.
Isolate passengers suspicious of Ebola. ☐

F **Flu vaccine**[4]
Take Flu vaccine prior to travel. ☐

U **Use tissues**[1]
Use tissues to wipe off the suspected infectious areas. ☐

F **Faucet**[5]
Faucets can be infectious. Use tissues. ☐

L **Lavatory seat**[1]
Lavatory seat can be infectious. Use toilet paper to cover the seat before you sit ☐

Y **Yikes!!**[6]
Doorknobs and handles are also infectious. Use tissues to handle the handles! ☐

Remember

		Answer	Patient Initials

A **Airline passengers**[7]

Watch out for any sick airline passenger.

☐

B **Buy**[8]

Buy your own drink (BYOD)!

☐

C **Cover**[6]

Cover your mouth!

☐

D **Discard**[6]

Discard the tissue immediately.

☐

Caregiver Initials_____

Bibliography

1. Prevention, Ebola (Ebola Virus Disease), Centers for Disease Prevention and Control. 2015 7/22/2015 [cited 2016 9/11/2016];

2. Hand Hygiene in West African General (Non-ETU) Healthcare Settings. Ebola (Ebola virus Disease), Centers for Disease Control and Prevention. . 2014 9/13/2014 [cited 2016 9/11/2016];

3. Signs and Symptoms. Ebola (Ebola Virus Disease), Centers for Disease Control and Prevention. 2014 11/2/2014 [cited 2016 9/11/2016];

4. Interim Recommendations for Influenza Vaccination and Post-exposure Chemoprophylaxis to Prevent Influenza Virus Infection in People Being Actively Monitored for Potential Ebola Virus Exposure, Notes on the Interim U.S. Guidance for Monitoring and Movement of Persons with Potential Ebola Virus Exposure, Risk of Exposure, Ebola (Ebola Virus Disease), Centers for Disease Control and Prevention. 2016 02/18/2016 [cited 2016 9/11/2016];

5. Hand Washing, Ebola, Centers for Disease Control and Prevention. [cited 9/11/2016;]

6. Q&As on Transmission, Ebola (Ebola Virus Disease), Centers for Disease Control and Prevention. 2015 11/14/2015 [cited 2016 9/11/2016];

7. Preventing Spread of Disease on Commercial Aircraft: Guidance for Cabin Crew, Managing Ill Passengers/Crew, Airline Guidance, Quarantine and Isolation, Centers for Disease Control and Prevention. 2016

8. Food and Water Safety, Resources for Travelers, Resources, Home, Centers for Disease Control and.

Patient Notes_____
Patient Drawings_____

Checklist for Ebola Precautions: ABCDEFG

49. Checklist for Ebola Precautions

ABCDEFG™

Patient Name_____
Caregiver Initials_____

Answer   Patient Initials

A Appearance[1]
Check your appearance in the mirror. ☐

B Boots. Buddy[1, 2]
Wear your boots.
Buddy to observe you. ☐

C Cover all surfaces[1-4]
Impermeable gown and first layer of gloves. ☐

D Disposable N95[1-3, 5]
Disposable N95 respirator or a powdered air purifying respirator. ☐

E Eyes, Ears and Nose cover[1-4, 6]
Full faced shield instead of goggles.
Surgical hood to cover the head and neck. ☐

F Full body cover[1, 2]
Full body second layer of waterproof apron that covers the opening of boots. ☐

G Gloves[1, 2, 4]
Gloves to cover the outer layer. ☐

Bibliography

1. Hageman, J.C., et al., Infection Prevention and Control for Ebola in Health Care Settings - West Africa and United States. MMWR Suppl, 2016. 65(3): p. 50-6.

2. Kouassi, D.P., et al., [Preparation of healthcare workers against the threat of Ebola virus disease in Ivory Coast]. Sante Publique, 2016. 28(1): p. 113-22.

3. Vetter, P., et al., Ebola Virus Shedding and Transmission: Review of Current Evidence. J Infect Dis, 2016.

4. Kerstiens, B. and F. Matthys, Interventions to control virus transmission during an outbreak of Ebola hemorrhagic fever: experience from Kikwit, Democratic Republic of the Congo, 1995. J Infect Dis, 1999. 179 Suppl 1: p. S263-7.

5. Mekibib, B. and K.K. Arien, Aerosol Transmission of Filoviruses. Viruses, 2016. 8(5).

6. Shantha, J.G., S. Yeh, and Q.D. Nguyen, Ebola virus disease and the eye. Curr Opin Ophthalmol, 2016.

Patient Notes_____
Patient Drawings_____

Checklist for Signs of Inflammation: Respectful

50. Checklist for Signs of Inflammation

ReSPeCTFul[TM]

Patient Name_____
Caregiver Initials_____

		Answer	Patient Initials

R Re
Redness[1]
Did you notice blue color of your legs or toes?
☐

S
Swelling[2]
Did you notice any swelling over the area?
☐

P Pe
Pain[3, 4]
Do you have pain over the area?
☐

C
Calor[5]
Do you feel warmth over the area?
☐

T
Is temperature same as heat?[6]
Do you have fever?
☐

F Ful
Functional loss[7]
Do you feel any difficulty using the affected part?
☐

Bibliography

1. Stevens, D.L., et al., Practice guidelines for the diagnosis and management of skin and soft tissue infections: 2014 update by the infectious diseases society of America. Clin Infect Dis, 2014. 59(2): p. 147-59.

2. Bisno, A.L. and D.L. Stevens, Streptococcal infections of skin and soft tissues. N Engl J Med, 1996. 334(4): p. 240-5.

3. Ellis Simonsen, S.M., et al., Cellulitis incidence in a defined population. Epidemiol Infect, 2006. 134(2): p. 293-9.

4. Mikhail, I.S. and G.S. Alarcon, Nongonococcal bacterial arthritis. Rheum Dis Clin North Am, 1993. 19(2): p. 311-31.

5. Chartier, C. and E. Grosshans, Erysipelas: an update. Int J Dermatol, 1996. 35(11): p. 779-81.

6. Liu, C., et al., Clinical practice guidelines by the infectious diseases society of america for the treatment of methicillin-resistant Staphylococcus aureus infections in adults and children. Clin Infect Dis, 2011. 52(3): p. e18-55.

7. Margaretten, M.E., et al., Does this adult patient have septic arthritis? Jama, 2007. 297(13): p. 1478-88.

VitalChecklist™

ABC of URINE™

Patient Name_____
Caregiver Initials_____

	Answer	Patient Initials

A **Altered Mental Status**
Do you know elderly patients with urine infections can be confused? ☐

B **Burning sensation or painful micturition[1]**
Do you have pain while passing urine? ☐

C **Cloudy Urine**
What is the color of your urine? ☐

O **Odor**
Do you have any smell in your urine? ☐

F **Frequency**
Do you urinate more than usual?[3] ☐

U **Urgency[4]**
Do you need to rush to the restroom when you feel the urge to pass urine? ☐

R **Retention[5]**
Do you have any trouble passing urine?
Did you notice any inability to pass urine? ☐

I **Incontinence[6, 7]**
Have you had accidents with your bladder? ☐

N Nocturia

Do you need to wake up at night more frequently to urinate?

□

E Enuresis[8]

Did you ever pass urine in bed at night?

□

Caregiver Initials_____

Bibliography

1. Jones, C., J. Hill, and C. Chapple, Management of lower urinary tract symptoms in men: summary of NICE guidance. Bmj, 2010. 340: p. c2354.

2. Mariani, A.J., et al., The significance of adult hematuria: 1,000 hematuria evaluations including a risk-benefit and cost-effectiveness analysis. J Urol, 1989. 141(2): p. 350-5.

3. Haylen, B.T., et al., An International Urogynecological Association (IUGA)/International Continence Society (ICS) joint report on the terminology for female pelvic floor dysfunction. Int Urogynecol J, 2010. 21(1): p. 5-26.

4. Nygaard, I., Clinical practice. Idiopathic urgency urinary incontinence. N Engl J Med, 2010. 363(12): p. 1156-62.

5. Marshall, J.R., J. Haber, and E.B. Josephson, An evidence-based approach to emergency department management of acute urinary retention. Emerg Med Pract, 2014. 16(1): p. 1-20; quiz 21.

6. Rogers, R.G., Clinical practice. Urinary stress incontinence in women. N Engl J Med, 2008. 358(10): p. 1029-36.

7. Abrams, P., et al., Fourth International Consultation on Incontinence Recommendations of the International Scientific Committee: Evaluation and treatment of urinary incontinence, pelvic organ prolapse, and fecal incontinence. Neurourol Urodyn, 2010. 29(1): p. 213-40.

8. Neveus, T., et al., The standardization of terminology of lower urinary tract function in children and adolescents: report from the Standardisation Committee of the International Children's Continence Society. J Urol, 2006. 176(1): p. 314-24.

Checklist for Urinary Symptoms: ABC of Urine

Patient Note

52. Checklist for Skin Wounds

How to measure skin wounds? Skin Wounds™

Patient Name_____
Caregiver Initials_____

Answer

Patient Initials

S | Site of the wound[1]

Describe the location of the wound?

☐

K | Keep calm and look, touch and measure

Look at the wound and touch the wound to evaluate for the blanchable and non-blanchable wounds. Ask for the pain.

☐

I (In) | In the wound bed; Infection or cause of the wounds

What do you see in the wound bed? Do you see fat, muscle, tendons or necrosis? Do you see any infections

☐

W | Wound Size-- Length, Breadth, Depth and Margin

Length, breadth and depth should be measured. Margins should be described.

☐

O | Onset of wounds

What is the duration of this wound? Any other ulcers?

☐

Ulcer Staging and Undermining or tunneling | Now it is called Pressure Injury[2]

Stage 1 – Skin intact but with non-blanchable redness(3)
Stage 2 – Partial-thickness loss of skin with exposed dermis.
Stage 3 – Full-thickness loss of skin, in which adipose (fat) is visible in the ulcer and granulation tissue and epibole (rolled wound edges) are often present
Stage 4 – Full-thickness skin and tissue loss with exposed or directly palpable fascia, muscle, tendon, ligament, cartilage, or bone in the ulcer.
Unstageable Pressure Injury: Obscured full-thickness skin and tissue loss
Deep Tissue Pressure Injury: Persistent non-blanchable deep red, maroon or purple discoloration

Necrosis

Do you see any black color in the wound bed?

Discharge or Device

Amount of discharge

Type of discharge:
- Serous
- Haemoserous
- Sanguinous
- Purulent

Color of discharge
Consistency
Medical Device Related Pressure Injury

Surrounding skin

Always look and touch the surrounding skin--Color, Temperature, Hair and Nail Growth, Edema

Caregiver Initials_____

Bibliography

1. Grey JE, Enoch S, Harding KG. Wound assessment. BMJ. 2006;332(7536):285-8.

2. Gray M, Edsberg L, Black J, Goldberg M, McNichol L, Moore L, et al. National Pressure Ulcer Advisory Panel (NPUAP) announces a change in terminology from pressure ulcer to pressure injury and updates the stages of pressure injury | The National Pressure Ulcer Advisory Panel - NPUAP: NPUAP; April 13, 2016Category: Hot Topics, Press Releases. Bookmark the permalink. [Available from: http://www.npuap.org/national-pressure-ulcer-advisory-panel-npuap-announces-a-change-in-terminology-from-pressure-ulcer-to-pressure-injury-and-updates-the-stages-of-pressure-injury/.

3. Cuddigan J. Stage 1 Pressure Injury: Non-Blanchable Erythema of Intact Skin NPUAP3/3/2017 [Wound Assessment]. Available from: http://www.npuap.org/wp-content/uploads/2017/03/Cuddigan-Janet-Stage-1.pdf.

4. DeMarco S. Wound and Pressure Ulcer Management.

Section H

Cancer

Patient Notes_____
Patient Drawings_____

Checklist for Cancer: Crowns of Hope

Write your list of problems here and talk to your healthcare provider

VitalChecklist™

Patient Name_____
Caregiver Initials_____

Side effects of cancer drugs. All medications do not have same side effects. Talk to your doctor about this. Your doctor may reduce your medication or change it.

	Answer	Patient Initials

C Crown

Hair loss[1]

Have you noticed any hair loss? This is the most common cause of stress. You may have hair fall out from eyelashes and eyebrows also.

☐

C

Chemo Brain[2]
Cognitive Dysfunction[3]
Clots[4, 5]

Have you noticed any confusion or mental fogging?
Have you noticed any issues with memory? Do you forget?
Do you have swelling in the legs? Do you have any shortness of breath? Clots in the lungs can cause shortness of breath.

☐

R

Red blood cells are low[6,7]
Radiology
Renal and Kidneys[8]

Ask your doctor about low red blood cells and hemoglobin. Shortness of breath can happen due to anemia. Bone marrow may not produce RBC. Talk to your doctor about results of X-Ray, MRI, CT-Scan, and PET scan.
What is your kidney function? BUN, creatinine, GFR. How about liver function test?

☐

O **Osteoporosis**[9, 10]

☐

When was your latest DEXA scan results? When did you get Vitamin D3 levels checked?

W **White blood cells are low**[11]
Weight Loss[12]

☐

Talk to your doctor about low white blood cells and infections. Do you cough, have headache, or burning sensation while passing urine?
Talk to your doctor about weight loss. Tell your caregiver about mouth ulcers, change in taste sensation, swallowing issues, diarrhea.

N **Nerves**[12]
Nails[14]
Nausea[15, 16]

☐

Have you noticed any numbness and tingling? Any problems with sensation.
Nails can become brittle and may have white lines on them. They may have ridges also.
You may have nausea and/or vomiting. Drink ample water.

S **Skin**[17]
Sexual dysfunction and decreased libido[18, 19]
Shortness of breath[20]

☐

Skin may become dry and you may have rashes.
Sexual dysfunction and decreased libido
May be due to infection or clots.

O **Fatigue**[21, 22]
of **Fever**[23, 24]

☐

You may feel tired and may not have energy to do things.
You may have high fever or low fever. Report high fever to your doctor. Make sure to make a log book of the same.

Caregiver Initials_____

H Heart's Ejection[25, 26]
Hearing loss[27]

Do you have chest pain, shortness of breath, swelling in the legs or feel dizzy?
Talk to your doctor about hearing loss and your caregiver may reduce the dose of medications

☐

O Other tests

Get your complete blood count, complete metabolic profile, thyroid tests, urine tests.

☐

P Pain[28]
Platelets are low[29]

Do you have pain? Can you point where are you feeling pain? On a scale of 0 to 10, how will you grade your pain.
What are platelets? Talk to your doctor if you have nosebleeds, bleeding gums, and bruising?

☐

E Erectile dysfunction[19]

Men with prostate cancer can have issues with ED. Other cancers can also cause this problem.

☐

H Have hope, not depression[30, 32]
Hope

Have hope and courage to fight this cancer. Side effects may be overwhelming and may cause depression, but hang in there.

☐

Caregiver Initials_____

Bibliography

1. Paus R, Haslam IS, Sharov AA, Botchkarev VA. Pathobiology of chemotherapy-induced hair loss. Lancet Oncol. 2013;14(2):e50-9.

2. Ahles TA. Brain vulnerability to chemotherapy toxicities. Psychooncology. 2012;21(11):1141-8.

3. Wefel JS, Kesler SR, Noll KR, Schagen SB. Clinical characteristics, pathophysiology, and management of noncentral nervous system cancer-related cognitive impairment in adults. CA Cancer J Clin. 2015;65(2):123-38.

4. Pinzon R, Drewinko B, Trujillo JM, Guinee V, Giacco G. Pancreatic carcinoma and Trousseau's syndrome: experience at a large cancer center. J Clin Oncol. 1986;4(4):509-14.

5. Edwards RL, Morgan DL, Rickles FR. Animal tumor procoagulants: registry of the Subcommittee on Haemostasis and Malignancy of the Scientific and Standardization Committee, International Society of Thrombosis and Haemostasis. Thromb Haemost. 1990;63(1):133-8.

6. Asbell SO, Leon SA, Tester WJ, Brereton HD, Ago CT, Rotman M. Development of anemia and recovery in prostate cancer patients treated with combined androgen blockade and radiotherapy. Prostate. 1996;29(4):243-8.

7. Pedersen-Bjergaard J. Radiotherapy- and chemotherapy-induced myelodysplasia and acute myeloid leukemia. A review. Leuk Res. 1992;16(1):61-5.

8. Launay-Vacher V, Oudard S, Janus N, Gligorov J, Pourrat X, Rixe O, et al. Prevalence of Renal Insufficiency in cancer patients and implications for anticancer drug management: the renal insufficiency and anticancer medications (IRMA) study. Cancer. 2007;110(6):1376-84.

9. Yu TM, Lin CL, Chang SN, Sung FC, Huang ST, Kao CH. Osteoporosis and fractures after solid organ transplantation: a nationwide population-based cohort study. Mayo Clin Proc. 2014;89(7):888-95.

10. Maalouf NM, Shane E. Osteoporosis after solid organ transplantation. J Clin Endocrinol Metab. 2005;90(4):2456-65.

11. Freifeld AG, Bow EJ, Sepkowitz KA, Boeckh MJ, Ito JI, Mullen CA, et al. Clinical practice guideline for the use of antimicrobial agents in neutropenic patients with cancer: 2010 update by the infectious diseases society of america. Clin Infect Dis. 2011;52(4):e56-93.

12. Davis MP, Dreicer R, Walsh D, Lagman R, LeGrand SB. Appetite and cancer-associated anorexia: a review. J Clin Oncol. 2004;22(8):1510-7.

13. Argyriou AA, Kyritsis AP, Makatsoris T, Kalofonos HP. Chemotherapy-induced peripheral neuropathy in adults: a comprehensive update of the literature. Cancer Manag Res. 2014;6:135-47.

14. Kim IS, Lee JW, Park KY, Li K, Seo SJ, Hong CK. Nail change after chemotherapy: simultaneous development of Beau's lines and Mees' lines. Ann Dermatol. 2012;24(2):238-9.

15. Wilbur MB, Birrer MJ, Spriggs DR. CLINICAL DECISIONS. Chemotherapy-Induced Nausea and Vomiting. N Engl J Med. 2016;375(2):177-9.

16. Warr DG. Chemotherapy-and cancer-related nausea and vomiting. Curr Oncol. 2008;15(Suppl 1):S4-9.

17. Fabbrocini G, Cameli N, Romano MC, Mariano M, Panariello L, Bianca D, et al. Chemotherapy and skin reactions. J Exp Clin Cancer Res. 2012;31:50.

18. Miller K, Bober S. How cancer treatment affects sexuality in women | Dana-Farber Cancer Institute - YouTube You Tube Video: Dana-Farber Cancer Institute; Jun 12, 2012 [sex, cancer and woman]. Available from: https://www.youtube.com/watch?v=0zmIH-JHeFw&feature=youtu.be.

19. Miller K, Bober S. How cancer treatment affects sexuality in men | Dana-Farber Cancer Institute - YouTube Dana-Farber Cancer Institute: You Tube; Jun 12, 2012 [Sex, cancer and men]. Available from: https://www.youtube.com/watch?v=0ON6La1-xXc&feature=youtu.be.

20. Thomas S, Bausewein C, Higginson I, Booth S. Breathlessness in cancer patients - implications, management and challenges. Eur J Oncol Nurs. 2011;15(5):459-69.

21. Campos MP, Hassan BJ, Riechelmann R, Del Giglio A. Cancer-related fatigue: a practical review. Ann Oncol. 2011;22(6):1273-9.

22. Iop A, Manfredi AM, Bonura S. Fatigue in cancer patients receiving chemotherapy: an analysis of published studies. Ann Oncol. 2004;15(5):712-20.

23. Krzyzanowska MK, Walker-Dilks C, Morris AM, Gupta R, Halligan R, Kouroukis CT, et al. Approach to evaluation of fever in ambulatory cancer patients receiving chemotherapy: A systematic review. Cancer Treat Rev. 2016;51:35-45.

24. Bodey GP. The changing face of febrile neutropenia-from monotherapy to moulds to mucositis. Fever and neutropenia: the early years. J Antimicrob Chemother. 2009;63 Suppl 1:i3-13.

25. Conrad AL, Gundrum JD, McHugh VL, Go RS. Utility of routine left ventricular ejection fraction measurement before anthracycline-based chemotherapy in patients with diffuse large B-cell lymphoma. J Oncol Pract. 2012;8(6):336-40.

26. Suter TM, Ewer MS. Cancer drugs and the heart: importance and management. Eur Heart J. 2013;34(15):1102-11.

27. McHaney VA, Thibadoux G, Hayes FA, Green AA. Hearing loss in children receiving cisplatin chemotherapy. J Pediatr. 1983;102(2):314-7.

28. Koltzenburg M, Torebjörk HE, Wahren LK. Nociceptor modulated central sensitization causes mechanical hyperalgesia in acute chemogenic and chronic neuropathic pain. Brain. 1994;117 (Pt 3):579-91.

29. Kuter DJ. Managing thrombocytopenia associated with cancer chemotherapy. Oncology (Williston Park). 2015;29(4):282-94.

30. Pasquini M, Biondi M. Depression in cancer patients: a critical review. Clin Pract Epidemiol Ment Health. 2007;3:2.

31. Die Trill M. Psychological aspects of depression in cancer patients: an update. Ann Oncol. 2012;23 Suppl 10:x302-5.

32. Jim HS, Small B, Faul LA, Franzen J, Apte S, Jacobsen PB. Fatigue, depression, sleep, and activity during chemotherapy: daily and intraday variation and relationships among symptom changes. Ann Behav Med. 2011;42(3):321-33.

Talk to your doctor about cancer screening

Patient Notes_____
Patient Drawings_____

Section I

Abdomen

VitalChecklist™

Patient Name_____
Caregiver Initials_____

Answer | Patient Initials

L — Liver cancer[1]
Do you know 10%-25% of patients with cirrhosis progress to liver cancer?

☐

I — Infection or spontaneous bacterial peritonitis[2]
Do you know ascitic fluid can become infected?
High death rates are associated with those who with infected ascetic fluid.

☐

V — Varices[3]
Dilated veins at the lower end of the esophagus or in the stomach can bleed. If they rupture, it may result in death.

☐

E — Encephalopathy[4, 5]
Estrogen catabolism decreases[6]
Toxic metabolites may affect the brain, but can also cause: mental confusion, poor concentration, rigidity, hyperreflexia, musty odor of breath.
Increased estrogen causes spider angiomas, palmar erythema, gynecomastia, testicular atrophy.

☐

R — Renal or Hepatorenal syndrome[7]
Do you have low urine output, low blood pressure or kidney failure?

☐

C — Coagulopathy[8]
Do you bruise or bleed easily? This happens when there is decreased production of clotting factors.

☐

A Ascites[9]

Do you have fluid in your abdomen?

P Portal Hypertension[3, 10]

Do you have bright red bleeding in the stool or in the
vomit? Do you have black colored stool?

☐

Caregiver Initials_____

Bibliography

1. Forner A, Llovet JM, Bruix J. Hepatocellular carcinoma. Lancet.

2. Such J, Runyon BA. Spontaneous bacterial peritonitis. Clin Infect Dis.

3. Biecker E. Gastrointestinal Bleeding in Cirrhotic Patients with Portal Hypertension. ISRN Hepatol.

4. Romero-Gomez M, Boza F, Garcia-Valdecasas MS, Garcia E, Aguilar-Reina J. Subclinical hepatic encephalopathy predicts the development of overt hepatic encephalopathy. Am J Gastroenterol.

5. Khungar V, Poordad F. Hepatic encephalopathy. Clin Liver Dis.

6. Gordon GG, Olivo J, Rafil F, Southren AL. Conversion of androgens to estrogens in cirrhosis of the liver. J Clin Endocrinol Metab.

7. Gines P, Guevara M, Arroyo V, Rodes J. Hepatorenal syndrome. Lancet.

8. Caldwell SH. Management of Coagulopathy in Liver Disease. Gastroenterol Hepatol (N Y).

9. Gines P, Fernandez-Esparrach G, Arroyo V, Rodes J. Pathogenesis of ascites in cirrhosis. Semin Liver Dis.

10. Aller MA, Arias JL, Cruz A, Arias J. Inflammation: a way to understanding the evolution of portal hypertension. Theor Biol Med Model.

11. What's Your Cap? â" Know when to put a lid on drinking. 2017

How do you discuss gastrointestinal symptoms with your doctor? An easy way to tell your story.

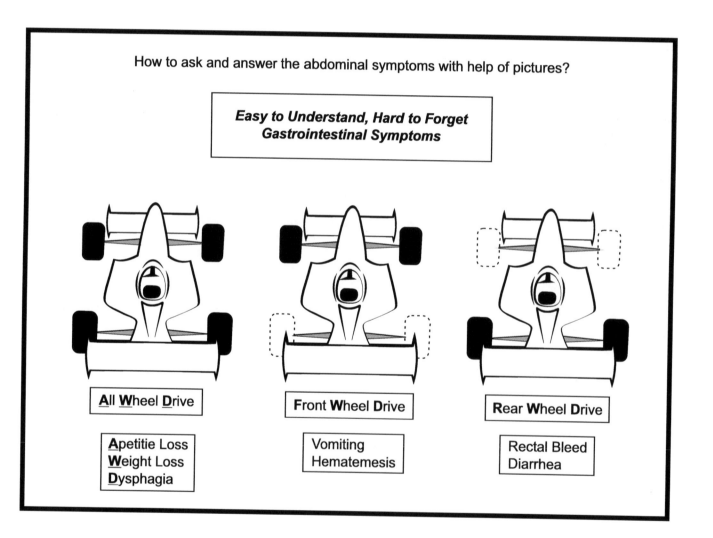

VitalChecklist™

Do you have Stool FLOATERS?™

Patient Name_____
Caregiver Initials_____

	Answer	Patient Initials

S Stringy ☐

T Thin and smooth stool ☐

O Oily stool ☐

O Or watery stool ☐

L Loose stool ☐

M (Mushy) Do you have mushy stool? ☐

M (Mucus) Any mucus in the stool? ☐

F (Floaters) Floaters or Steatorrhea [stee-at-uh-ree-uh][1, 2] Steatorrhea: >7g of fecal fat per day while consuming 100 g of dietary fat per day; Fecal Elastase < 100 microgram /g stool [3] ☐

Does your stool float? Having higher fat content in the stool will make stool float; these are called FLOATERS.

F **Frequency**[4]
Diarrhea is defined as increase in volume and weight of the stool

Do you have more bowel moments?
How many times have you passed bowel moments?
If you have large volume diarrhea then it is an upper intestinal tract problem. If you have small volume diarrhea then it is left colon or rectum problem.

☐

L **Lose weight**[4]

Have you lost weight?

☐

O **Odor**[6]

Do you have foul smell?

☐

A **Abdominal pain or cramps**[4, 7]

Do you have belly pain, bloating and swelling?

☐

T **Texture or type of stools**

Can you describe the texture or type of the stools?

☐

E **Excessive gas or flatulence**[7]

Do you pass more gas than usual?

☐

R **Rumbling or gurgling in the abdomen**

Do you have any gurgling in the belly?

☐

S **Sticky stool**[8]

Does your stool stick to the toilet bowl?

☐

Caregiver Initials_____

Bibliography

1. The definition of steatorrhea 2017

2. DiMagno EP, Go VL, Summerskill WH. Relations between pancreatic enzyme outputs and malabsorption in severe pancreatic insufficiency. N Engl J Med.

3. Pongprasobchai S. Maldigestion from pancreatic exocrine insufficiency. J Gastroenterol Hepatol.

4. Whitcomb DC, Lehman GA, Vasileva G, Malecka-Panas E, Gubergrits N, Shen Y, et al. Pancrelipase delayed-release capsules (CREON) for exocrine pancreatic insufficiency due to chronic pancreatitis or pancreatic surgery: A double-blind randomized trial. Am J Gastroenterol.

5. TA W. Clinical Methods: The History, Physical, and Laboratory Examinations. Walker HK HW, Hurst JW,, editor. Boston: Butterworths; 1990 1990.

6. Samer Alkaade MaAAV, MD. A Primer on Exocrine Pancreatic Insufficiency, Fat Malabsorption, and Fatty Acid Abnormalities. AJMC Managed Markets Netwrok. 2017.

7. Fieker A, Philpott J, Armand M. Enzyme replacement therapy for pancreatic insufficiency: present and future. Clin Exp Gastroenterol.

8. Struyvenberg MR, Martin CR, Freedman SD. Practical guide to exocrine pancreatic insufficiency – Breaking the myths. BMC Med. 152017.

Section J

Eye

VitalChecklist™

PUPILLARY™

Patient Name_____
Caregiver Initials_____

Answer   Patient Initials

P   Pupillary Dilation[1]

Pupil mid-dilated (4-6mm) and reacts poorly to light
Exacerbates symptoms
Can be caused by low-level or dim light

☐

U   Unusual Halos[1]

Described as halos or rainbows around lights
May be accompanied by headache and vomiting

☐

P   Peripheral vision loss[1]

Must evaluate as patient may not notice loss of
peripheral vision
Precedes loss of central vision

☐

I   Intraocular pressure increase[1]

Itching
Conjunctival redness
Corneal edema or cloudiness
Shallow anterior chamber

☐

L   Low level light is a problem[2]

Causes dilation of eye and exacerbates symptoms

☐

L   Lens displacement[1]

Anteriorly displaced lens rests against iris
Results in block of aqueous humor flow

☐

A   Acute Pain[3]

Severe eye pain with angle closure glaucoma

☐

R Redness of the eyes [1]

Conjunctival redness suggests a rapid rise in
intraocular pressure in the setting of glaucoma

☐

Y Years > 60 [1]

Age > 60 is a risk factor that predisposes to primary
angle closure glaucoma

☐

Caregiver Initials_____

Bibliography

1. @NatEyeInstitute. Facts About Glaucoma: @NatEyeInstitute; 2015 [Available from: https://nei.nih.gov/health/glaucoma/glaucoma_facts.

2. Leibowitz HM. The red eye. N Engl J Med. 2000;343(5):345-51.

3. Mantravadi AV, Vadhar N. Glaucoma. Prim Care. 2015;42(3):437-49.

VitalChecklist™

Do You See Halos at Night™

Patient Name_____
Caregiver Initials_____

	Answer	Patient Initials

D *Do*

Double vision

Often an early symptom
May clear as the cataract enlarges

☐

Y *You*

Yellow

Seeing bright colors as faded or yellow
Gradual change from clear lens to yellow-brown
Note difficulty with reading
May have difficulty with color recognition

☐

S *See*

Sensitivity to light

May complain of glare
Lights may appear too bright (eg headlights and lamps)

☐

H *Halos*

Halos around bright lights

Around headlights and street lamps
Usually appear in dim or dark settings

☐

N *Night*

Loss of night time vision

Difficulty seeing at night or in low-light situations
May experience light scattering at night

☐

Bibliography

1. @NatEyeInstitute. Cataract: @NatEyeInstitute; 2015 [Available from: https://nei.nih.gov/health/cataract/.

2. Bollinger KE, Langston RH. What can patients expect from cataract surgery? Cleve Clin J Med. 2008;75(3):193-6, 9-200.

VitalChecklist™

Patient Name_____
Caregiver Initials_____

	Answer	Patient Initials

Distorted vision[1]
Gradual loss of vision in one or both eyes
Drastic decrease in visual acuity
Burred vision
Scotomas- Partial loss of vision or blind spot
Sudden distortion of straight lines
☐

Dark Patches[1]
Scotomas affecting central vision
Shadows or missing areas of vision
☐

Recognition[1]
Due to blurred or distorted visual field
Note changes in recognition of faces, traffic signs, text, or other activities of daily living
☐

Age[2,3]
Prevalence increases with age
Starting at age 50
More pronounced over age 65
☐

Color and Contrast insensitivity[1]
Difficulty differentiating one dark color from another or one light color from another
☐

Curvy and wavy lines[1]
Straight lines appear wavy on Amsler grid evaluation
Other straight edges appear curved
Note changes in the appearance of window blinds, doors, telephone poles.
☐

		Answer	Patient Initials

U Urgent ophthalmic evaluation[1]

Obtain history including:
Rate of vision loss
Which eye(s) involved
Type of vision loss (near, far, both)
Acute vision loss requires urgent evaluation

☐

L Lacking Light[1]

Rely on brighter light to perform fine visual acuity tasks
(e.g. reading)
May require magnifying lens for reading

☐

A Acute Vision Loss[4]

Requires urgent ophthalmologic evaluation
Drastic decrease in visual acuity two levels or more

☐

R Reading difficulty[1]

Due to blurred vision, decreased visual acuity,
decreased light utilization, etc

☐

Caregiver Initials_____

Bibliography

1. @NatEyeInstitute. Facts About Age-Related Macular Degeneration National Eye Institute: @NatEyeInstitute; 2015 [Available from: https://nei.nih.gov/health/maculardegen/armd_facts.

2. Klaver CC, Wolfs RC, Vingerling JR, Hofman A, de Jong PT. Age-specific prevalence and causes of blindness and visual impairment in an older population: the Rotterdam Study. Arch Ophthalmol. 1998;116(5):653-8.

3. Weih LM, VanNewkirk MR, McCarty CA, Taylor HR. Age-specific causes of bilateral visual impairment. Arch Ophthalmol. 2000;118(2):264-9.

4. Quillen DA. Common causes of vision loss in elderly patients. Am Fam Physician. 1999;60(1):99-108.

Section K

Arts Plus Medicine

"A picture is worth a thousand words"

In this era of technology, we have apps, websites, three dimensional pictures, and models to explain the disease process to patients. In addition to the above-mentioned tools, we have pamphlets and booklets for improving health literacy. Above all, it is a mandate from the insurance company to give patient education material.

Do you think by giving the reading material and pamphlets, patients health literacy will improve? One of my USMLE Step 2 Clinical Skills students drew pictures for his Standardized Patients in the exam and later I came to know that he passed his exam with flying colors. Interestingly, in this exam we don't have any pamphlets or models, and medical students have to explain the disease process and available treatments with words. However, in addition to words, my students use pictures and checklists to explain medical concepts to patients.

An AHA moment!

If my students are making standardized patients happy with the pictures and checklists, I should be using the same in my practice. As a result of the revelation, I started using pictures for my real-life patients. In the next section, I have explained the basic two-dimensional pictures health caregivers can draw and utilize to explain concepts to their patients. If you are a patient, you can utilize the following images with google images and/or YouTube videos to understand your disease process. If you are a caregiver, I will explain this concept of pictures in detail in my next book—Doctor in no hurry!

Let's improve Patient Experience Scores together!

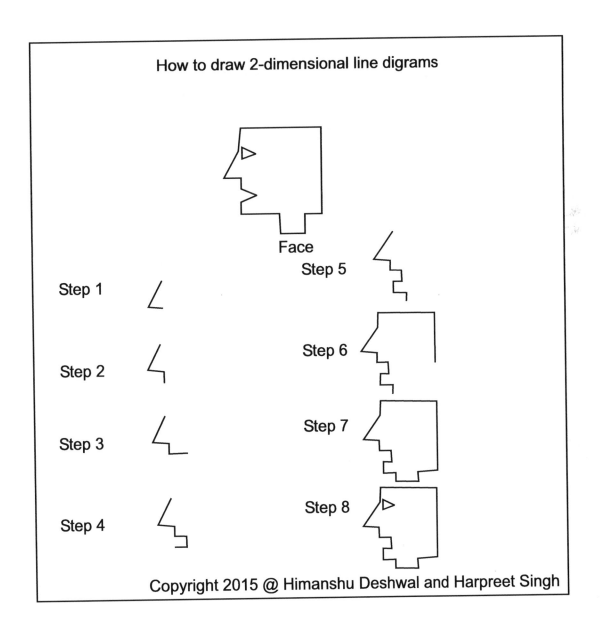

How to draw 2-dimensional line digrams

Face

Step 5

Step 1

Step 2

Step 3

Step 4

Step 6

Step 7

Step 8

Figure: 1

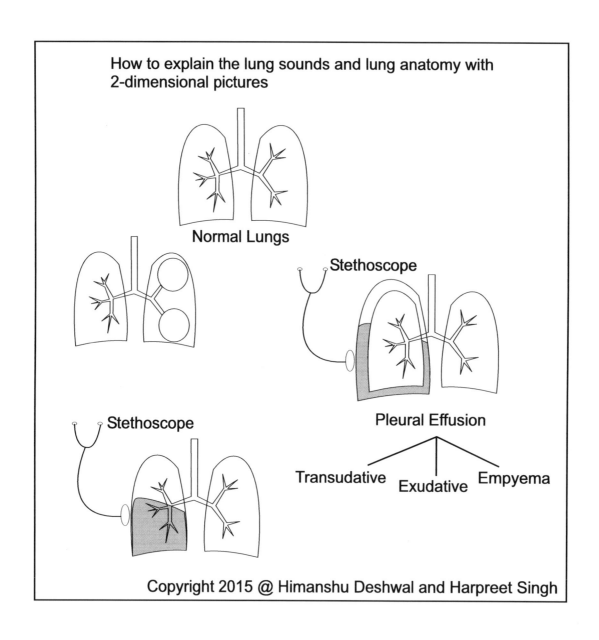

Figure: 2

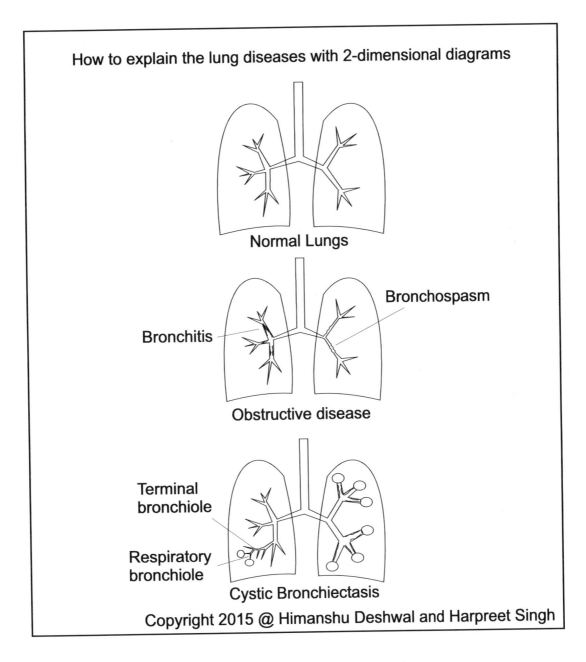

How to explain the lung diseases with 2-dimensional diagrams

Normal Lungs

Bronchitis

Bronchospasm

Obstructive disease

Terminal bronchiole

Respiratory bronchiole

Cystic Bronchiectasis

Figure: 3

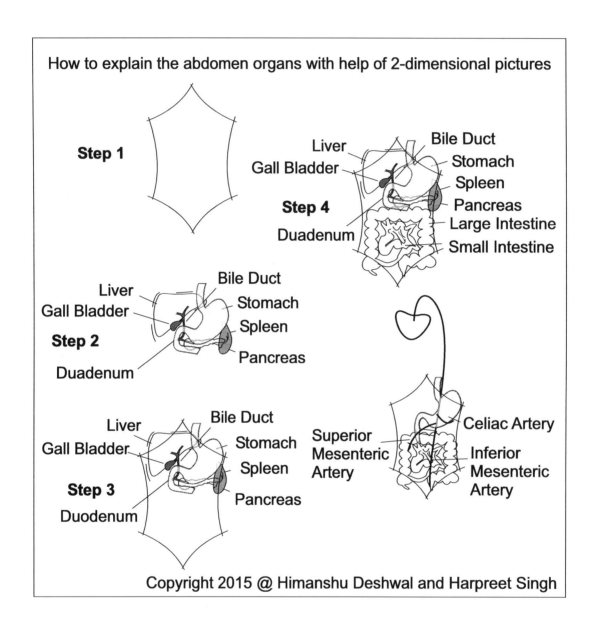

How to explain the abdomen organs with help of 2-dimensional pictures

Step 1

Step 2
Liver
Gall Bladder
Bile Duct
Stomach
Spleen
Pancreas
Duadenum

Step 3
Liver
Gall Bladder
Bile Duct
Stomach
Spleen
Pancreas
Duodenum

Step 4
Liver
Gall Bladder
Bile Duct
Stomach
Spleen
Pancreas
Large Intestine
Small Intestine
Duadenum

Superior
Mesenteric
Artery
Celiac Artery
Inferior
Mesenteric
Artery

Figure: 4

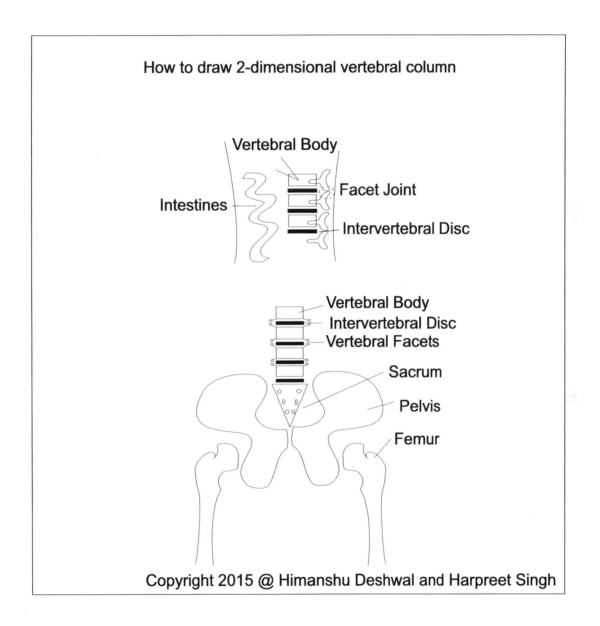

How to draw 2-dimensional vertebral column

Vertebral Body

Facet Joint

Intestines

Intervertebral Disc

Vertebral Body
Intervertebral Disc
Vertebral Facets

Sacrum

Pelvis

Femur

Figure: 5

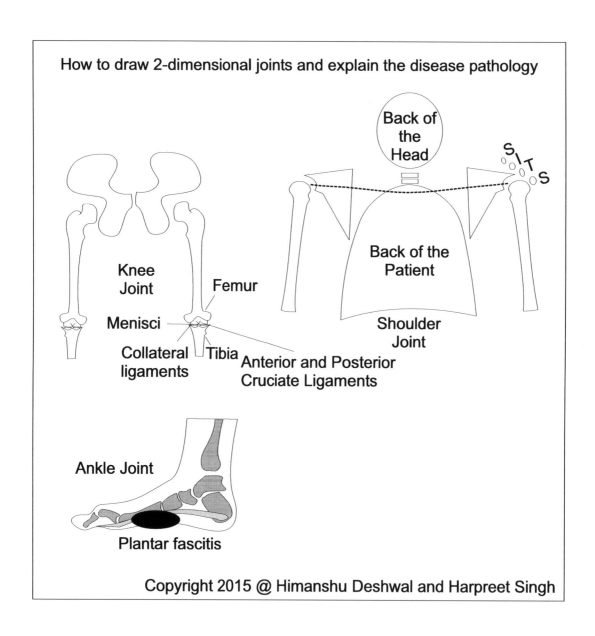

How to draw 2-dimensional joints and explain the disease pathology

Back of the Head

S I T S

Back of the Patient

Shoulder Joint

Knee Joint

Femur

Menisci

Collateral ligaments

Tibia

Anterior and Posterior Cruciate Ligaments

Ankle Joint

Plantar fascitis

Figure: 6

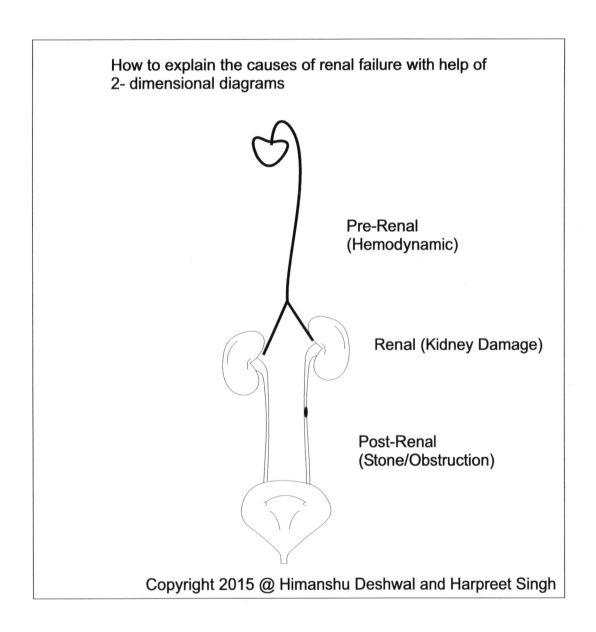

How to explain the causes of renal failure with help of 2- dimensional diagrams

Pre-Renal (Hemodynamic)

Renal (Kidney Damage)

Post-Renal (Stone/Obstruction)

Figure: 7

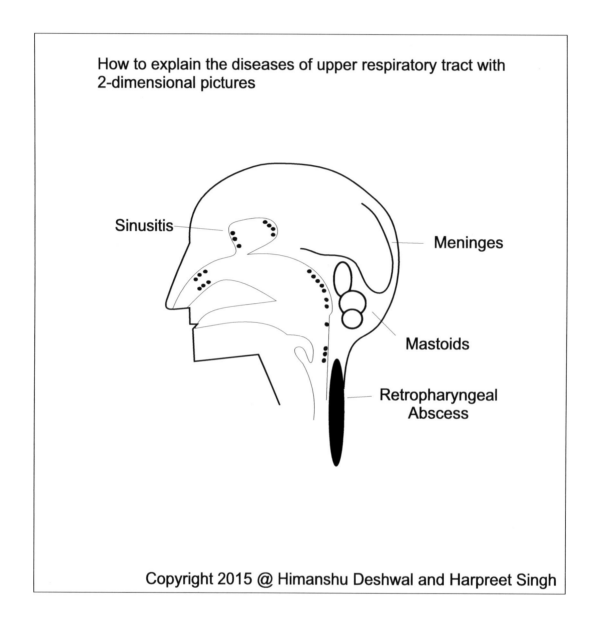

How to explain the diseases of upper respiratory tract with 2-dimensional pictures

Sinusitis

Meninges

Mastoids

Retropharyngeal Abscess

Figure: 8

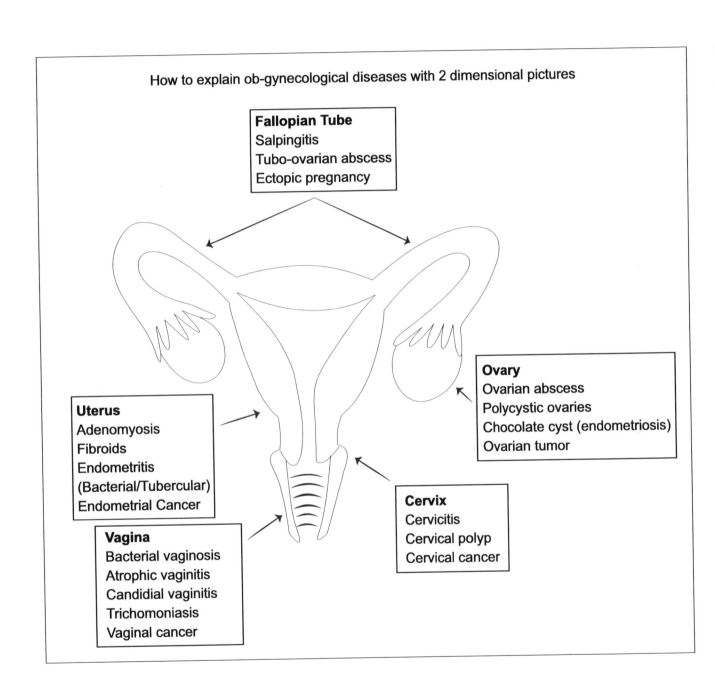

How to explain ob-gynecological diseases with 2 dimensional pictures

Fallopian Tube
Salpingitis
Tubo-ovarian abscess
Ectopic pregnancy

Ovary
Ovarian abscess
Polycystic ovaries
Chocolate cyst (endometriosis)
Ovarian tumor

Uterus
Adenomyosis
Fibroids
Endometritis
(Bacterial/Tubercular)
Endometrial Cancer

Vagina
Bacterial vaginosis
Atrophic vaginitis
Candidial vaginitis
Trichomoniasis
Vaginal cancer

Cervix
Cervicitis
Cervical polyp
Cervical cancer

Figure: 9

221

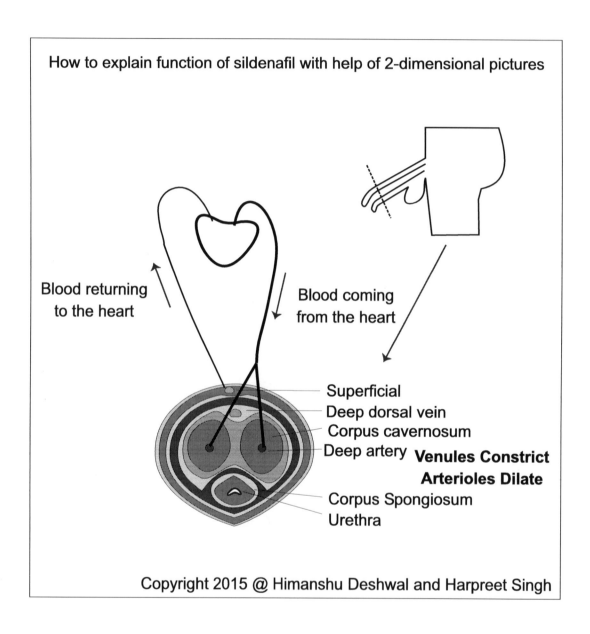

How to explain function of sildenafil with help of 2-dimensional pictures

Blood returning to the heart

Blood coming from the heart

Superficial
Deep dorsal vein
Corpus cavernosum
Deep artery **Venules Constrict**
Arterioles Dilate
Corpus Spongiosum
Urethra

Figure: 10

How to draw and discuss the problems of the abdomen with help of pictures

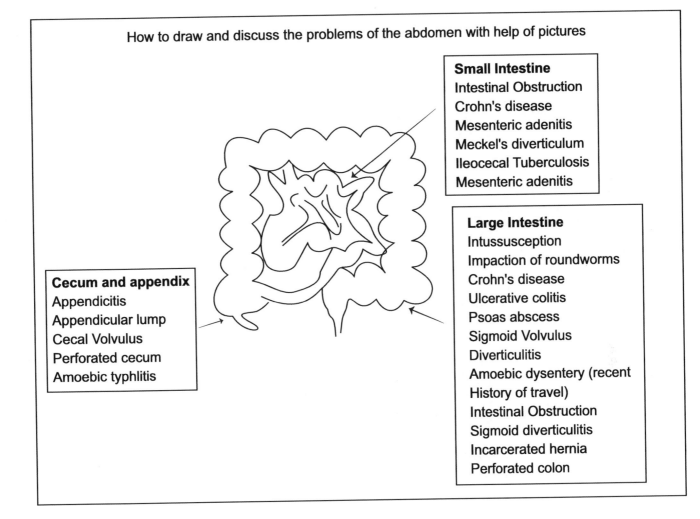

Small Intestine
Intestinal Obstruction
Crohn's disease
Mesenteric adenitis
Meckel's diverticulum
Ileocecal Tuberculosis
Mesenteric adenitis

Large Intestine
Intussusception
Impaction of roundworms
Crohn's disease
Ulcerative colitis
Psoas abscess
Sigmoid Volvulus
Diverticulitis
Amoebic dysentery (recent
History of travel)
Intestinal Obstruction
Sigmoid diverticulitis
Incarcerated hernia
Perforated colon

Cecum and appendix
Appendicitis
Appendicular lump
Cecal Volvulus
Perforated cecum
Amoebic typhlitis

Figure: 11

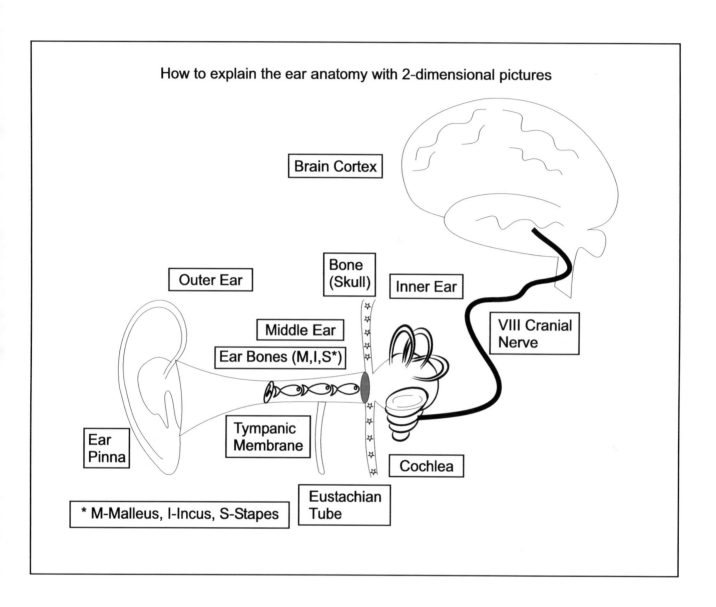

Figure: 12

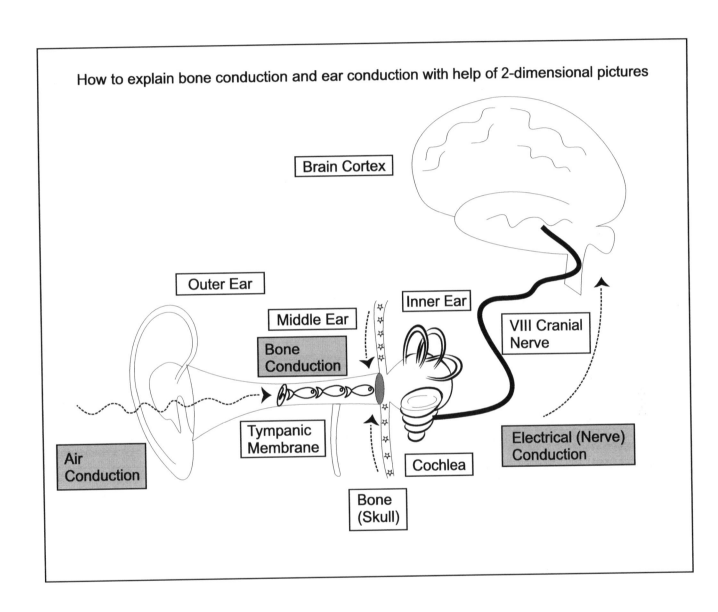

How to explain bone conduction and ear conduction with help of 2-dimensional pictures

Brain Cortex

Outer Ear

Inner Ear

Middle Ear

VIII Cranial Nerve

Bone Conduction

Tympanic Membrane

Electrical (Nerve) Conduction

Air Conduction

Cochlea

Bone (Skull)

Figure: 13

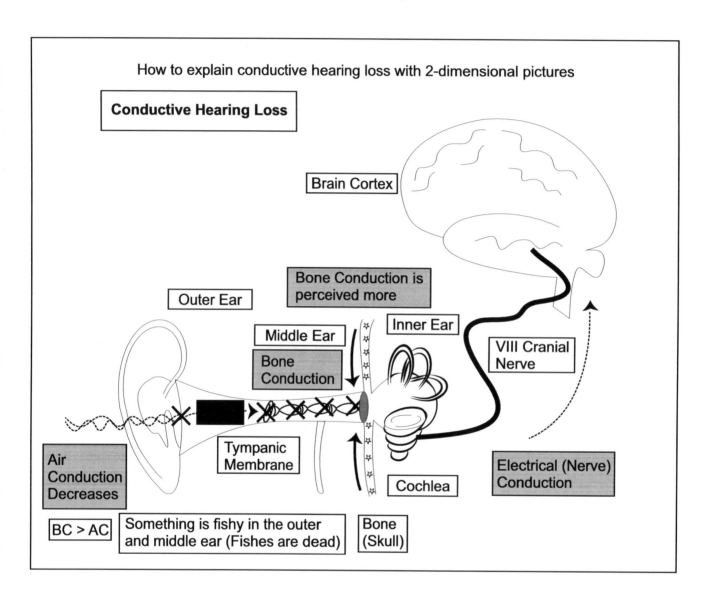

Figure: 14

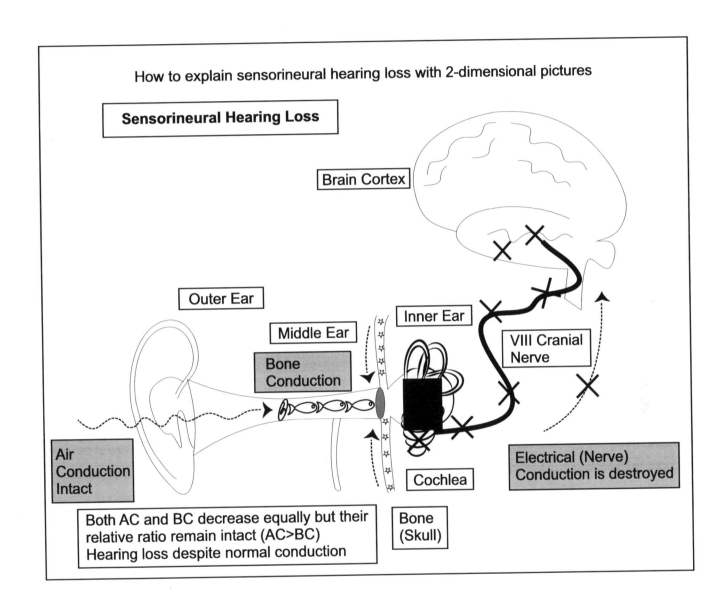

Figure: 15

227

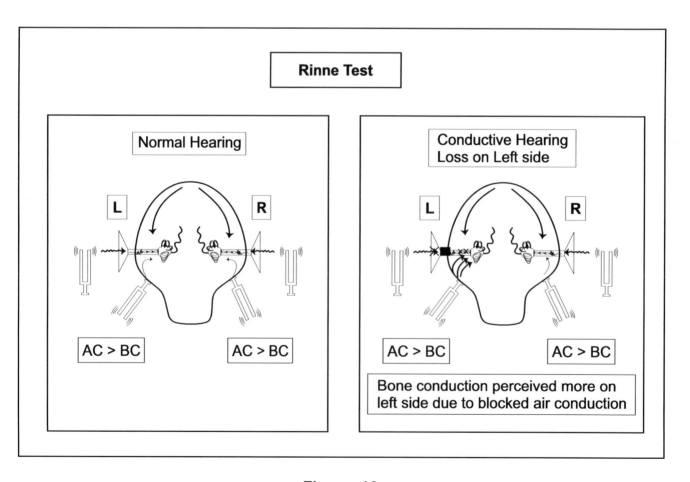

Figure: 16

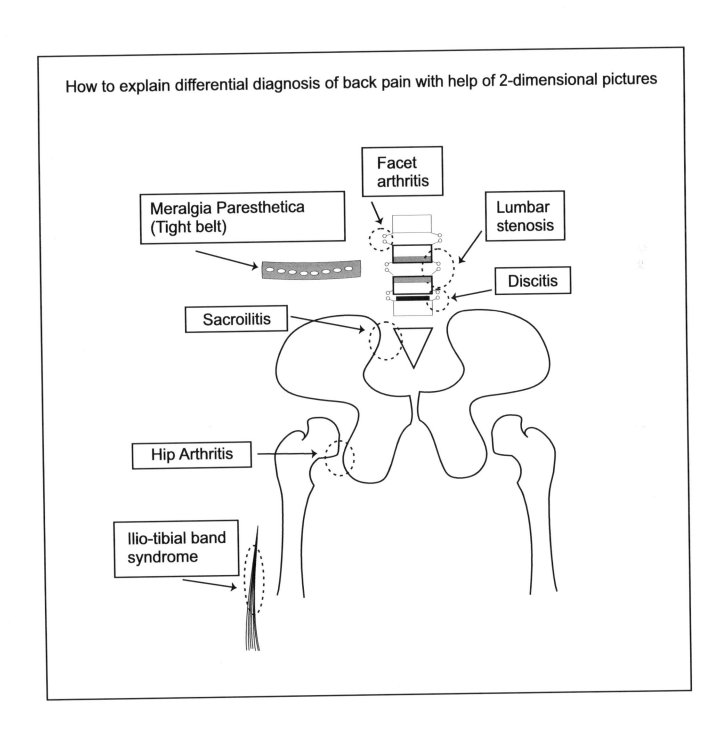

How to explain differential diagnosis of back pain with help of 2-dimensional pictures

Facet arthritis

Meralgia Paresthetica (Tight belt)

Lumbar stenosis

Discitis

Sacroilitis

Hip Arthritis

Ilio-tibial band syndrome

Figure: 17

How to explain differential diagnosis of cauda equina syndrome with help of 2-dimensional pictures

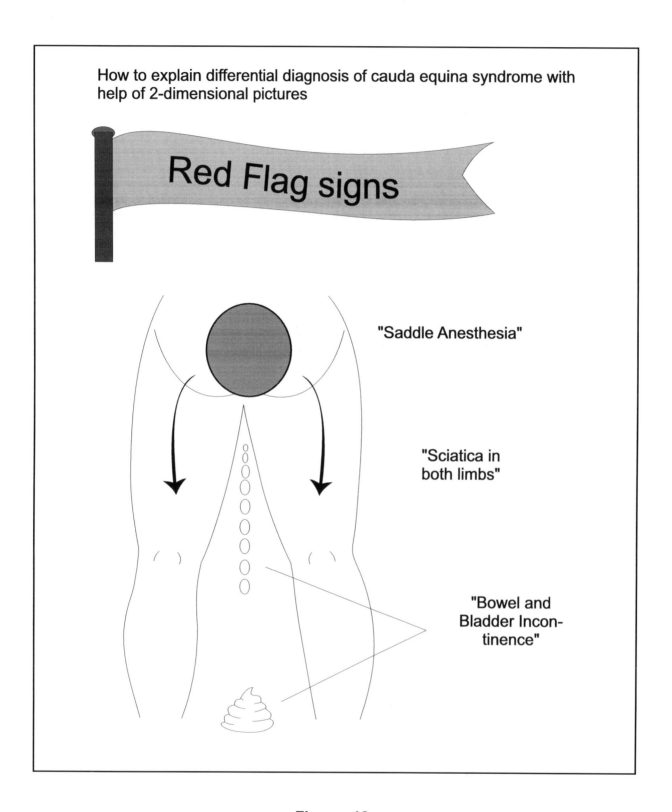

Figure: 18

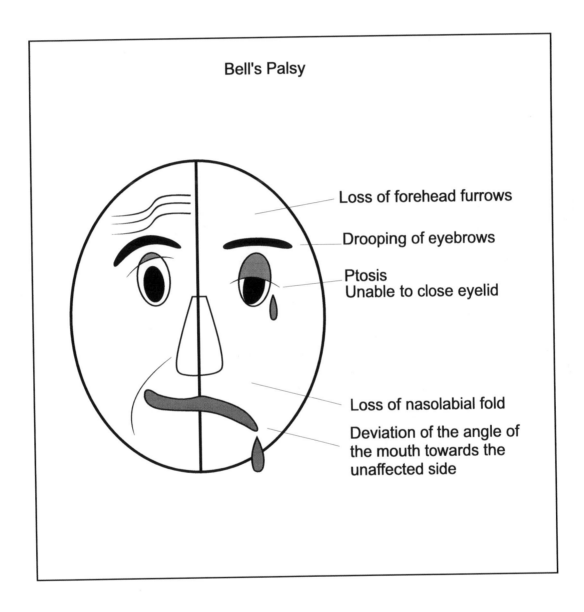

Figure: 19

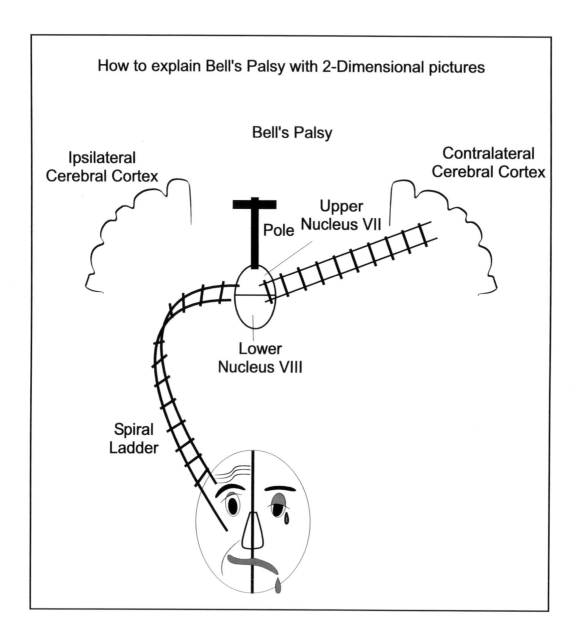

Figure: 20

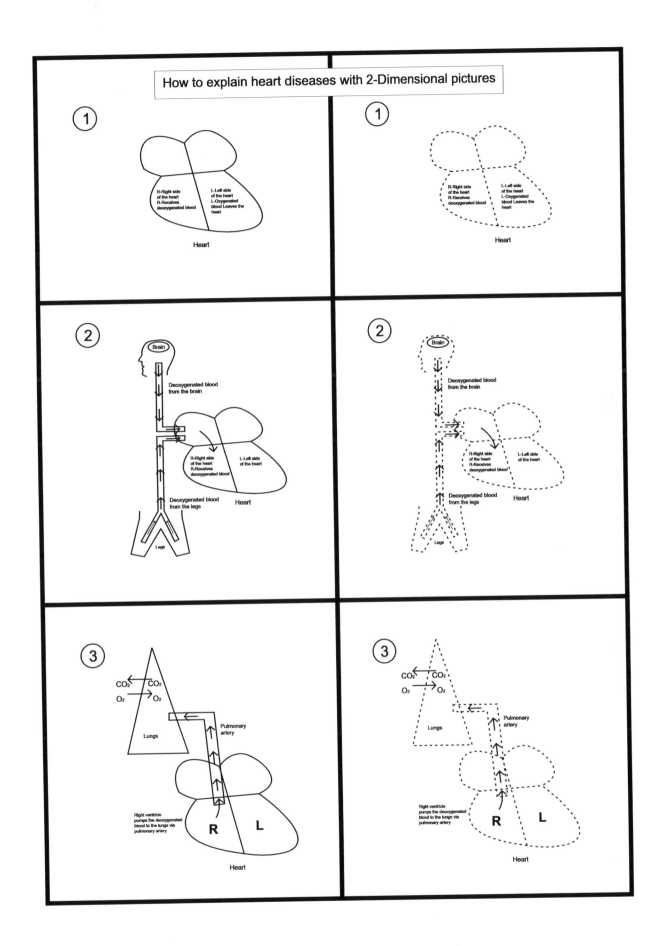

Figure: 21

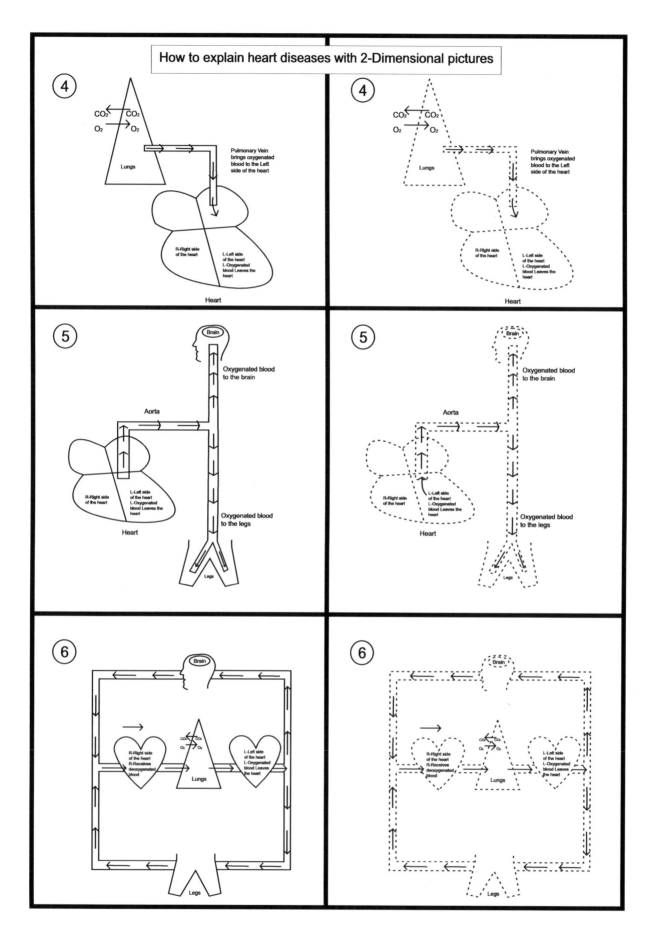

Figure: 22

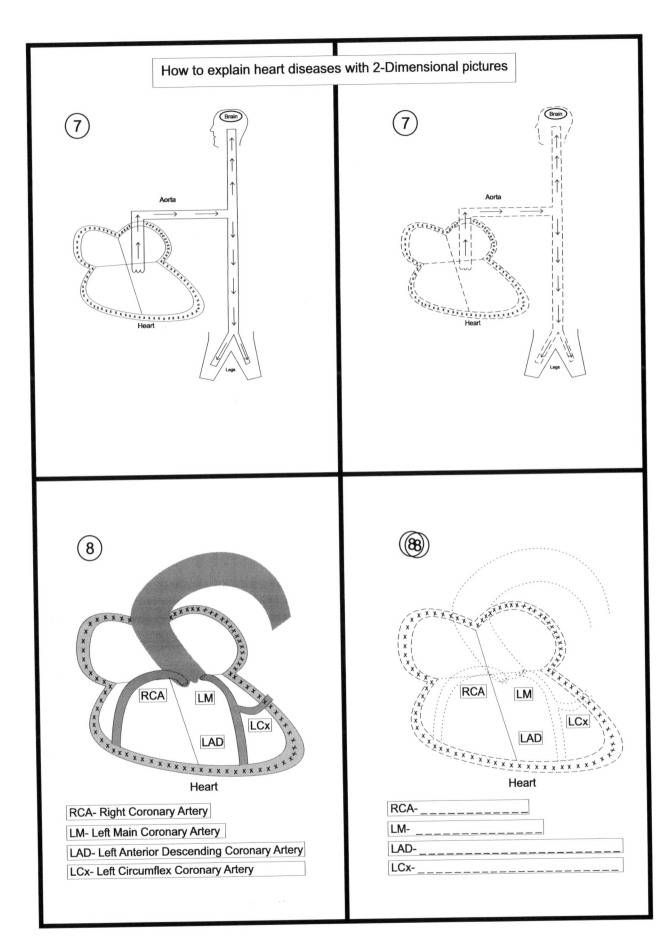

How to explain heart diseases with 2-Dimensional pictures

RCA- Right Coronary Artery

LM- Left Main Coronary Artery

LAD- Left Anterior Descending Coronary Artery

LCx- Left Circumflex Coronary Artery

RCA- _ _ _ _ _ _ _ _ _ _ _ _

LM- _ _ _ _ _ _ _ _ _ _ _ _ _

LAD- _ _ _ _ _ _ _ _ _ _ _ _ _ _ _ _

LCx- _ _ _ _ _ _ _ _ _ _ _ _ _ _ _

Figure: 23

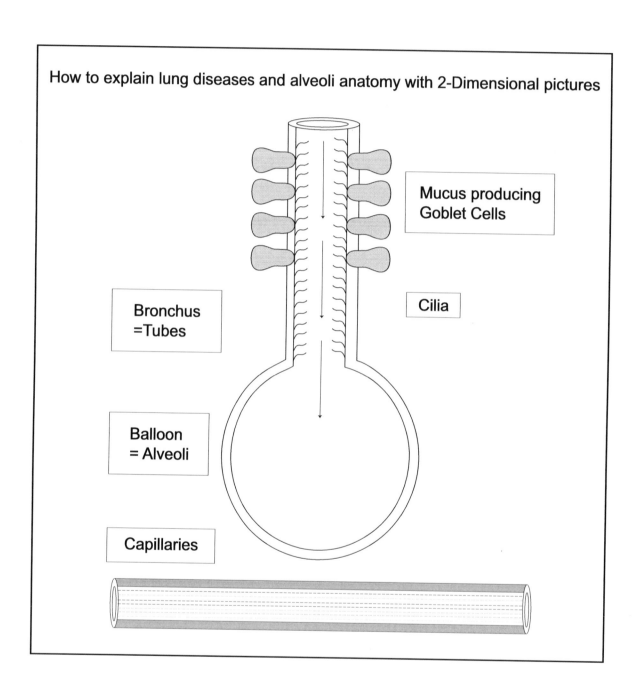

How to explain lung diseases and alveoli anatomy with 2-Dimensional pictures

Mucus producing Goblet Cells

Bronchus =Tubes

Cilia

Balloon = Alveoli

Capillaries

Figure: 24

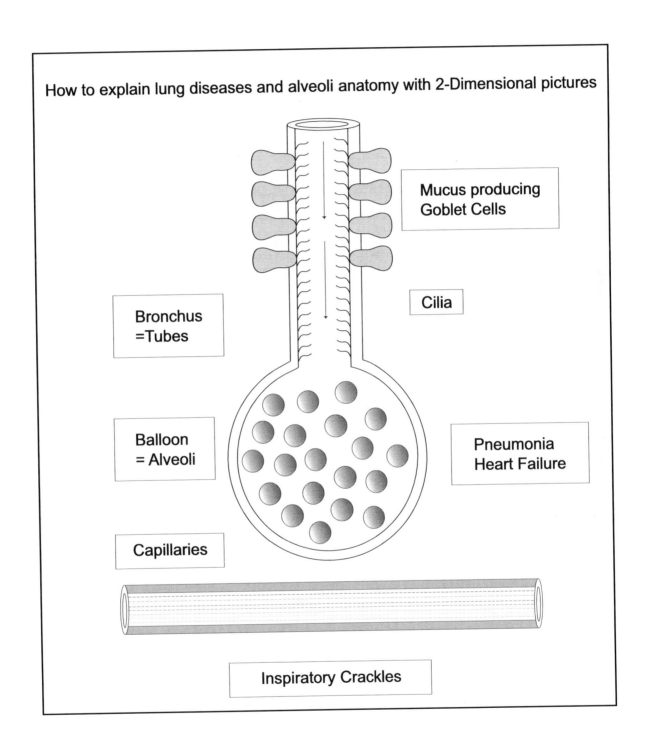

How to explain lung diseases and alveoli anatomy with 2-Dimensional pictures

Mucus producing Goblet Cells

Cilia

Bronchus =Tubes

Balloon = Alveoli

Pneumonia Heart Failure

Capillaries

Inspiratory Crackles

Figure: 25

How to explain lung diseases and alveoli anatomy with 2-Dimensional pictures

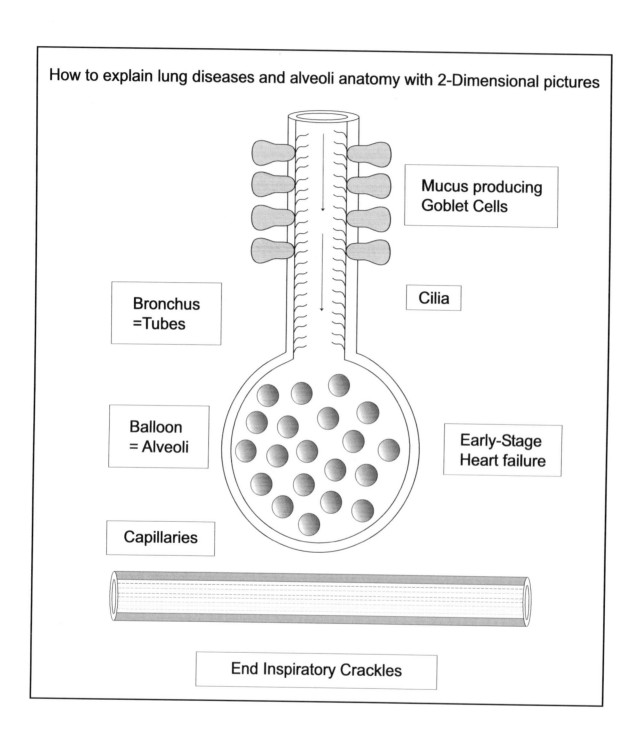

Mucus producing Goblet Cells

Cilia

Bronchus =Tubes

Balloon = Alveoli

Early-Stage Heart failure

Capillaries

End Inspiratory Crackles

Figure: 26

How to explain lung diseases and alveoli anatomy with 2-Dimensional pictures

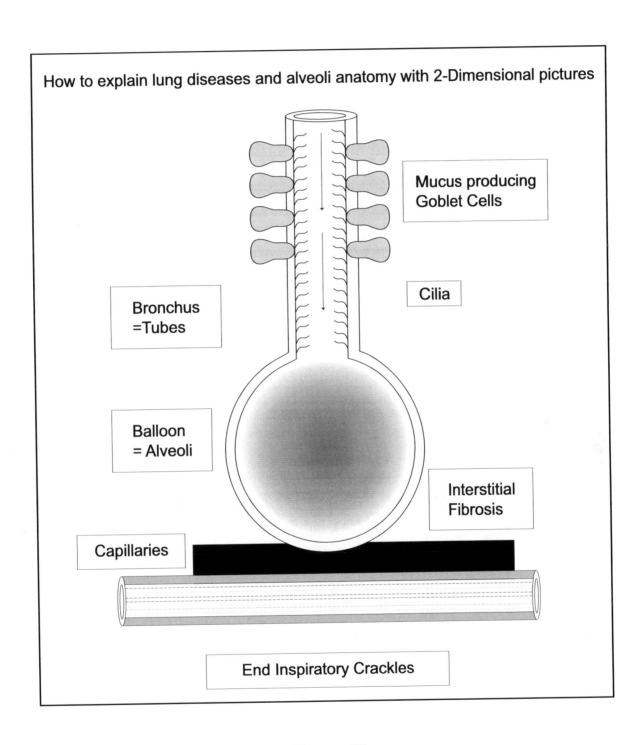

Mucus producing Goblet Cells

Cilia

Bronchus =Tubes

Balloon = Alveoli

Interstitial Fibrosis

Capillaries

End Inspiratory Crackles

Figure: 27

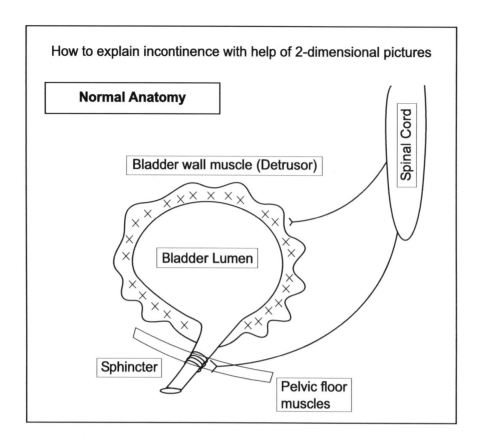

Figure: 28

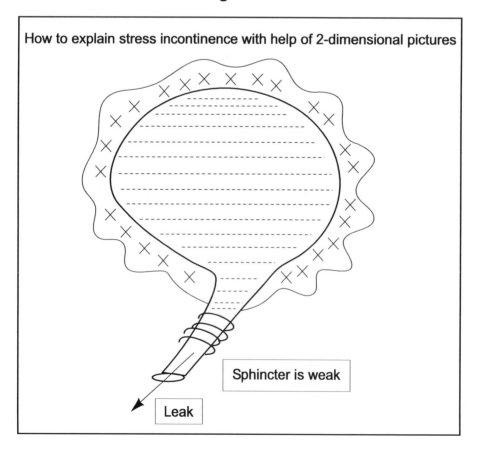

Figure: 29

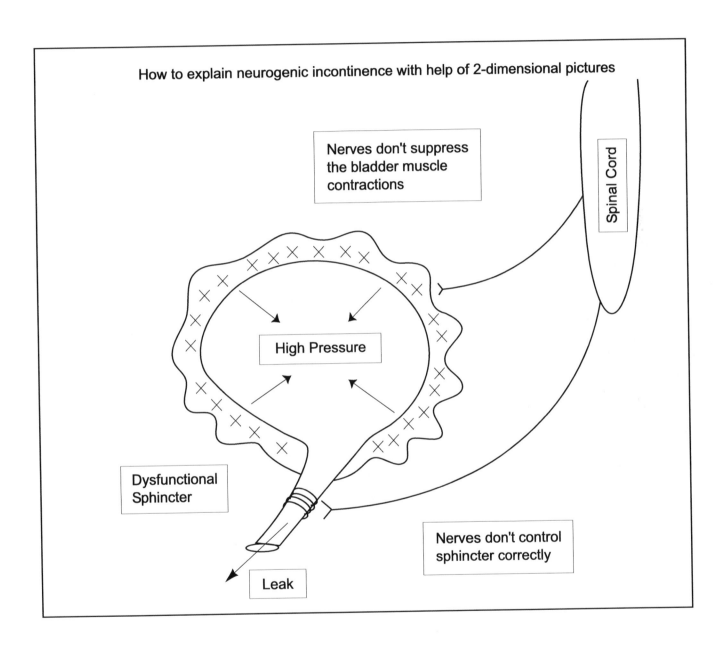

Figure: 30

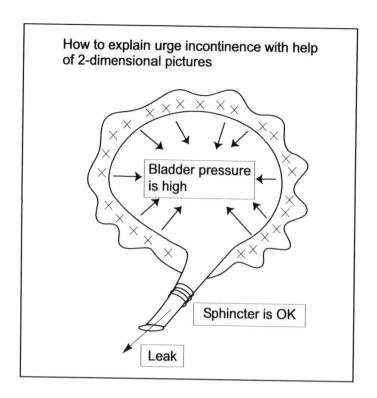

Figure: 31

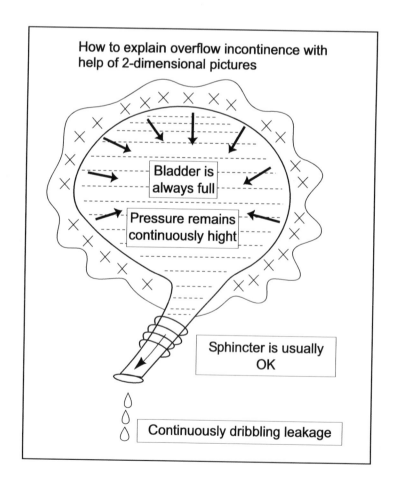

Figure: 32

How to explain differential diagnosis of chest pain with help of 2-dimensional pictures

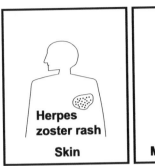
Herpes zoster rash
Skin

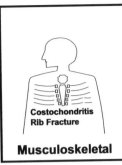
Costochondritis Rib Fracture
Musculoskeletal

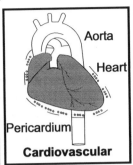
Aorta
Heart
Pericardium
Cardiovascular

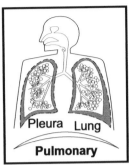
Pleura Lung
Pulmonary

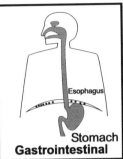
Esophagus
Stomach
Gastrointestinal

Figure: 33

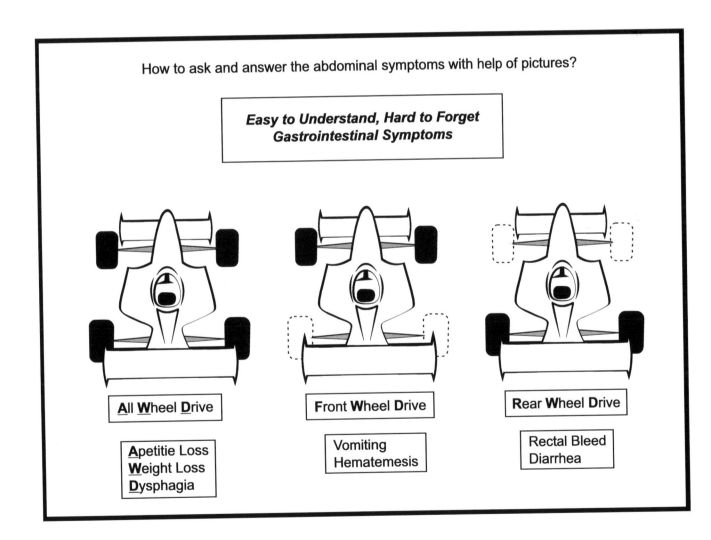

How to ask and answer the abdominal symptoms with help of pictures?

Easy to Understand, Hard to Forget
Gastrointestinal Symptoms

All **W**heel **D**rive

Front Wheel Drive

Rear Wheel Drive

Apetitie Loss
Weight Loss
Dysphagia

Vomiting
Hematemesis

Rectal Bleed
Diarrhea

Figure: 34

How to explain differential diagnosis of kidneys, ureters, bladder with help of 2-dimensional pictures

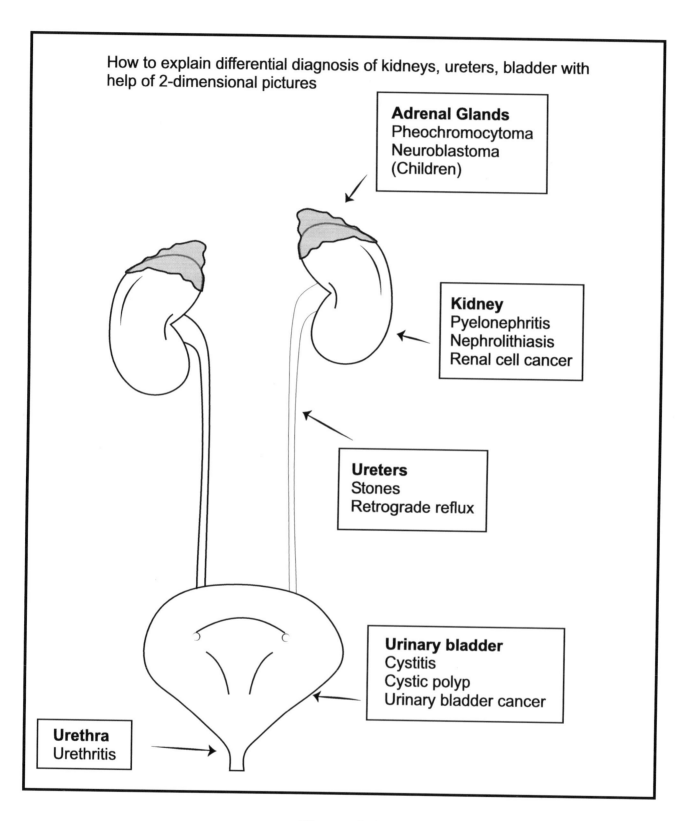

Adrenal Glands
Pheochromocytoma
Neuroblastoma
(Children)

Kidney
Pyelonephritis
Nephrolithiasis
Renal cell cancer

Ureters
Stones
Retrograde reflux

Urinary bladder
Cystitis
Cystic polyp
Urinary bladder cancer

Urethra
Urethritis

Figure: 35

How to explain differential diagnosis of abdominal pain with help of 2-dimensional graphs

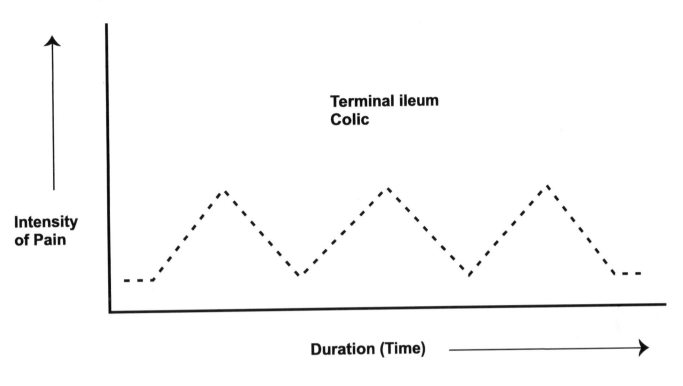

How to explain differential diagnosis of abdominal pain with help of 2-dimensional graphs

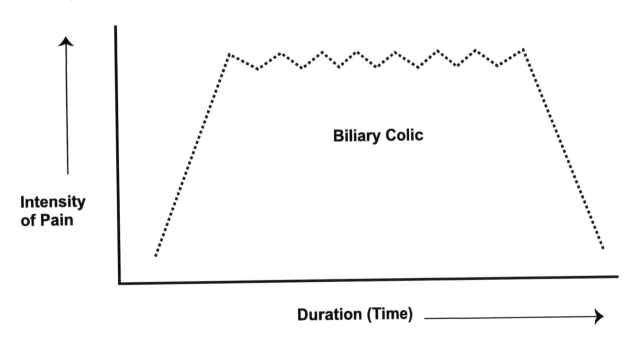

Figure: 36

How to explain differential diagnosis of abdominal pain with help of 2-dimensional graphs

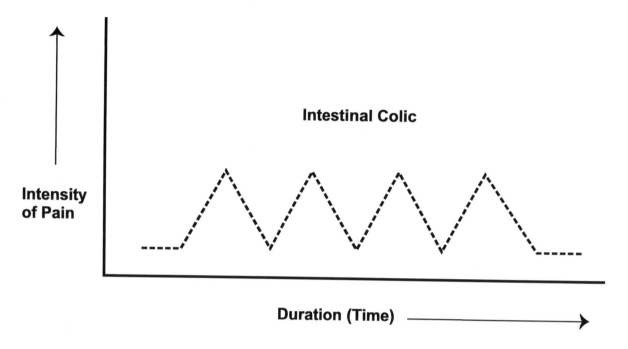

How to explain differential diagnosis of abdominal pain with help of 2-dimensional graphs

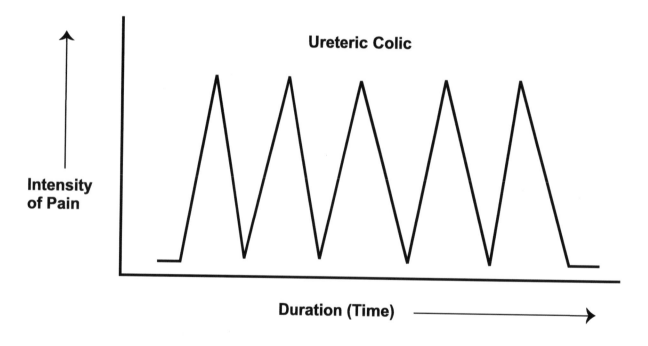

Figure: 37

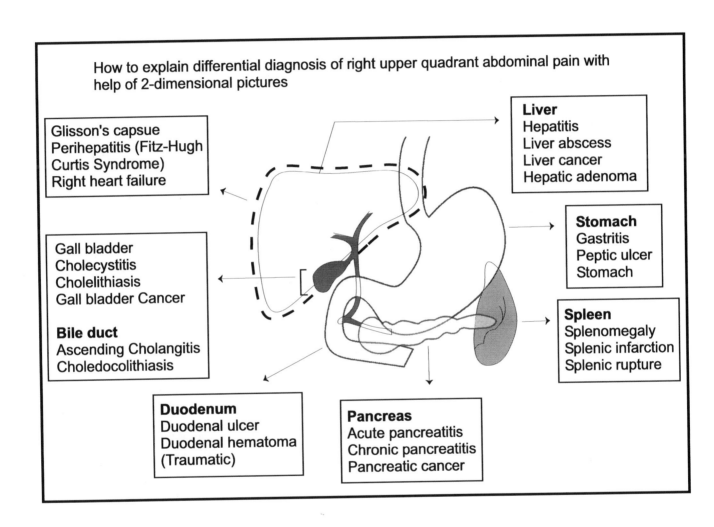

How to explain differential diagnosis of right upper quadrant abdominal pain with help of 2-dimensional pictures

Liver
Hepatitis
Liver abscess
Liver cancer
Hepatic adenoma

Glisson's capsue
Perihepatitis (Fitz-Hugh Curtis Syndrome)
Right heart failure

Stomach
Gastritis
Peptic ulcer
Stomach

Gall bladder
Cholecystitis
Cholelithiasis
Gall bladder Cancer

Bile duct
Ascending Cholangitis
Choledocolithiasis

Spleen
Splenomegaly
Splenic infarction
Splenic rupture

Duodenum
Duodenal ulcer
Duodenal hematoma
(Traumatic)

Pancreas
Acute pancreatitis
Chronic pancreatitis
Pancreatic cancer

Figure: 38

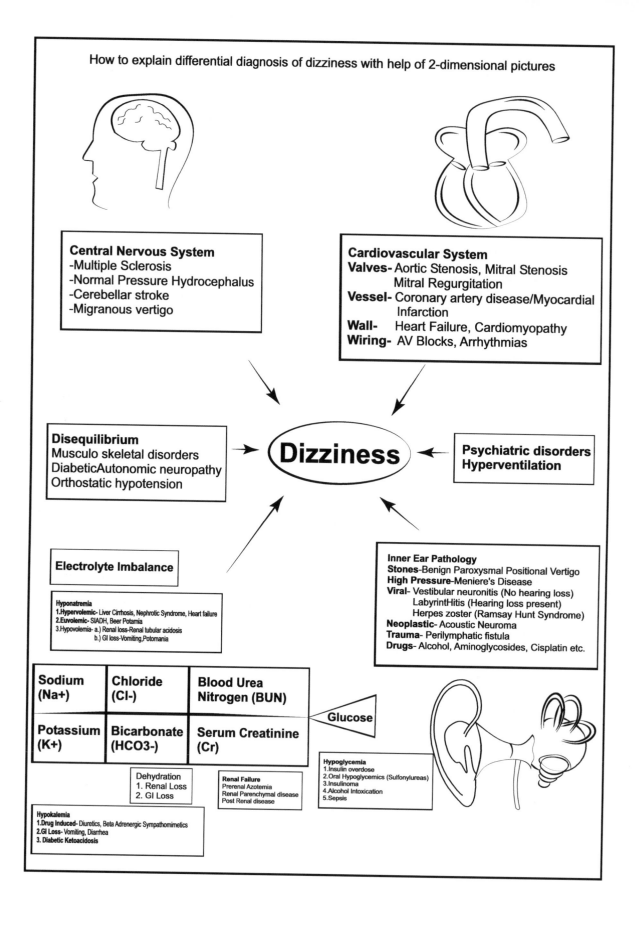

Figure: 39

How to explain differential diagnosis of headache with help of 2-dimensional pictures

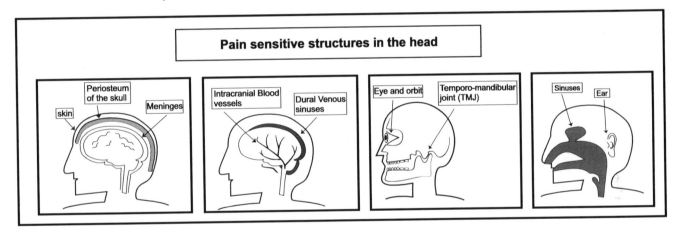

Figure: 40

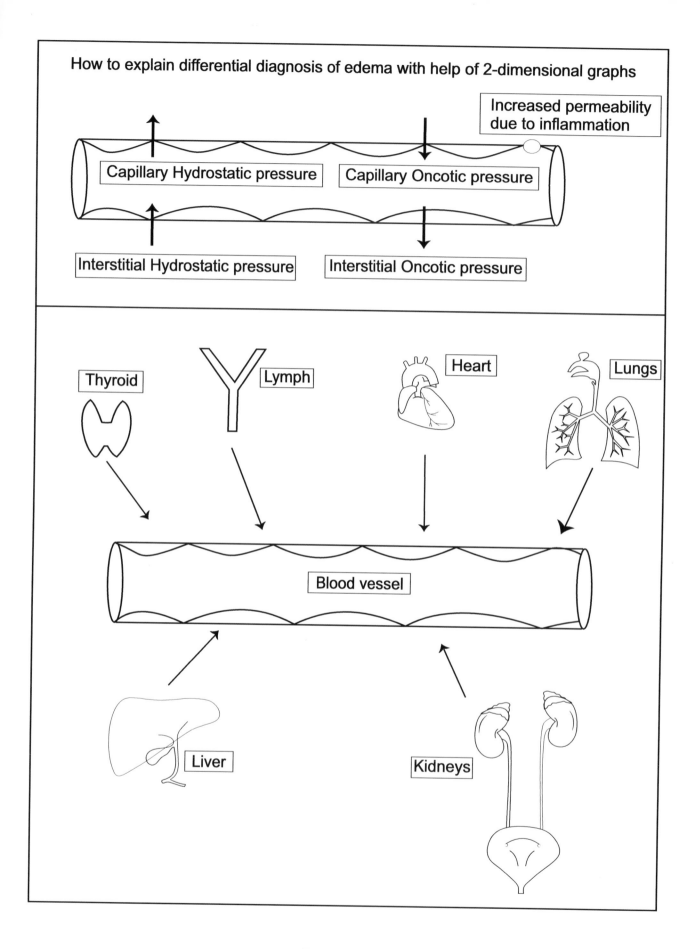

Figure: 41

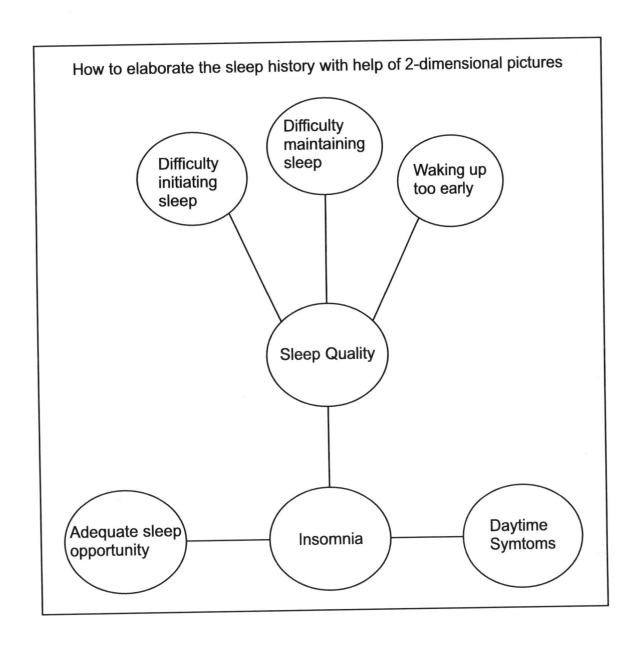

How to elaborate the sleep history with help of 2-dimensional pictures

Think of three groups when you are asking sleep history

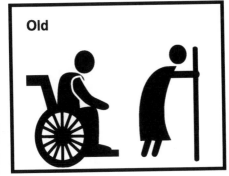

Figure: 42

251

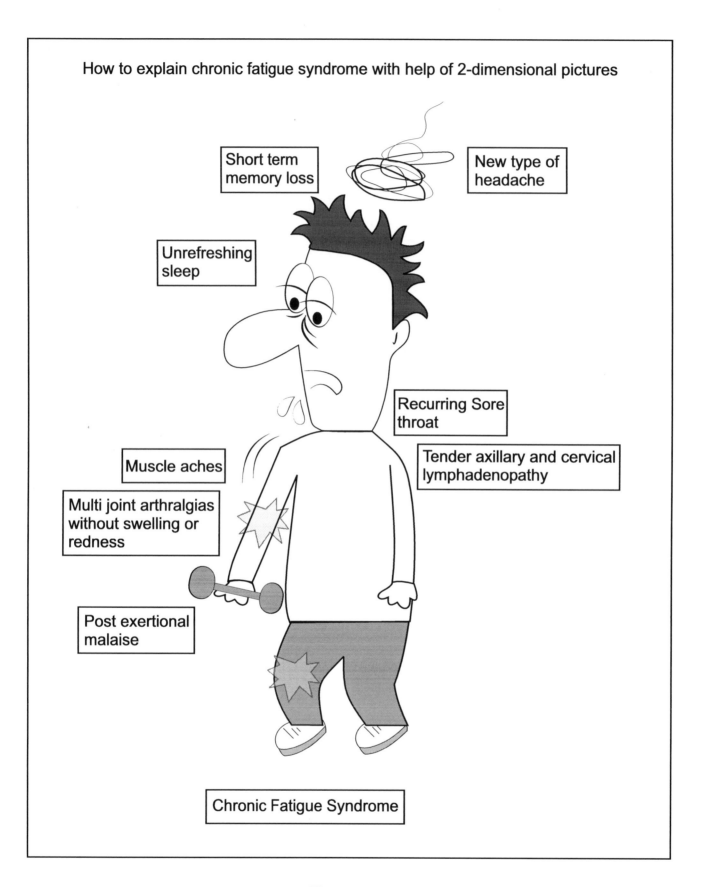

Figure: 43

How to explain differential diagnosis of shortness of breath with help of 2-dimensional pictures

Central and Neuromuscular
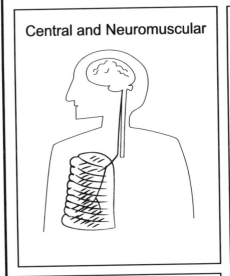

Pulmonary
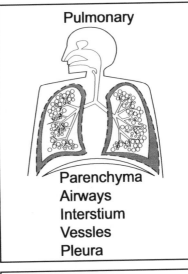

Parenchyma
Airways
Interstium
Vessles
Pleura

Cardiovascular
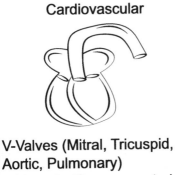

V-Valves (Mitral, Tricuspid, Aortic, Pulmonary)
V-Vessels (Coronary arteries)
W-Walls (Cardiac muscles)
W-Wire (Electrical conduction of the heart)

Hematological
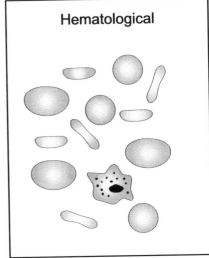

Metabolic

Deconditioning
Sedentary lifestyle
Obesity Hypoventilation syndrome
(Pickwickian syndrome)

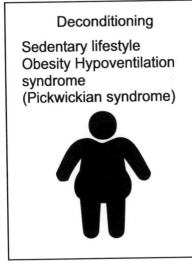

Figure: 44

He is very kind and caring, takes the time to answer all your questions and educates you in areas you are questioning—G. H.

We were lucky to have found Dr. Singh for my father as my dad was extremely ill and had been misdiagnosed by other doctors. We've been blessed to have found Dr. Singh because he truly cares about his patients and their situation. He is very kind, extremely knowledgeable, enthusiastic and patient. He answers all questions, is very responsive to all concerns and puts the care of his patients first. He is an EXCELLENT doctor!— V

I love Dr.Singh he listens to your problems he always makes me feel better when I leave his office—T. T.

He has helped me and my family for several years now. He uncovered a problem with my daughter that no one else was able to find. I can't tell you how much I appreciate Dr. Harpreet in my life. I highly recommend him!— -K.F.

Very complete— Tim V in big Rapids, MI

Dr, Singh has good bed side manners, a little humor, and will take the time to explain and teach about diseases, procedures, etc. He is very kind and polite to his patients. I would definitely recommend him to anyone looking for a good internist.— M.A. in Big Rapids,

Dr. Singh is wonderful. He takes the time to listen to you, making real world suggestions to improve your health. He is very thorough and clear with instructions.— L.B. in Big Rapids

Dr. Singh is the most caring, compassionate doctor I've ever met. He doesn't rush through your appointment. He listens to your concerns and explains things so you understand. I have and will continue to recommend Dr. Singh to all my friends.— J.G. in Canadian Lakes

Hba1c is down; weight is down. Your Scan and Spot Nutrition Facts program works. It helps to track the daily consumption of food. Taking Dr. Harpreet Singh's class/seminar and seeing graphics help me understand the program.—G. P. in Big Rapids, MI

Dr. Singh takes time with his patients to answer any and all questions that his patient may have and makes sure you understand all of it before leaving his office. He is very dedicated to all of his patients. That is what I love about this doctor! He is the best doctor I have seen so far over the years.— M.B. in Mecosta ,MI

Dr Singh has superior knowledge of the entire medical field. I have had many visits with him, some of which resulted in surgery. One that I wish to comment on was a Hernia Repair diagnosed by Dr Singh. I followed his diagnosis with three specialists who insisted I didn't have a Hernia problem. Dr. Singh knew I did and I knew I did so I tried a fourth surgeon who confirmed Dr Singh's diagnosis and I followed up with surgery correcting the problem. Excellent diagnosis and successful surgery.— H.L. in Stanwood, MI

Always patient. Active listener. Takes his time. Is in no rush for me to leave. Excellent and knowledgeable. He's been a savior for my wife.— L.M. in White Cloud, MI

Excellent doctor. Great patient skills. I'd recommend him to everyone. Takes time to listen. Never in a hurry.— B.M. in White Cloud, MI

I highly recommend Dr. Singh, he takes time with every patient, he listens to your concerns and always does a complete exam at each visit. He makes you, as a patient, feel important . You may have a 45 min wait to see him but it's worth it and means he is not rushing through the patient before you and you know he is not going to rush through your appointment!! I have full trust in Dr. Singh !!!—K in Leroy, Mi

Great doctor. Excellent bedside manner and ability to explain diagnoses. Expect to wait 30-120 minutes to see him though because he isso thorough that he is often an hour behind your appointment time. If you want quicker service, book your appointment as early in the day as possible. If you need an excuse to leave work early and kill a few hours, however, book your appointment 2pm or later because I've often waited until 5:30-6pm to talk to him with a 3pm appointment time.—Anonymous, Big Rapids, MI

Dr. Singh is both an excellent doctor and person. He has been able to help me with medical issues I have dealt with for some time. Very friendly and knowledgeable. Explains treatment options and use of medications very well. Dr. Singh is the A-team of doctors.— N.M. in Big Rapids, MI

From 270 pounds to 201 pounds since I started seeing Dr. Singh. This is all in 1 year. We are very happy. Now we read lot of labels. Grocery bills have gone down because we are not buying processed food. His teaching of labels with checklist and pictures have been helpful,— BKS in Hersey, MI
Lost 28 pounds on Scan and Spot Diet. I have taught Dr. Singh's diet to my friend and she has also lost 7 pounds in 3 weeks. I appreciate Dr. Harpreet Singh for all the help. My life has improved and I can walk and exercise long distance. My overall health has improved to much. I was taking many pain medications and now almost none because of the weight loss. I feel good.—-OH in Grand Rapids, MI

Thanks to Dr. Singh my life has been dramatically changed for the better. After finding out I have a gluten and wheat allergy we discussed the best option for me to better my health. Since that day I have lost 21 lbs! I couldn't ask for a better doctor.— M.M. in Big Rapids, Mi

I am quite pleased with Dr. Singh. He is thorough, and seems genuinely interested in his patients. He is very pleasant, and takes his time during appointments, though that sometimes makes him late for the next appointment(s). This seems to have improved in the last six months.— S.K. in Big Rapids, MI

My spouse and I are patients of Dr. Singh and we could not be ANY happier! He's the best doctor we've ever had; kind, thoughtful and considerate and gives us as much time as we need to ensures that we thoroughly understand. Our medicines and overall care are carefully considered and well managed. I have many major medical issues and my health has improved greatly because of Dr. Singh He discovered that I am allergic to wheat. After 3 months of not eating wheat-my skin has healed and all of my digestive problems are gone-I FEEL GREAT!— J.M. in Mecosta, MI

I have been working with Dr. Singh for a little over two years now. I feel that given my age, the results are far better than I anticipated! I have dropped from 323 pounds, down to 242, my blood pressure is now 140/72, as compared to 190/100, my cholesterol, bad is down to normal, good is/has improved, and most important to me, is my HG A1C has dropped from a high of 8.4 down to 6.3 (for the last year, below 7.0) not perfect, but on the way... Bottom line, Thanks, Dr. Singh and staff!!— H.D. West in Barryton, Michigan

I met with Dr. Singh to establish a G.P. to help me pull together all the information I was getting from my 5 specialty doctors as I felt like all my separate symptoms were related. Dr. Singh was VERY thorough and immediately narrowed down the area that he felt was the cause (something my specialists had never addressed). He showed me what tests to order & set a plan in motion. I would highly recommend him to anyone looking for a doctor who will work with you instead of just prescribing a band aid.—L.G. in Grand Rapids, MI

I started seeing Dr.Singh in February 2016. I have lost 40 pounds my blood pressure is lower by 20 points. My BMI has decreased by 4 points, Triglycerides have gone down from 528 to 177. His Scan and Spot diet works. I have learned to read nutrition labels. So happy for myself. I am getting close to getting new pants.— D.H in Big Rapids, MI

Dr. Singh is thorough. He has improved my health. He spends time and is thorough. He is friendly. We learned how to eat healthy. Scan and Spot diet works. He brings God and faith into the discussion— R.L. in Big Rapids, MI

I have lost 40 pounds, Hba1c was 10.7 and is now 6.7. Lost 3 inches off my waist. Dr. Singh's Scan and Spot diet works. Most importantly, I had to change my wardrobe..— RS in Ypsilanti

Dr. Singh is a very good doctor. I had a close family member who was suddenly ill. She has stroke like symptoms but kept getting progressively worse. He was able to find the dx of CJD. (Creutzfeldt Jacob Disease). It was   terminal, but it helped the family to know what was going on with our family member—M.R. in Big Rapids

Started seeing Dr. Singh 9 months ago in December 2015. Hba1c was 13.4 and weight was 316 pounds. Now after 9 months on Scan and spot diet and watching (iCrush) diabetes video on Youtube, I am more in tune with diabetes. Now Hba1c is 6.9 and I weigh 263 pounds. My vision has gotten better.— K in Mecosta MI

Dr. Singh is very knowledgeable, caring and respectful. He has a genuine concern for the patients well-being. I would recommend to anyone.— G.T. in Leroy, MI

Dr. Singh is very thorough. He always listens to your concerns. He takes his time with every patient and I really appreciate that. I would highly recommend him if you're looking for a good, caring doctor.— J.H. in Big Rapids, Mi

Dr. Singh is a rare breed of doctor. who truly cares about his patients to a point, that you can't help but thank God for him, due to his desire to heal people and educate them to understand the cause of their sickness. He leaves no stone unturned in his desire to raise the quality of one's health concerns. His dietary knowledge alone has helped me go from 236 lbs. down to 198 lbs. His bedside manner is excellent as well as his communication skills. He listens very well.— J.W & S.W.

He reminds of the side effects of smoking every time I see him. Nobody has shown the side effects like that. He showed me checklist and diagrams for quitting smoking. Now, I have quit smoking.— RH

Very kind and caring doctor. Takes as much times as you need and wants to know anything that might be bothering you. Not just the problem you were in there for. He treats the whole person.— D in Big Rapids, MI

Wonderful doctor. My first visit with him was just to get prescriptions renewed, but on the basis of my medical history and drugs I was prescribed he ordered some lab work and found that I had a very treatable condition that could be controlled by a temporary medicine and change in diet. I am now off medicine for arthritis, asthma and acid reflux and feel much better. Thank you Dr. Singh- C in Big Rapids, Mi

I highly recommend Dr. Singh for all of your health needs. He has treated me for several months for diabetes. He was the first person, after more than 10 years working with other doctors and specialists, to tell me that diabetes can be defeated by a combination of weight loss and exercise. Guided by him, I have now lost about 50 pounds, have noticed that several symptoms of diabetes have decreased, and that some prescription pills that I used to take are no longer necessary.—Anonymous, Big Rapids, MI

Always a pleasure to visit Dr. Singh. He takes the time to make sure he understands what I am concerned about. His staff are helpful and welcoming.— Sheridan, MI

Dr. Singh is a caring and knowledgeable health professional. I appreciate his expertise and thoroughness. He uses diagnostic tools often to make sure there is information for making careful decisions.— J.T. in Big Rapids, MI

Without the expert examination and attention that Dr. Singh gave my husband we wouldn't have found his kidney cancer. Previous doctors missed this entirely. He saved my husband's life and we are still seeing Dr. Singh and receiving excellent care.—L.O. in Big Rapids, MI

Dr Singh is such a very intelligent andkind physician. Each office visit, I'm more impressed with his skill of blending all his knowledge. I have recommended Dr. Singh to anyone that will listen. Spectrum Hospital has a real asset in. Dr H. Singh— M.D. in Ma Costa, MI

Best Doctor I ever encountered in my life. He is VERY thorough and knowledgeable! The extensive examinto the problems my daughter was having was above andbeyond any exam I have ever been involved in in my life and I'm 57 years old. At no time did we feel like we were hurried by Dr. Singh. In addition, he is compassionate of his patients & makes real connections. I can't sing, Dr. Singh's praises more.— M.B. in Croswell, MI

Dr. Singh has given me the best advice to improve my health. Scan and Spot diet very easy to follow. I lost 48 lbs in a year. Was in size 16, now size 6. Had terrible gastric reflux since I was a teenager now off all medications and taking 1 teaspoon of tummeric root a day as an anti-inflammatory per Dr. Singh. Thank you Dr. Singh for all your medical advise and the Scan and Spot diet. Karen— K.A. in Big Rapids, MI

Excellent doctor. He has been through a lot with me and my surgeries and he has never given up on me. I have been through lot of doctors and by far he is the best caregiver that I have had and I thank him very much for taking time with me.— J.H. Big Rapids, MI

Dr. Singh is very caring and attentive. He is most descriptive and explains how systems work relative to my complaint. His 100% focus on me as a patient is truly reassuring. This man is THE "go to" Doctor.— M.B. in Chase, MI

Dr. Singh was very concerned about my condition and took the time to explain to me what I needed to do to get well and listened to my concerns and answered my questions—Anonymous

My father started seeing Dr. Singh after being hospitalized for lung & heart issues. While we most times do have to wait a considerable amount of time past our appointment time, we understand that Dr. Singh spends a great deal of time with us making sure we understand what is going on. We never feel like we'rebeing rushed through an appointment.— L.R. in Reed City | Feb 10, 2017

Professional care; great team-work by staff; received educational materials to coincide with my health needs. Confident in regard to quality care.— P.B. in Stanwood, MI

For more testimonials visit www.healthgrades.com or end of this book

Health Caregivers Testimonial

Nurse Recommendation

Because of Dr. Singh's style of medicine and his dedication to his patients, more and more of my family members have become his patients. Why, you might ask? What is so different about how Dr. Singh takes care of them? Let me tell you.

It all started with my cousin who needed a new doctor because of her increasing symptoms, yet to be diagnosed. Dr. Singh took her history, did the usual tests and diagnosed her with congestive heart failure. But something wasn't right. In spite of treatment, she was getting worse. So he donned his detective hat and kept looking. Does your doctor do that?

Long story short, he kept looking until, truly just in time, he found the reason behind her increasing fatigue and pain. It had nothing to do with her heart, she had plasma cell leukemia! Using his knowledge, listening skills and unwillingness to stop with the apparent, he saved her life, literally. In less than 24 hours, she went from diagnosis to first chemotherapy treatment, unheard of in this rural, isolated community. There is no doubt in her and her family's mind that he saved her life. The disease was progressing so rapidly at that point that we would have lost her within hours.

Over the next year of treatment ups and downs, and we've had our share, he has been there, reaching out to her and her family, even when the focus of treatment was provided by others. The concept of "Patient centered" is how he practices. He doesn't wait for you to come to him; if there is a concern, or he hasn't seen you, he contacts you. Does your physician call you to see how you are doing? Send you a text? Visit you at your house when you can't come to him? Dr. Singh does.

By using his Core Measures approach, Dr. Singh connects with the patient and the family. Using simple drawings, taking the time to sit right in front of you, eyeball to eyeball, and talk about the real issues of your situation, providing you with the level and intensity of information you need and can handle at the moment, Dr. Singh connects with his patients and their families to guide them through the very complicated maze of American Health Care.

I am honored to know Dr. Singh and to have him care for my family. I am grateful that there are still physicians in practice that remember why they are doing what they are doing. He gives me hope for the future of health care in the USA. We need thousands of Dr. Singh's. I hope you become one of them!

Sincerely,

Sue, RN, MSN

NURSE Recommendation

I would like to acknowledge the time Dr. Singh has taken to speak with the patients and their families on our unit this week. Not only has he called or sat down with each family member that asked, but he also called the family of each patient he saw without anyone asking him to. This makes such a difference for families and the RN's caring for them. Thank you, Dr. Singh for the time and the compassion you gave.

Jennifer XXXXX , RN

<u>NURSE Recommendation</u>

Both Dr. Singh and Lisa spent all morning on the unit caring for not one, but two of our patients that were in crisis. They were not even assigned to these patients, but came up to help anyway. They did an excellent job treating the patients and were wonderful with speaking with their families. We could not have asked for more and cannot thank you both enough.

Natalie XXXXX RN

<u>NURSE Recommendation</u>

Dr. Singh,

It has been a pleasure getting to know you and working alongside a physician such as you. You have demonstrated a terrific sprit with such respect and compassion for patients and colleagues alike. "It is true, life is really generous to those who pursue their personal legend." Paulo Coelho

Lisa XXXXX, RN

Britney XXXXX, RN

Dr. Singh,

We are extremely grateful for your help in the matter of XXXX XXXXX. It was a great relief to find some-one who shared our sense of urgency and need for compassionate care of our patient. I sometimes feel that many in the medical profession have lost the sense of service that supposedly would have brought them into this field in the first place.

Thank you for caring for our patients, and thank you retaining our faith,

David L. Pastoor, MD

Dr. Singh,

I just wanted to thank you so much for taking me under your wing. You are a great doctor and I learned a lot. I really enjoyed the teaching time we had together and I appreciate your time (I know its valuable). Thank you for the consistent encouragement and the great advice! Christina

---

April 7, 2009

Dear Harpreet Singh, MD;

Our records indicate that during the 2008 academic calendar year; you served as a clinical preceptor for the Grand Valley State University Physician Assistant Student. As an expression of our sincere gratitude for your services, we are giving you a certificate of appreciation. We look forward to contin-ued relations with you for our students and for the future of health care. We are also looking at ways to strengthen our program and ask you to email any feedback to us at pas@gvsu.edu. If there is anything that we can do for you, please do not hesitate to contact us.

Respectfully;

Wallace D. Boeve, EdD, PA-C

Program Director

Physician Assistant Studies

College of health professions

Grand Valley State University

March 26,2010

Dear Harpreet Singh, MD;

Our records indicate that during the 2009 academic calendar year, you served as a clinical preceptor for the Grand Valley State University Physician Assistant Student. As an expression of our sincere gratitude for your services, we are giving you a certificate of appreciation. We look forward to continued relations with you for our students and for the future of health care. We are also looking at ways to strengthen our program and ask you to email any feedback to us at pas@gvsu.edu. If there is anything that we can do for you, please do not hesitate to contact us.

Respectfully;

Wallace D. Boeve, EdD, PA-C

Program Director

Physician Assistant Studies

College of health professions

Grand Valley State University

Dr. Singh,

Thank you so much for all the work you are doing —both with yourself and your practice style, as well as that with your present PA's/NP's. I appreciate your willingness to teach as opportunities present themselves. I hope you are able to see the benefits of the changes you have made. Thank you for your continued commitment.

Emily, HOWM

Dr. Singh,

Thank you for your commitment to education & for all the time & energy you put into the case studies for journal club. Your willingness to do that is hugely valuable to me & HOWM as a group.

Thank you again. Keep smiling,

"It gives me great pleasure to be writing a reference for Dr. H. Singh. I have enjoyed knowing Dr. Singh and working with him these past years. As a Physician Recruiter, I come in contact with physicians of all specialties, shapes, and sizes, and I can tell you that Dr. Singh's clinical skills and bedside manner are among the finest. In my opinion, anyone would be in good hands if Dr. Singh was handling them as a physician or in any business venture. I continue to be amazed at his great outlook on life in general and can tell you his reputation with patients is wonderful. This is thanking Dr. Singh for the pleasure of knowing him, and wishing him success in the future."

Cindi Whitney-Dilley

Whitney Recruitment, LLC

"Of all the years of going to doctors, he's one of the best I've met! He is considerate, reasonable, and understands. He does everything he can to help you. He wants to help me, not just give me pills."

XXXXX

"Just a token of thanks for the excellent care given to me at the hospital."

XXXXXX

Dr. Singh,

I don't know how to describe my gratefulness or express my appreciation for the care you gave my wife in the emergency room the day of her stroke.

I thought after her 13-year battle with cancer, chemo, multiple surgeries, and radiation we were prepared for anything. I was wrong. I thank God that you were the doctor in Emergency on December 26, 2010.

You gave exceptional and immediate care to ensure my wife's survival. You kept my family and me up to speed on her prognosis and what was being done for her during the most frightening and difficult time of our lives. You did this with a gentleness, kindness, and compassion that I will always be grateful for.

Even after being told by the head neurologist that we should not expect much in the way of my wife speaking again, you continued to say she was young and capable of recovery beyond what we could imagine. Your care and communication went way above and beyond what was required.

Your help and follow-up continued with us long after she was out of your care and living in a rehab facility.

You are a wonderfully talented doctor, but more importantly, a wise, kind, compassionate, and confident caregiver. I feel you did everything you could for not just XXXXX, but for our whole family as well. My wife and I will be always grateful and have a special place in our hearts for you. Almost one year later, XXXXX is home- living, speaking, driving, and being the wonderful Mom and wife she always was.

I thank God and you every day for this second chance. I am forever in your debt.

Sincerely,

XXX XXXXXXXX

Dearest Dr. Singh,

God Bless you; I will never forget you, as you took time to hold my hand and comfort me, which I needed so bad that day. I was so scared that I wouldn't make it through.

If I am ever re-admitted, I hope that you will be my doctor. You are truly a god send. I pray for you daily.

XXXXX and XXXXX XXXXX

Dear Mr. XXXXX,

The attending physicians, primarily Dr. Grey and Dr. Singh, were thorough in their care and their explanations and were unending in the compassion displayed. Dr. Harpreet Singh's support went far beyond her doctor. He rapidly became a friend and confidant. When the diagnosis of cancer occurred, he personally called my brothers in California and Hawaii, leaving his personal cell phone number to make sure they had all their questions answered. We recognize that the surgical course my mother followed was unusual for someone 92-years-old, but Dr. Singh assured all she was strong enough to come through with expectations of quality time ahead.

During her convalescence in the XXX unit, she was continuously supported and encouraged by the entire staff. Since her transfer to rehab, she has grown continually supported and encouraged by the entire staff. Since her transfer to rehab, she has grown continually stronger and returned to her apartment the day of Thanksgiving. She's got ways to go, but that journey gets shorter every day.

Again, thank you and your staff from the entire XXXX Family. The care and compassion of your staff are truly appreciated.

Sincerely,

XXXX Family

Dear Dr. Singh,

Thank you for making my Christmas "merry" by healing my eye. May God bless you as much as you have blessed XXXX through your knowledge, good care, and comfort. Your kindness towards XXXX as well as to us, was a true blessing.

XXXXX sisters,

XXXX XXXX

XXXX XXXX

Dear Dr. Singh,

Thank you for being so kind to our family. We felt so confused and lost until you came to us.

We appreciate that you took the time to show and explain XXXX CT scan to our family. We also appreciated you giving us printouts. It was comforting to have when things were quiet at home so we could look over the information you gave us and try to digest it. It just felt good having something to hold on to.

We can't thank you enough for coordinating everything. People would say they would be right back, but never returned. You always returned when you said, which was very comforting to our family. You were so dependable, and our family needed someone to rely on.

We also appreciated the fact that you coordinated things with your brother at XXXXXXXXXXXX. Knowing you were setting everything up for XXX made us all feel better, because we knew it would be done correctly and we would be kept informed. The surgery did not go the way we were hoping for, but you taking time to stop by to see XXX and our family at XXXXXXXXX Hospital meant so much to us.

Our family would never forget you and how wonderful you were to us.

We enjoyed meeting your brother. Please thank him from us for getting XXX in so quickly to see him. We all appreciated the sense of humor ("yank it out") you showed us. We are still laughing about it. It's nice to have something to smile about.

Thank you for being so caring.

XXXX XXXX and Family

"I am writing to thank Dr. Harpreet Singh for all his help and assistance. You are the best! From the bottom of my heart, I sincerely appreciate you. I am glad you were on duty."

XXX XXXX

To XXXX XXXXX,

I just wanted you to know that the care my friend XXXX XXXXX received at XXXXX XXXXX XXXXX campus from Dr. Harpreet Singh was wonderful! The change he has made in her medication and his total devotion to her as his patient has significantly improved her health condition. Ms. XXXXX would like to keep Dr. Singh as her physician when she is discharged from the hospital.

In my many years of being a geriatric nurse, I have never met another physician like him, so I can understand why XXXX XXXXX has so much confidence in Dr. Singh. XXXX is 91-years-old and deserves the continuity of care and peace of mind that Dr. Singh's attention would allow her. Please consider making an exception to Dr. Singh's contract so that my friend, XXXX XXXXXXX, can be cared for by a physician that truly cares about her as a geriatric patient, is knowledgeable about her geriatric conditions, and can put a smile on her face that says it all. Why couldn't Dr. Singh be both?

I look forward to hearing back from you and can be reached XXX-XXX-XXXX,XXX-XXX-XXXX, or at the following address;

XXXX XXXXX

Grand Rapids

Sincerely,

XXXXX XXXXXXX

To Dr. Singh,

Some impart wisdom or comfort and care. Some point out the path, and some take you there. Some warm the heart with a human touch. You have all these gifts. Thank you so much for your excellent care and concern for XXXXX XXXXXX and his family during his stay at XXXXXXX from 10-20-10 to 11-1-10.

XXXX XXXXX XXXXX

Dr. Singh,

Thank you for taking such good care of my dad when we brought him from Florida to XXXXXXX. You were so kind & gentle; you really helped him to adjust!

My dad is home, still on an IV antibiotics & with a drainage tube due to the pleural effusion. He does feel great, though!

Blessings,

XXXX XXXXX

Oct/8/05

Dear Dr. Singh,

It is with both pride and pleasure that I write you this note. You were one of my attending physicians during my stay at XXXXXXX Health Center. I was also given a dual chamber pacemaker by Dr. XXXXXXX. I truly appreciate your professional medical services and appropriate communication. You and your personality have helped me to attain health status.

Thank you so much.

XXX XXXX

XXX-XXX-XXXX

Dear Dr. Singh,

Thank you so much for all of your care, advice, and kindness! XXXXX HOSPITAL patients are so lucky you are there! Being there with my sick mom was so stressful for us and you made both of us feel better just by your presence … good vibes from a good guy! Take care …be good.

Thank you,

XXX XXXXXX

"I am honored to be able to write a testimonial for Dr. Singh. He has given me the necessary tools to succeed in my weight loss journey. He explained things step by step and used drawings, which helped me to better understand. At each visit he would supply new information and assign me a new task to complete. He showed me how to keep a food journal, read labels, and make better food choices when shopping. I never felt overwhelmed when given a new task to complete. Other doctors said to lose weight, but never took the time to explain how and then follow through. Because of Dr. Singh, I have lost almost 30 lbs. He is kind, caring, and sensitive to his patients. I thank him from the bottom of my heart. Without him it wouldn't have been possible."

Jan 27,2013

I gladly write this letter for Dr. Harpreet Singh. On a personal level, he is pleasant, congenial, honest, and a good family man. I have seen him on a professional level as well. I strongly feel he is thorough in his evaluation, very knowledgeable regarding medicine, and feel he gives "good patient care. " He was very helpful on the professional level with education I needed about my health. He was clear in his direction of care and made my exam very comfortable. I have enjoyed getting to know him. I would not hesitate to seek care from him and would recommend him to others.

If you would like to discuss this recommendation further, I would be glad to talk with you. Please feel free to contact me.

Thank you

Sincerely,

Steven P. Delaney

Court Administrator, Magistrate- District Court, Mecosta County

"My first encounter with Dr. Harpreet Singh came by chance & at a very low point in my life. I wasn't able to see my practitioner at the time, so I went ahead & booked with him. It was important that I keep the ball rolling, as I knew I needed help. As a healthcare professional myself, I found myself over-whelmed on the job, tired and drained of the things that truly matter...Compassion, Hope, Kindness & Empathy. Soon you realize you cannot give to others what you are not giving to yourself.

The stress of my job had gotten so bad, I just bottomed out. Working long hours in a very stressful environment, with little to no support from mgmt, trying to satisfy an insatiable employer, left me very depressed and defeated. It was time for me to take care of myself. Dr Singh was the answer to many prayers. He listened to me helped and me see things in other perspectives so that I could move forward and become stronger...physically, mentally, & emotionally.

He always amazes me with his thought processes. He sees outside the box on many levels, includ-ing spiritually. He does not fit the mode of a "pill doctor." Sure, he recognizes prescription mgmt in his practice, but he does so much more. He is a great teacher and is known for drawing pictures with explanations. When you leave the office, you feel informed and confident in your choices. That's the feeling I want in my heath management.

If the business of healthcare continues in the direction of business and not healthcare, it is apparent that the stresses will continue to target the people working in it. There will be more anger, more de-mands, less patience, and less support.

Thank goodness for the people who continue to put the CARE in healthcare. We may stumble, but we get up & keep going every day. To make a difference, to care for those you love, to do the right thing in this world. Dr. Singh is one of these people. If ever you should stumble, no matter who you are or what you do, Dr. Singh will help you get back on track. He certainly made a difference for me."

XXXX XXXXX

"Dr. Singh has shown his continued concern by contacting me several times to find out how I'm doing and where my labs are going. I feel he is such a knowledgeable doctor and cares about my illness. Now days, so many doctors just walk in and out of patients' lives. We believe God is in charge of our lives and that he worked through Dr. Singh that day. We will forever be grateful to have had Dr. Singh walk into ours. He truly cares about his patients."

X.X

"I do have to say, 'Dr. Singh who is on the floor of the hospital,' is one of the best doctors you have had in a very long time. He listens to your complaints and does what he thinks is best for the patient."

XXX

Dr. Singh,

"I thank my God through Jesus Christ for you …" Your care for my husband, Joe, while he was hospitalized was "over the top." Thank you so much for your patience with all of our questions. It helped a lot to be heard and understood. The world of "blood clots" was a "foreign land" for us, and it helped tremendously to be able to really talk with you! As much as we wish you were an outpatient doctor, your services are invaluable to inpatient care. We wish every doctor was more like you! Thank you again, Dr. Singh, for everything!

XXXX XXX

To Whom It May Concern,

I just wanted to do a special thank you to Dr. Singh. He was very caring and right on top of my care. I had back surgery on Nov.13, 2008. I needed units of blood and got really sick. Dr. Singh took the extra mile, even calling while at home during the night to check on me. Thank God for people like him who put the patients 1st.

Thank you,

XXXX XXXX

I am writing to thank Dr. Harpreet Singh for all of his help & assistance. You are the BEST! From the bottom of my heart, I sincerely appreciate you. I'm glad you were on duty.

XXXX XXXXX

Thank you for taking such good care of my dad when we brought him from Florida to XXXXXXX. You were so kind & gentle; you really helped him to adjust!

My dad is home, still on an IV antibiotics & with a drainage tube due to the pleural effusion. He does feel great, though!

Don't tell the patient "what" they should do about their disease, tell them "why" they must do it.

-Harpreet Singh MD

Inspiration

I would like to first acknowledge Dr. Girish Juneja and Rashmi Juneja, who gave me the chance to serve the Big Rapids Community. Had I decided not to work in Big Rapids, I may not have come across the business books I avidly listened to, ultimately inspiring my topic of focus; patient experience. In listening to patients. I discovered that patients were being told to ask questions, but lacked the education as to "how to ask questions." It was at this moment that I decided to develop a patient educational tool to help improve the healthcare process. I am grateful to Don Katz, founder of Audible App, who made the Audible platform so that I could listen to these books.

- Simon Sinek (Start with Why, Leaders Eat Last)
- Atul Gawande MD (The Checklist Manifesto)
- Captain Chesley "Sully" Sullenberger (Highest Duty)
- Peter Pronovost (Safe Patients, Smart Hospitals)
- Anthony Robbins (Money, Awaken the Giant Within)
- John Medina (Brain Rules)
- Kelly McGonigal (The Willpower Instinct)
- Mel Robbins (The 5 Second Rule)
- Ken Robinson Ph.D. (Creative Schools)
- Malcolm Gladwell (Outliers, David &Goliath, Blink, The Tipping Point)
- Benjamin Graham (The Intelligent Investor)
- Elizabeth Cohen (The Empowered Patient)
- Sanjay Gupta MD (Vital Signs on CNN)
- Nicholas Christakis (Connected)
- Vicki Halsey (The Hamster Revolution)
- Tim Burress (The Hamster Revolution)
- Mike Song (The Hamster Revolution)
- Mahan Khalsa (Let's Get Real or Let's Not Play)
- W. Chan Kim, Renee Mauborgne (Blue Ocean Strategy)
- Michael Porter (Competitive Strategy)
- Joan Magretta (Understanding Michael Porter)
- Angela Duckworth (Grit)
- George Anders (The Rare Find)
- Amit Sood MD (The Mayo Clinic Guide to Stress-Free Living)
- Jason Fung MD (The Obesity Code)
- Robert T. Kiyosaki (Rich Dad Poor Dad)
- David Allen (Getting Things Alone)
- Chip Heath, Dan Heath (Decisive, Made it Stick)
- Michael Bungay Stanier (The Coaching Habit)
- Perry Marshal (80/20 Sales and Marketing, Ultimate Guide to Google Adwords)
- David Linden (Touch)
- Jeff Cobb (Leading the Learning Revolution)
- Jeffery Liker (The Toyota Way)
- Charles Duhigg (The Power of Habit, Smarter Faster Better)
- Claude Hopkins (Scientific Advertising)
- Mark Cuban, Kevin O'Leary, Lori Griener, Daymond John, Robert Herjavec (Shark Tank)
- Steve Jobs (Apple)
- Walter Isaacson (Steve Job)
- Clayton Christensen (The Innovator's Dilemma, The Innovator's Prescription)

- Peter Drucker (Management)
- Jim Collins (Good to Great, Great by Choice)
- Morten T. Hansen (Great by Choice)
- Dave Ramsey (Entreleadership)
- Steven Levy (In the Plex)
- Sherry Turkle (Alone Together)
- Michael Gerber (The E-Myth Revisited)
- Joel Comm (The Adsense Code)
- Eliyahu Goldratt (The Goal, Critical Chain, It's not Luck)
- Jeff Cox (Velocity, The Goal)
- Suzan Bergland (Velocity), Dee Jacob (Velocity)
- Josh Kaufman (The Personal MBA)
- Linda Galindo (The 85% Solution)
- Alice Schroeder (The Snowball)
- Christopher Steiner (Automate This)
- Howard Schultz (Onward)
- Neal Gabler (Onward, Walt Disney)
- Neil Fiore (The Now Habit)
- Thomas Hager (The Now Habit)
- Daniel Bor (The Ravenous Brain)
- Ann Handley (Content Rules)
- C.C. Chapman (Content Rules)
- Timothy Ferris (The 4-Hour Workweek)
- Fred Reichheld (The Ultimate Question)
- Seth Godin (Purple Cow)
- V.S. Ramachandran (The Tell-Tale Brain)
- Jon Gertner (The Idea Factory)
- Stephen Covey (The 7 Habits of Highly Effective People)
- Shama Hyder Kabani (The Zen of Social Media Marketing),
- Larry Julian (God is my CEO)
- Jonah Berger (Contagious)
- Robert M. Sapolsky (A Primate's Memoir)
- Blake Master (Zero to One)
- Peter Thiel (Zero to One)
- James Merlino (Service Fanatics)
- Stephen J. Dubner (Freakonomics)
- Steven D. Levitt (Freakonomics)
- Warren Berger (A More Beautiful Question)
- Dale Carnegie (How to Win Friends & Influence People)
- Vani Hari (Food Babe)
- JJ Sutherland (Scrum)
- Jeff Sutherland (Scrum)
- Eric Reis (The Lean Startup)
- Fred Lee (If Disney Ran Your Hospital)
- Tony Hsieh (Delivering Happiness)
- Mark Sanborn (You Don't Need a Title to Be a Leader)
- Michael Raynor (The Innovator's Manifesto)
- William Davis (Wheat Belly)
- Roger Dooley (BrainFluence)
- Nancy F. Koehn (Oprah, Leading with Heart)
- Douglas Conant (Touch Points)

- Mette Norgard (TouchPoints)
- Marcus Lemonis (The Profit)
- Daniel Pink (Drive)
- Norm Brodsky, (Street Smarts)
- Bo Burlington (Street Smarts, Built to sell)
- Nigel Holis (The Global Brand)
- Dave Logan (Tribal Leadership)
- John King (Tribal Leadership)
- Halee Fischer-wright (Tribal Leadership)
- Travis Bradberry (Emotional Intelligence 2.0)
- Jean Greaves (Emotional Intelligence 2.0)
- Abraham Varghese (Cutting for Stone)
- Toby Cosgrove (The Cleveland Clinic Way)
- Shep Hyken (The Cult of the Customer, Moments of Magic, The Amazement Revolution, Amaze Every Customer Every Time)
- Anthony Back (Practical Patient Literacy)
- James Tulsky (Practical Patient Literacy)
- Robert Arnold (Practical Patient Literacy
- Mark Graban (Lean Hospitals)
- Neil Patel (Hustle)
- Jonas Koffler (Hustle)
- Patrick Vlaskovits (Hustle)
- Lisa Nichols (Abundance Now)

There were many other thought-provoking leaders, TED talks, book and videos that have inspired me throughout this process. I am incredibly indebted to Pubmed.gov, Uptodate.com, Webmd.com and Mayoclinic.org for providing an excellent resource for our patients. Above all, I am thankful to my patients who provided their candid feedback. This would not have been possible without the standardized patients who portrayed clinical scenarios for my medical students. The words of Sheri Jo still ring in my ears; "Dr. Singh, by being a standardized patient, I am a better patient and ask more relevant questions from my doctors, as I am always prepared." Though Sheri Jo left us at the age of 42 due to cancer, she gave me an idea to start a patient education initiative.

Many colleagues and medical students have asked the question: "If patients ask more questions, will it, in turn, delay the care of other patients?" However, if you map the lean flow of the patient from the waiting area to their discharge, it has repeatedly been shown patients with poor health literacy cost more to the hospitals, clinics and insurance companies. How do they cost more? Patients who do not ask questions in the initial stage of the process, end up asking "by the way, doctor" questions. This forces doctors to log back into their electronic health system and do an addendum to the chief concern, followed by a history of presenting illness and may result in having to examine the patient all over again. All of this needs to be documented in assessment and plan to meet the ICD 10 coding guidelines. If this delay happens for every patient, this will result in an added hour at the end of the day. If patients are encouraged to ask questions to the medical assistants, it would streamline the process, reducing the number of "doorknob questions."

I believe in lean management and saving healthcare dollars. My definition of L.E.A.N Patient Experience is: Listening, Educating, Activating and eNgaging with the patients. Improving health literacy ultimately helps to better the patient experience and improve patient satisfaction scores.

Many physicians have left a mark on me and have helped me to develop my own patient experience, client experience, or customer experience model. Some of the most influencial are Dr. Paul Singh, Dr. Conrad Fischer, Dr. A.K. Handa, Dr. Vivek Pandey, Dr. Tejinder Mander, Dr. Timothy Fritz, Dr. Jeffery Wilt, Dr. Mimi Emig, and Dr. Timothy Daum who all taught me how to respect and take care of the people around me. This is just a few of the many doctors who have influenced me through this journey. For a complete list, take a sneak-peak of my communication and clinical skills book for medical students—Road to USMLE Step 2 CS. I am indebted to my students especially Dr. Ankur Sinha, Dr. Himanshu Deshwal, Dr. Avantika Singh, and Dr. Krishna Adit Agarwal who contributed in my first book—Road to USMLE Step 2 CS.

My L.E.A.N. Patient Experience wouldn't have been successful if I was not blessed by my spiritual teacher Nirankari Baba Hardev Singh Ji, who taught me a message of love, respect and harmony. Though he is not with us anymore, his message lives on in my heart, which I have inculcated in my daily medical practice.

Imagine a 12-year-old kid who couldn't even pronounce his name and was bullied because of his acne and obesity. Imagine a sixth grader who feared to speak in front of his class because of his stuttering. Now, imagine a kid who had no friends and was spanked throughout his childhood. Imagine a kid who borrowed shoes from his older brother and in order to fit into these shoes, had to fill them with pieces of paper. Now, you do not have to go far to find this kid. This child was me, a young boy who suffered from situational depression from all that I battled. I did not fit in with my other classmates because I was teased, bullied, beaten and not popular to say the least. Up until 19 years of age, I stuttered and was not even able to speak my name—Harpreet. Now, imagine somebody gives you a chance of a lifetime to speak in front of a congregation of about 200 people. Here I stammer and have difficulty verbalizing my thoughts, but was asked to speak in front of a large crowd for which I did for twelve and half minutes. This moment ultimately changed the trajectory of my life. From not being able to speak, to becoming an orator: I owe this blessing to Nirankari Babaji, who gave me the opportunity to speak. I now have a radio show, conduct health and wellness seminars and above all love communicating with patients.

What my Guruji taught me was not only how to speak and communicate, but more importantly, inner awareness. The message of love and respect e has taught me is something that I teach my medical students in Vital Checklist Communication and Clinical Workshop's and extending to my patient education and patient experience initiative. Now, I am being coached by Nirankari Satguru Mataji to follow the path of righteousness. She has sacrificed her health, her family, her children and above all, her time. She has taught us how to walk-the-walk by setting an example herself. Now, I seek blessings from my patients, family members, and loved ones so that I can follow this path of loving my fellow human beings and helping my patients.

This would not have been possible without the sacrifices of my mother—Ajit Kaur who inspires me to this day. I came from a humble background and had only two pairs of pants as I embarked on my journey through school. My mother walked for miles in the sweltering Indian summer heat so that she could save money for our families educations. It took lots of hard labor to continously burn charcoal stoves as gas (which can become expensive), get up at 4 o'clock to cook meals for my five siblings and then lose my dad at a young age. These were just some of the struggles and sacrifices she made. Behind every successful man is a woman, mine was undoubtedly my mother. this saying holds very true, but I would like to extend that phrase by adding that, "Behind every super- successful man are women." Writing books, creating patient education tools and spending time away from the family would not have been possible without the sacrifice of my wife—Aroma.

Thank you, and God bless! Let's improve patient experience.

This humble self,

Harpreet Singh

Dr. Singh's Vision
DrSinghMD.com
HAPPY PATIENTS
Start with WHY
People don't buy what you do, they buy why you do it - Simon Sinek

for caregivers and
healthcare professionals

VitalChecklist.com

Simon Sinek's Golden Circle, Start with why : how great leaders inspire everyone to take action. New York: Portfolio, 2009

for health + wellness
and disease prevention

iCrush.org

IMPROVE HCAHPS AND CGCAHPS SCORE
MAKING "BEST-TO-UNIQUE" HEALTH CAREGIVERS
IMPROVE HELATH LITERACY

ENGAGE AND IMPROVE PATIENT SATISFACTION
MAKING SMART PATIENT SMARTER
IMPROVE PATIENT EDUCATION

Timeline

2009: Started teaching communication and clinical skills to medical students. Name of the company was under the name "99 Percentile"

2010: Taught in Physician assistant school

2011: Inspired by Atul Gawande's book—The Checklist Manifesto. Changed the name from 99 Percentile to Vital Checklist.

2011-2012: Medical Director of a small hospitalist program in Three Rivers Health

2012- Present: Internal Medicine Doctor in Primary Care Practice

2014: (iCrush) 5k for Diabetes in Big Rapids

2015: (iCrush) Multiple Sclerosis in Grand Rapids

2013-2016: Wrote a book with his team members Road to USMLE Step 2 Clinical Skills book

2017 Onwards: Vital Checklist transitioning to a Lean Patient Experience Portal. Make Unique Doctors, Nurse's, Physician Assistants and Nurse Practitioners. Previously, our focus was medical students, physician assistant students and nurse practitioner students.

How the idea of patient education initiatives came to mind?

I became a standardized patient. A standardized patient is a patient who portrays the clinical scenario for my medical students. Putting myself in the patient's shoes helped me to really gauge what is going through the patients mind. In addition, I trained my team members to be standardized patients (SP's). These SP's repeatedly told me that they were better patients and attested to asking the right questions to their health caregivers. I determined that if I could teach standardized patients, that I could also train patients also to ask questions.

A lot of C-Suite people have asked me the question: " Will training people to ask more questions delay the care of other patients." This is what I face on daily basis in the volume-based healthcare system. More patients equates to more money. However, if it were your mom, dad or loved one, would you really want a doctor that was working in a hurry? Checking the boxes and giving pamphlets to patients is not going to take us anywhere. Thinking that this methodology is patient education is a misconception. My conscience never allowed this, does yours? If I do a sloppy or rushed job, it results in me losing sleep at night . Training people upfront with the appropriate questions to ask is a far better approach than the "by the way" doctor tactic. Let's dissect this and begin with the "why" of this problem. If patients have "doorknob questions", this will delay the care because a medical professional must then log back into the electronic healthcare chart and do an addendum to the note, which is time-consuming and thus causes a delay in patient care. If the patient was prepared with the appropriate questions, they could have asked their questions to the medical assistant or nurse practicioner receiving answers and, thus saving the doctor a substantial amount of time. If the medical assistant or nurse doesn't know, the answer to the question can then be answered by the doctor in a timely fashion and may be helpful for the doctor to diagnose the disease and recognize the disease efficiently.

Institute of Medicine published a book—Health Literacy: A prescription to end confusion, recommended actions to be taken by the patients for the betterment of their health.

LeanPEX.com
LEANPATIENT™ EXPERIENCE

LISTEN   EDUCATE   ACTIVATE   eNGAGE

CERTIFICATION COURSE
BY

iCrush.org is a health, wellness, chronic disease prevention portal where we will educate patients via our online portal and community workshops.

Why of iCrush.org? Patient Education in the native language

How will we educate the patient? Vital Checklist, two-dimensional art, YouTube Videos, Workshops and 24/7 Awareness touch points

What will happen? Patient education leads to activation and engagement, thus increasing the awareness of the disease.

(iCRUSH) Diabetes Healthcare Presentation by Dr Singh

475 views

Savingslegs.com	Savingslegs.org
ShoesandSocksoff.com	

I saw a patient who had shortness of breath and erectile dysfunction. When I examined the patient, he had dry gangrene on his second toe of his left foot. About 2 months prior, my patient had a negative stress test. When I asked him about his foot examination, he reported that his feet were examined many years prior. It was at this moment that I thought of starting a Saving Legs Movement where patients were be encouraged to take off their shoes and socks off in the clinic for easy examination. Shoes and Socks off is not only a call to action but also an acronym to remember symptoms of peripheral artery disease.

Health, Wellness and Chronic Disease Management is a tool for patients to memorize "things to do" for easy prevention. We are currently developing an app to help streamline this initiative.

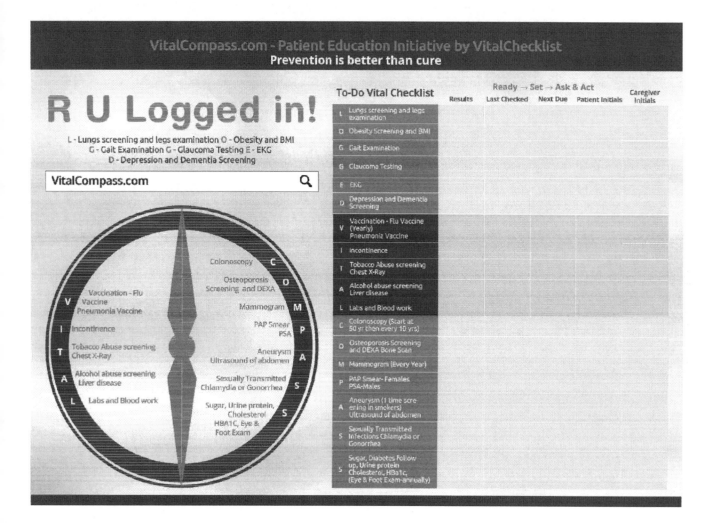

Diabetes is a worldwide disease and the first step to solving this problem is health literacy. I have designed an innovative Vital Checklist—(iCrush) Diabetes; we can provide patient education in different languages. (iCrush) Diabetes is a call to action to crush this disease and remember "things-to-do" about the complications of this disease. Every day patients will receive a text message and will be reminded of the key points.

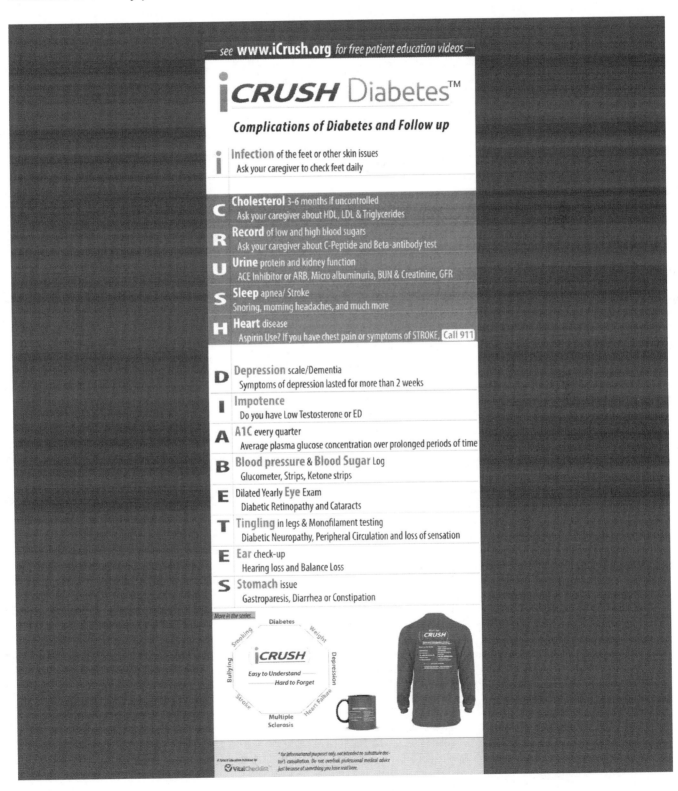

Reading nutrition labels is the toughest thing for patients. Everybody is harping on "food is medicine, " but when it comes to understanding and teaching the nutrition, we pay very little attention to our patients regarding their diet. If we want to change our patients eating habits, it must be implemented when they are young and in school. Nutritional education should happen in schools where kids are in the initial process of forming the good and unhealthy eating habits. I have devised a unique Scan and Spot approach to reading nutrition labels for children and adults, which will help them to overpower obesity, diabetes, hypertension and heart failure and other dreaded disease.

We are looking for the like-minded people to partner with us and help us take this scan and spot nutrition facts curriculum to the schools, clinics and treat obesity.

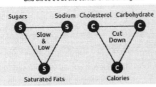 Presents **FATTOJI**

BUY RIGHT, EAT RIGHT & FEED RIGHT
For more information and patient education videos visit: icrush.org

Prevent	Prevent	Prevent	Promote	Reduce
Childhood Obesity	Adult Obesity	Chronic Disease	Health & Wellness	Healthcare Cost

According to this research "Longitudinal trends in obesity in the US from adolescence to the third decade of life", published in Obesity Journal conducted by Dr. Penny Gordon Larsen et al. states that 13.3% of adolescents were obese in 1996. By 2008, obesity prevalence increased to 36.1%. Ninety percent of obese adolescent remained obese in their adulthood in 2008. Let's (iCrush) Childhood Obesity and save healthcare dollars.

TRIANGLE OF JUNK (TOJ)

Step 1: Draw two inverted triangles. Write three s's and three c's at the corner of the triangles.

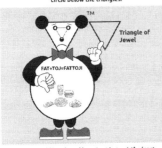

Sugars — Sodium — Cholesterol — Carbohydrate
Slow & Low — Cut Down
Saturated Fats — Calories

Step 2: Add fat to triangle of junk by adding a big circle below the triangles.

Triangle of Jewel

FAT+TOJ=FATTOJI

Step 3: Add hands and legs. Last but not the least, add a bow tie to make Fattoji

MAKING OF THE FATTOJI

SOUP NUTRITION FACTS

Serving Size 1 cup (240mL)
Serving Per Container About 2

Amount Per Serving

Calories 250   Calories from Fat 140

	%Daily Value*
Total Fat 15g	**23%**
Saturated Fat 6g	30%
Cholesterol 10mg	**3%**
Sodium 1,080mg	**45%**
Total Carbohydrate 21g	**7%**
Dietary Fiber 2g	7%
Sugars 1g	
Protein 8g	

- Vitamin A 0% • Vitamin C 0%
- Calcium 4% • Iron 15%

*Percent Daily Value are based on a 2,000 calorie diet. Your daily values may be higher Or lower depending on your calorie needs.

Calories:	2,000	2,500
Total Fat	Less than	65g	80g
Sat Fat	Less than	20g	25g
Cholesterol	Less than	300mg	300mg
Sodium	Less than	2,400mg	2,400mg
Total Carbohydrate		300g	375g
Dietary Fiber		25g	30g

Calories per gram:
Fat 9   Carbohydrate 4   Protein 4

GREEN FATTOJI | AMBER FATTOJI | RED FATTOJI

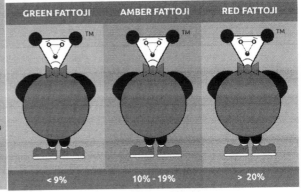

< 9% | 10% - 19% | > 20%

Patient Education Initiatives started by Dr. Harpreet Singh MD

 VitalChecklist™ | iCRUSH Diet™ | Shoes Socks OFF™ | iCRUSH ™ | iCRUSH Diabetes™ | VitalCompass™ | LEAN Patient Experience

---

 iCRUSH Obesity™ /  iCRUSH Diabetes™

Innovator, Radio Show Host, Author, Speaker, USMLE Coach, Patient Educator, Chief Experience Officer, Internal Medicine Physician

i	**Insulin resistance and Impaired glucose tolerance** May develop into Type 2 Diabetes Mellitus	**i**	**Infection of the feet or other skin issues** Ask your caregiver to check feet daily
C	**Cholesterol and Cardiovascular** May have heart disease and cholesterol issues? Obesity may also result in some kinds of cancer	**C**	**Cholesterol 3-6 months if uncontrolled** Ask your caregiver about HDL, LDL & Triglycerides
R	**Respiratory** May develop asthma	**R**	**Record of low and high blood sugars** Ask your caregiver about C-Peptide and Beta-Auto antibody test
U	**Urinary and Kidneys** May have stress incontinence; Proteinuria; May have kidney disease (Glomerulosclerosis)	**U**	**Urine protein and kidney function** ACE inhibitor or ARB, Micro albuminuria, BUN & Creatinine, GFR
S	**Sleep Apnea** May develop sleep apnea	**S**	**Sleep apnea/Stroke** Snoring, morning headaches, and much more
H	**Hypertension & Headaches** May have blood pressure issues & Pseudotumor cerebri	**H**	**Heart Disease** Aspirin Use? If you have chest pain or symptoms of Stroke, call 911
O	**Orthopedic and arthritis** May have Blount disease and arthritis; Joint pain, Pain	**D**	**Depression scale/Dementia** Symptoms of depression lasted for more than 2 weeks
B	**Body image** May have poor esteem, depression, anxiety, and depression	**I**	**Impotence** Do you have Low testosterone or ED
E	**Endocrine** May develop polycystic ovarian disease. Irregular Menstrual Disorder	**A**	**A1C every quarter** Average plasma glucose concentration over the prolonged periods of time
S	**Social Isolation** Teasing, Bullying, poor self-esteem	**B**	**Blood pressure & blood sugar log** Glucometer , Strips, Ketone Strips
I	**Inflammation and Cancer** Inflammation in the body may result in cancer O:Ovarian; B: Breast; Es: Esophagus; I: Intestine; T: Thyroid;	**E**	**Dilated Yearly Eye Exam** Diabetic Retinopathy and Cataracts
T	**Thyroid and Obesity: How are they related?** Is obesity cause or complication of hypothyroidism?	**T**	**Tingling in legs & Monofilament testing** Diabetic Neuropathy, Peripheral Circulation and loss of sensation
		E	**Ear check-up** Hearing loss and balance loss
Y	**Y are you dull, down and depressed** Are you depressed or sad because of Obesity?	**S**	**Stomach issue** Gastroparesis, Diarrhea or Constipation

KETOGENIC FATTOJI

Very Low Carbohydrate Diet
Scan & Spot Sugar, Carb & Added Sugar

S	Sugar
Ca	Carb
A	Added Sugars
N	Nutrients/Ingredients

Types of Sugars: Sucrose, High-Fructose, Glucose, Half Fructose, Beet, Cane Sugars, Corn Syrup, Fructose Sweetener, Molasses, Anhydrous, Dextrose, Crystal, galactose, surcose, disacchride, Maltose, Malted Grain, Oligrosaccharides, Poly-saccharides, Glycerol, Sugar Alcohols, Subsitites Sugar, Sucralose, (Not A Complete List)

WHY
If you **BUY Right!** You will **EAT Right!**
Don't decide about your food at the **DINING TABLE!** Instead, DECIDE when **BUYING** your groceries.

HOW
Decode Nutrition Facts in a quick **GLANCE**
Don't get **CONFUSED** by the **FLASHY** Labels

WHAT
SCAN the Nutrition Labels cautiously &
SPOT the Nutrition Facts efficiently.
Learn the
EASY to understand, **HARD** to forget Facts.

Adapting Simon Sinek's wonderful theory of "Start with Why" and Golden Circle

WHAT / HOW / WHY

Don't just tell the patients
WHAT to do... but tell
them **WHY** to Do

Visit **iCrush.org** for more Patient Empowerment Tools
Phone: 269-818-1000
Email: drsingh@icrush.org

- Dr. Harpreet Singh has started LEAN Patient Experience course for physician assistants, nurse practitioners, health caregivers, hospitals and clinics. Invite Dr. Singh to speak drsingh@vitalchecklist.com
- Dr. Harpreet Singh has started health and wellness workshop for schools, colleges and businesses. Invite Dr. Singh to speak drsingh@icrush.org
- Buy Dr. Singh's ROAD TO USMLE Step 2 CS book and How to be a BAD patient?

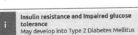

Have you heard LDL is a lousy cholesterol and HDL stands for healthy cholesterol? Is this the right explanation.

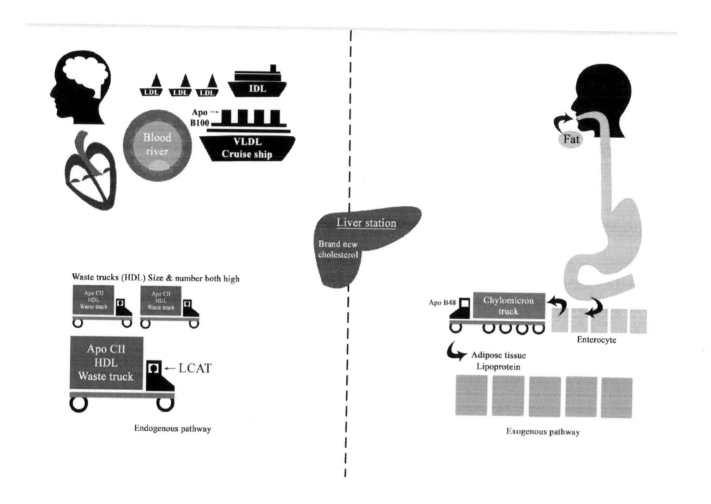

(iCrush) This tool, which encapsulates mental health, stress, depression, bipolar disorder and suicide was developed to help streamline communication with people, children and teenagers. More research is needed, and we are looking to collaborate with various organizations to help us develop this tool.

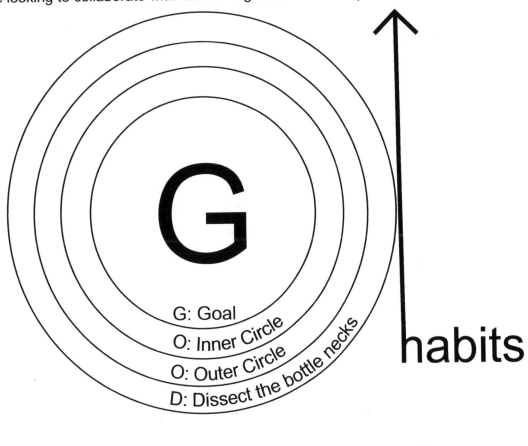

G: Goal
O: Inner Circle
O: Outer Circle
D: Dissect the bottle necks

habits

NurseHandoff.com	Easy, bedside Nurse to Nurse Communication and handoff tool

Have you ever noticed a nurse carrying a scratch piece of a paper in her pocket? Why in this era of technology is a nurse still carrying a scrap piece of paper?

Often, I have received many answers:

- Something to write on
- When a doctor calls, I need to see it quickly
- I can't go from one patient to the other
- In situations of code, I need a ready reference point
- Bedside communication with patients is much easier
- Handoff is much easier

I felt the need to devise an easy tool for the nurses with whom I work.

	Patient Name / Room number	Pain scale	Patient Name / Room number	Pain scale	Patient Name / Room number	Pain scale
i Incision(s)	☐ clean ☐ dry ☐ intact	1 2 3	☐ clean ☐ dry ☐ intact	1 2 3	☐ clean ☐ dry ☐ intact	1 2 3
D Dressings / Drains		4		4		4
O Orientation x 3 / Behavior		5 6 7		5 6 7		5 6 7
F Fall Risk / Trauma	Injury: Fracture | Dislocation | Intracranial | Crushing | Burn | Elect. Shock ☐ Fall Risk	8 9 X	Injury: Fracture | Dislocation | Intracranial | Crushing | Burn | Elect. Shock ☐ Fall Risk	8 9 X	Injury: Fracture | Dislocation | Intracranial | Crushing | Burn | Elect. Shock ☐ Fall Risk	8 9 X
L Lines / Catheter asso. infections		1 2		1 2		1 2
I Input / I/V Fluids		3 4		3 4		3 4
P Prophylaxis	☐ select prophylactic antibiotic ☐ start prophylactic antibiotic(1h) ☐ stop prophylactic antibiotic (24h)	5 6 7	☐ select prophylactic antibiotic ☐ start prophylactic antibiotic(1h) ☐ stop prophylactic antibiotic (24h)	5 6 7	☐ select prophylactic antibiotic ☐ start prophylactic antibiotic(1h) ☐ stop prophylactic antibiotic (24h)	5 6 7
F Foley / Catheter asso.Urine Tract inf.		8 9 X		8 9 X		8 9 X
L Look at Tele, Vitals & Neuro		1		1		1
O O2 & Respiratory Rx		2 3		2 3		2 3
P Pressure Sores / Ulcers		4 5 6		4 5 6		4 5 6
S Stools & Skin care		7 8		7 8		7 8
D Daily Weight		9 X		9 X		9 X
O On Isolation Precautions		ROM		ROM		ROM
Y Ygrella-allergY		Turn		Turn		Turn
O Oral Nutrition / NPO		Ambulate		Ambulate		Ambulate
U Urine Output		Chair		Chair		Chair
or do you have **?** **Fo** Foreign object **Bi** Blood incompatibility **A** Air embolism	Post-Operative: respiratory failure, wound dehiscence, iatrogenic pneumothorax, accidental lacerations, CLOTs if any ?	Commode BRP BR	Post-Operative: respiratory failure, wound dehiscence, iatrogenic pneumothorax, accidental lacerations, CLOTs if any ?	Commode BRP BR	Post-Operative: respiratory failure, wound dehiscence, iatrogenic pneumothorax, accidental lacerations, CLOTs if any ?	Commode BRP BR

www.vitalchecklist.com   hi@vitalchecklist.com   +1(855)500-VITAL

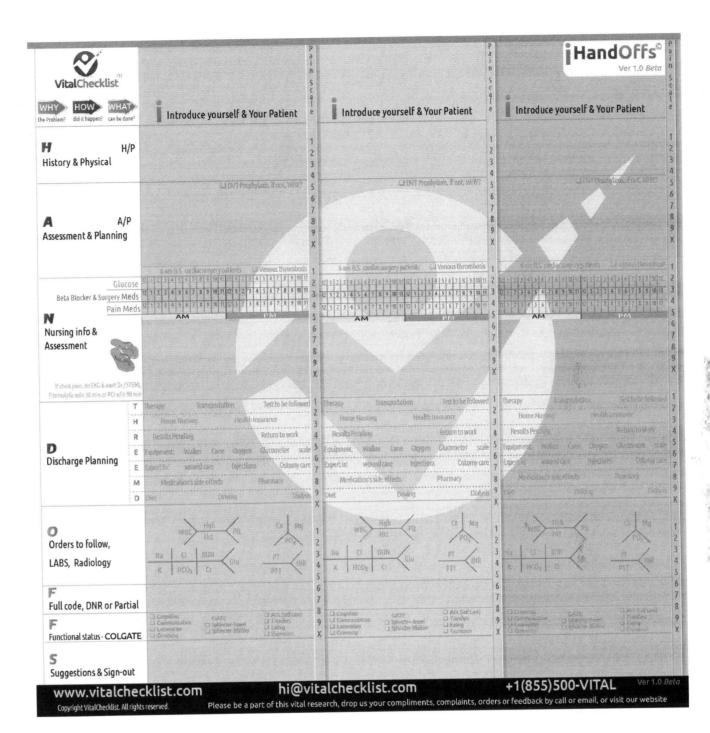

VitalChecklist

WHY the Problem? HOW did it happen? WHAT can be done?

H H/P
History & Physical

A A/P
Assessment & Planning

Glucose
Beta Blocker & Surgery Meds
Pain Meds

N
Nursing info & Assessment

If chest pain, do EKG & alert Dr / STEMI,
Fibrinolytic w/in 30 min or PCI w/in 90 min

D
Discharge Planning

O
Orders to follow,
LABS, Radiology

F
Full code, DNR or Partial

F
Functional status - COLGATE

S
Suggestions & Sign-out

iHandOffs
Ver 1.0 Beta

Introduce yourself & Your Patient
Introduce yourself & Your Patient
Introduce yourself & Your Patient

Pain scale 1 2 3 4 5 6 7 8 9 X

- Why does most of the communications between health caregivers and patients happen at the time of discharge from the hospital?
- Why do we print discharge instructions for patients only at the time of discharge?
- Should discussion about the "things-to-do" at home happen at the time of discharge only or start earlier?
- Should a patient receive printed paper earlier?
- Should patients rely on apps, websites, Google or Bing search engine?

Is every patient different? Some patients are visual learners while others learn better with audio, in regards to remembering instructions. Some patients need touchpoints for they are kinesthetic learners, while other patients need written material, for which they need to read themselves in order to retain the data. , Lastly, there are many patients that need to write in order to absorb and learn the discharge instructions. Just checking boxes and thinking communication has happened is not going to educate our patients. Chasing patients with post-discharge calls be sufficient enough either. Real-time talk is important and critical in order to effectively and efficiently treat our patients.

When the patient is in the hospital, we often overlook paying attention to the patient-provider communication and chase patients to get good patient satisfaction scores after being discharged. In order to achieve positive reviews, hospitals invest their energy and money into calling patients post discharge. Is this health literacy? The entire system needs to be overhauled. I have used Eliyahu Goldratt's Theory of Constraint to exploit this bottleneck methodology in the current discharge process. This is the weakest link in the process which inevitably increases the length of stay, decreased throughput, increases operational expense, needs for more inventory, increases emergency department boarding of patients and thus increasing ER wait times.

We have designed the Communication Cards and Communication Box to help patients overcoming these constraints. These can be given early in the admission for easy two-way communication.

How are Eliyahu Goldratt's five steps defined:

1. Identify the systems constraints
2. Decide how to exploit the constraints
3. Subordinate everything else to the exploitation of constraints
4. Elevate the system's constraint
5. If any constraints have been violated, repeat the process

How can you memorize these steps?

DrSinghMD	How to remember the steps?	
D	**Diagnose** the problem	
R	Past **records** of your problem	
S	**Step up** to get a maximum capacity	
In	Bring **In-line** everything around the constraint	
G	**Get** an upgraded investment for this constraint	
H	Stop **Hibernation** and challenge the status quo	
MD	**Measure data** repeatedly until improvement starts	

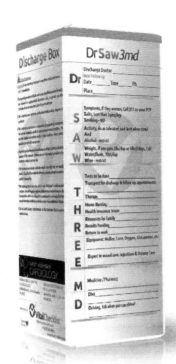

Vital Checklist in different languages

Spanish

Portuguese

Russian

Punjabi

Hindi

Marathi

Arabic

Urdu

Telugu

Malayalam

Tamil

Paingrade.com	An objective pain assessment tool

I saw a patient who told me that his pain was a 10/10 in intensity but could participates in a wide array of living activities. However, on the other spectrum, I saw patient whose pain was 4/10 in intensity but ended up being admitted to the ER. I am designing the pain scale to help patients present their clinical scenario in a better way for their health caregivers.

(Coming Soon)

What if U Fly?	How to prevent sickness while flying?

WHAT IF U FLY?

An innovative mnemonic to educate and memorize best practices towards

Prevention of FLU

iCRUSH

iCrush.org

W — Wash hands frequently

HAT — Hand Sanitizer (Approved by TSA)

I — ILL If you are sick, don't travel

F — Flu Shot every year

U — Use Tissue or towel

F — Turn off the Faucet with tissue

L — Lift up the Lavatory seat with tissue

Y — Yikes! Door Knobs/ handles can also spread infection; Use tissue to open or close

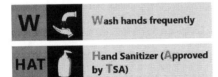
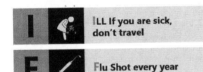
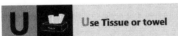
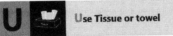
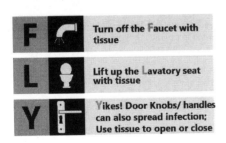

REMEMBER

A — Watch for sick Airline passengers

B — BYOD - Buy your own drink, don't share

C — Cover your Nose & Mouth with tissue while sneezing or coughing

D — Discard Tissue after use. Don't wipe nose with hands

A Patient Awareness Initiative by

VitalChecklist™

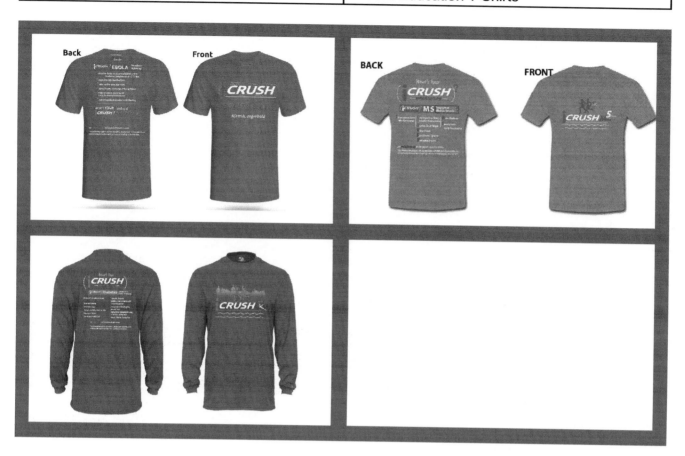

About Jasmine Hundal

Jasmine contributed to Vital Checklist by managing the bibliography and coordinating the endeavor.

Dr. Jasmine Hundal's interest in Medicine started early in her childhood when she faced the adversity of suffering all around her. There was lack of basic health care in the village in India where she was born and raised. This is what motivated her to become a doctor. She joined the one of the most prestigious medical colleges in the country, Armed Forces Medical College, located in Pune, where she completed her MBBS. Serving in the Indian Army, she became a regimental officer of the highest altitude but with the humblest attitude. She saw patients with gangrene, depression, and suicidal ideation due to isolation. She was the health caregiver, family caregiver, medical officer, and also a counsellor for the men serving in extreme conditions. After she got married, she moved to United States to serve humanity. Today she is an Internal medicine resident University of Missouri Healthcare and we believe that she will be an asset to any program she joins.

About Sreenivasan Shanmugam

Sreenivasan translated Vital Checklist into Tamil and coordinated the project.

Dr. Shreenivasan Shanmugam is a Primary Care Physician from India. He graduated from Vinayaka Missions Medical College, in Salem, India in 2013. His dream is to pursue residency in the United States of America. He is an optimistic and loving person, and he believes that a positive attitude is as important to healthcare as medicine. He is an optimistic and loving doctor also gives patients the desire to live a healthier life. Preventative medicine is a vital part of his approach. He loves listening to his patients about their concerns and helping them to the greatest of his ability. He believes hope is crucial on the pathway to recovery for a patient. Along with imparting hope, he desires to bestow knowledge to his patients.

About Igor Vaz

Igor translated Vital Checklist into Portuguese.

Dr. Igor Vaz is a physician in Brazil and also hold a bachelors degree in computer engineering. He is pursuing an Internal medicine residency position in the United States. He has a particular interest in patient education because he believes that medicine is both a biological and a social science. In his opinion, practicing medicine is about dealing with human beings that are in very fragile position. They are scared about their disease and when information is offered proactively, the patient is able to understand their condition and a good doctor can empower them to make decisions about their treatment and future. He also has an interest in research and received a Brazilian federal research grant for two and half years as a researcher assistant in the genetic department of Universidade Federal do Estado do Rio de Janeiro (UNIRIO). He is an author for Vital Checklist and a research assistant in a project involving post-bariatric surgery patients in intensive care units. He enjoys running and practicing Krav Maga in his spare time.

About Chintan Rupareliya

Chintan translated Vital Checklist into Gujarati and Russian

Dr. Rupareliya is an India based multilingual health care professional currently working as a researcher in Neurology. After getting his MD from Russia in 2012, Dr. Rupareliya came to the United States to pursue the graduate education in Healthcare Administration. Dr. Rupareliya completed his fellowship in Electroencephalography (EEG) and Epilepsy before applying for residency. Since then, he has been involved as a clinical research scholar in the field of Epilepsy. Dr. Rupareliya's area of clinical interest includes clinical neurophysiology, movement disorders, cerebrovascular disorders, and multiple sclerosis.

About Udhayvir Singh Grewal

Udhayvir translated Vital Checklist into Punjabi.

Dr. Udhayvir Singh Grewal is an intern at Government Medical College and Rajindra Hospital, in Patiala, India. He is in the initial phase of his professional career and is highly enthusiastic about educating patients and improving patient care experiences. Udhayvir is passionate about clinical research in oncology and infectious diseases. Strongly believing in the importance of good leadership skills in young physicians, he has served as the Vice President for Capacity Building, Medical Students' Association of India, and also as the Program Coordinator of Human Resources for Health Program, International Federation of Medical Students' Associations. Udhayvir is also a student member of the American College of Physicians and the American Society of Clinical Oncology.

About Dr. Shobita Anand

Shobita translated Vital Checklist into Marathi.

Dr. Shobita Anand is an M.B.B.S graduate from Dr. D Y Patil University Navi Mumbai. She is currently pursuing her diploma course in Diabetes Mellitus from Apollo Hospital Mumbai and involved Diabetes Mellitus research. She aims to pursue Internal Medicine in the United States. She is passionate about teaching and creating social awareness about current trends of diseases. Educating patients is her forte and has contributed her time to activate patients at DSNDP program (Dr. Shri Nanasaheb Dharmadhikari Pratishthan), a social awakening organization, which has made its place in Guinness Book of World Record. She has played a vital role in conducting health and child care camps. She is an active member of flood control camps and rehabilitation. Outside of medicine, she loves traveling and cooking Indian cuisines. To cap, Shobita is a connector and connects well with people, patients, and caregivers.

About Charu Arora

Charu translated Vital Checklist into Hindi,

Dr. Arora discovered his interest in becoming a doctor while he was in high school. A zealous lover of biological sciences, he enjoys interacting with people and bringing positive change to their lives. He was a clinical researcher at Harvard Medical School (Boston) and Children's Hospital of Los Angeles. He is a budding physician and has a deep inclination in Global Medicine. Charu is the founder and editor in chief of an online parenting blog called Peds4You, which is dedicated for the inclusive betterment children's health. Outside of academia and extracurricular activities, he loves to spend his time cooking gastronomic delights, singing Bollywood songs, and playing with his four-legged canine baby. He has had several research papers published in state and national level indexed journals. He is currently working in the clinical and research field as a primary physician in the institute of Neurosciences at a tertiary care teaching hospital in India. A social worker, blogger and debater, Charu is the author of a textbook, Pediatrics for Undergraduate Students, which is scheduled to be published very soon.

About Lissette Jimenez

Lissette translated Vital Checklist into Spanish.

Dr. Lissette Jimenez is an Internal Medicine Resident physician at White River Medical Center in Batesville, AR. She received her bachelor's degree in biology and graduated medical school from Universidad Iberoamericana in Santo Domingo, Dominican Republic. She has a passion for working in underserved communities and serving those in need. Her interest in medicine includes pursuing a fellowship in gastroenterology. In addition to this, she loves being involved in the educational aspect of medicine, especially teaching and advising medical students on their future endeavors.

About Omar M. Al-Janabi

Omar translated Vital Checklist into Arabic

Dr. Al-Janabi is a Ph.D. Candidate in Clinical and Translational Science / Neurology at the University of Kentucky College of Medicine. He received his bachelor in medicine and general surgery (M.B.Ch.B.) from Tikrit University College of Medicine and his master's degree in medical sciences from the University of Kentucky College of Medicine.He worked as a neurology resident physician for four years at Tikrit Teaching Hospital in Iraq. His clinical experiences have made him passionate about patient education and care, as it is considered one of the pillars of a successful health system. He also believes that patients can achieve the best outcome through proper education and guidance. In addition to his interest in patient education, he loves teaching medical students, and is currently conducting clinical research in the field of cerebrovascular disease, Alzheimer's disease and neuroimaging.

About Rehan Malik

Rehan translated Vital Checklist into Urdu

Dr. Rehan Malik is a Resident Physician at Mount Sinai Medical Center Miami, Florida. He has a passion for patient care, and is a strong believer in patient education for better patient compliance and health outcomes. With his background in preventive cardiology research, he has been a spokesperson at the community level in Miami-Dade for educating masses in adopting healthy behaviors and lifestyle strategies for CVD prevention. In this regard, Patient Education Guide (PEG), with its 12 different languages, support would be a stepping stone in solving the language and communication barrier in the diverse US Healthcare population.

About Dinesh Arora

Dinesh translated Vital Checklist into Punjabi

Dr. Dinesh Kumar has completed medical school from Government Medical College and Hospital in Patiala, India and proceeded to complete his general surgery residency from Christian Medical College and Hospital, India. Dinesh has worked as a Surgeon Consultant in General surgery at Christian Medical College & Hospital. Currently, Dinesh is pursuing a career as a general surgeon in United States and contributing in improving patient education. Dinesh is an Assistant Medical Author in Road to USMLE, Step 2 Clinical Skills and has a passion to help educate patients in layman language. Dinesh loves to serve in the medical field and wants to lead his life in this service.

About Meghna Kesireddy

Meghna translated Vital Checklist into Telugu.

Dr. Meghana Kesireddy is currently an Internal Medicine Resident physician at the University of Texas Medical Branch in Galveston, Texas. She graduated from Osmania Medical College in India. She has worked as a visiting medical student at Mayo Clinic, Case Western Reserve University, Grand Rapids Medical Health and Louisiana State University. She is particularly interested in practicing preventive medicine and empowering the patients to take charge of their health through effective patient education. Working for the 'Patient Education Guide' is her first step in the area of patient empowerment. She likes to be involved in medical education and clinical research. She looks forward to pursuing a fellowship in Hematology- Oncology after her residency. On a personal level, travelling all around the world and experiencing different cultures is one of her biggest dreams.

About Sai Koyoda

Sai translated Vital Checklist into Telugu.

Dr. Sai Krishna Koyoda is currently pursuing a residency in the Department of Internal Medicine at Monmouth Medical Center, NJ. He is an alumni of Osmania Medical College in Hyderabad, India. He is interested in research oriented patient care and is particularly passionate about futuristic medicine, immunology, and its related fields. He has been an awardee of Short term studentship, sponsored by Indian Council of Medical Research for his project, 'Study of Neural Modulation on Inflammation'. He was also the chief executive member of the Osmecon, undergraduate research symposium organizing committee. Outside of medicine, he loves philosophy, physics, and programming.

About Shahena Shreenivasan

Shahena translated Vital Checklist into Malayalam.

Dr. Shahena is a recent graduate from Vinayaka Missions Medical College in Salem, India. She is currently working as a Junior Resident in the ICU at VIMS Hospital in Salem, India. Her aim is to become an Attending Physician in the United States. She loves teaching medicine. She is a reliable, enthusiastic and responsible person who considers the medical profession as divine. Apart from her profession, she loves spending time with her family, especially with her two-year-old daughter. Her research interests include Stem Cells and Genetic Engineering.

About Shafi Rana

Shafi translated Vital Checklist into Punjabi.

Shafi Rana, an expert in Strategic Healthcare Operations and Quality Control, also takes interest in linguistics and understands the usage and importance of simplistic medical verbiage as it increases adherence and quality of care. Shafi holds a Bachelor of Science from St. Johns University in NY along with a Medical Doctorate from American University of Antigua - College of Medicine and a Master's in Business Administration from Davenport University.

About Noni Rana

Noni translated Vital Checklist into Punjabi.

Dr. Rana is a medical graduate of American University of Antigua with a Masters in Health Administration. He is currently working as a Director of Operations for one of the leading urgent care centers in New York. He is responsible for the financial performance of regional offices, strategic operations, patient safety, risk management and compliance. His primary role has been developing protocols for clinics to help divert and reduce unnecessary ER visits.

Dr. Harpreet Singh is a renowned medical doctor, co-host of Talk Medicine radio show on WBRN, medical author, speaker, creator of "Vital Compass" and "Shoes and Socks off in the Clinic", founder of "Vital Checklist" and "iCrush.org." He started his American Dream on September 23, 2003, with 54 dollars and an M.B.B.S degree from KMC, Manipal, India. After completing his residency, he worked as a hospitalist and was a Medical Director. He has excellent bedside manners and his passion for patients has gained him the title of *"Dr. House with a good personality."* Some of his patients call him a detective, and others investigator. One of his peers has referred him as the William Osler of 21'st century. Because of his love for patient-care and patient experience, he was appointed as Chief Experience Officer of Michigan Primary Care Partners.

When he is not seeing patients, he is teaching communication and clinical skills to medical students, physician assistants and nurse practitioners. He has taught physician assistants at GVSU and is a community adjunct faculty for medical students at Central Michigan University. His Vital Checklist Workshop is very popular among the medical student, and he has written a book—*Road to USMLE Step 2 CS.*

Dr. Singh's vision is to educate patients and help them to become proactive, which can <u>be achieved</u> by educating, activating and engaging them. Accomplishing this is not a simple task, and he is effectively using the technology to build the iCrush.org platform where he is posting his patient education videos, with the sole mission of making change in the healthcare system. He has started (iCrush) Lifestyle Institute where his focus is on health and wellness. He has organized (iCrush) 5k for diabetes, and (iCrush)5k for multiple sclerosis to educate and make people aware of this dreaded disease. With (iCrush) Lifestyle Institute, he is promoting workplace health and wellness to reduce medical costs, absenteeism, presenteeism and decreases musculoskeletal injuries with the goal of improving return on investment (R.O.I) and return on emotions (R.O.E.). Many attendees have praised him for his Scan and Spot Weight Loss Seminar.

His patients call him an "Artist Doctor" as he explains the disease process with the help of pictures. He has used art and technology to develop patient safety touchpoints to prevent chronic disease which <u>is housed</u> under VitalCompass.com. He dreams of starting his own Patient Education TV show one day where he can draw and explain the disease process and reach the masses.

Dr. Singh is a voracious reader and reads medical books, journal articles, and business books. This is what has inspired him to write and create mnemonics, checklists, and art for easy understandability and memory. He meditates, enjoys playing racquetball and is addicted to hot yoga. His ultimate goal is patient safety and making patients happy.

Invite Dr. Singh to speak to your organization. Email us at drsingh@vitalchecklist.com